Defending Priv...ᵥᵤ

DEFENDING PRIVILEGE

Rights, Status, and Legal Peril in the British Novel

~

Nicole Mansfield Wright

Johns Hopkins University Press
Baltimore

Johns Hopkins University Press
2715 North Charles Street
Baltimore, Maryland 21218-4363
www.press.jhu.edu

Library of Congress Cataloging-in-Publication Data

Names: Wright, Nicole, 1982– author.
Title: Defending privilege : rights, status, and legal peril in the
British novel / Nicole Wright.
Description: Baltimore : Johns Hopkins University Press, 2020. |
Includes bibliographical references and index.
Identifiers: LCCN 2019010078 | ISBN 9781421433738 (hardcover) |
ISBN 1421433737 (hardcover) | ISBN 9781421433745 (paperback) |
ISBN 1421433745 (paperback) | ISBN 9781421433752 (ebook) |
ISBN 1421433753 (ebook)
Subjects: LCSH: Literature and society—Great Britain—History—
18th century. | Literature and society—Great Britain—History—
19th century. | Law and literature—Great Britain—History—18th century. |
Law and literature—Great Britain—History—19th century. |
British literature—18th century—History and criticism. |
British literature—19th century—History and criticism.
Classification: LCC PR448.S64 W75 2020 | DDC 820.9/3554—dc23
LC record available at https://lccn.loc.gov/2019010078

A catalog record for this book is available from the British Library.

Special discounts are available for bulk purchases of this book.
For more information, please contact Special Sales
at specialsales@press.jhu.edu.

Johns Hopkins University Press uses environmentally friendly book
materials, including recycled text paper that is composed of at least
30 percent post-consumer waste, whenever possible.

For my parents, Marguerite Alejandro-Wright and Brian Wright,
and
For my husband, Rick Mansfield

CONTENTS

In his journal entry for Sunday, 12 February 1826, Walter Scott described surmounting the challenges he faced in composing his novel *Woodstock*: "When I lost myself in former days in some country to which I was a stranger—I always push[e]d for the pleasantest road and either found [it] or made it the nearest. It is the same in writing."* During my own journey as writer, as I navigate the literary terrain of that unfamiliar place—the past—a number of people have helped along the way. I am fortunate that previous travelers left trail markers, that others pointed the way or assisted in chopping through thickets, and still others made the journey lighter through their intellectual engagement and companionship.

Catherine Goldstead expertly steered my project through the pipeline from the very first stages. While she is wondrously efficient, I especially resonated with her intellectual curiosity and her talent for discerning where to bolster the analysis or enrich the argument. I am also indebted to her and to the marketing team for designing a gorgeous cover. Juliana McCarthy provided clear and patient advice on the process of preparing a book and put significant time into preparing the manuscript. Joe Abbott is a keen-eyed and gracious copyeditor, and my pages benefited from his efforts. Debby Bors and Kim Johnson kept the production of the book running smoothly. Becky Hornyak prepared my index with care.

Special thanks to Sandra Macpherson and Caleb Smith for coming to Boulder to offer commentary essential to developing my manuscript into a book. Their generous feedback helped me hone my ideas. I also thank the anonymous reviewers of my manuscript for suggestions that made the project stronger.

*Walter Scott, in *The Journal of Sir Walter Scott*, ed. W. E. K. Anderson (Oxford: Clarendon, 1972), 86–87.

At Yale, my advisers, Jill Campbell and Katie Trumpener, helped launch me into a career as a scholar. From Jill's first phone call to welcome me to the program, I knew that she and I were *simpatico*; conversations with her invariably sharpen my ideas. I marvel at Katie's capacity for cultivating new research directions.

Claude Rawson has for years demonstrated the generosity of mentorship and the rigorous critical acumen of a world-class scholar. I am impressed by the time, attention, and guidance he has given me as I have proceeded along the path of an academic career. I hope I can help those rising in the field as much as he has. Simon Stern, an indefatigable font of ideas, has been a supporter from the beginning. I do not know how he found the time to read my chapters with such care, but he did. Jenny Davidson welcomed me into the fold and took the time to give me useful feedback on my plan for the book. Margaret Anne Doody's enthusiastic response to an early presentation of my project—and her suggestions that became key to chapter 2—fueled my progress. Alison Conway gave helpful comments on my book proposal, demonstrating gracious mentorship. Lisa Regan has been a discerning reader of my work; with her X-ray vision, she sees beyond the words on the page to the underlying meaning, and her feedback has been indispensable. David Lobenstine combines a wordsmith's talents with a gift for discerning the larger significance of historical developments. I thank all of these interlocuters for the time they have kindly given to my ideas. Amyrose McCue Gill and Amanda Besch proofread the manuscript with diligent eyes.

The English Department at the University of Colorado, Boulder, is a lively and energizing place to work. In particular, Ramesh Mallipeddi generously provided insightful feedback as my project developed. Janice Ho offered valuable commentary on my draft, and discussions with her are always a pleasure. Teresa Toulouse gave copiously of her time to read my writing and engage with my ideas, and I was impressed by how swiftly she replied with substantive and perceptive written suggestions—spiced with a refreshing dash of wit. Members of the department's work-in-progress group—including Lori Emerson, Jason Gladstone, Emily Harrington, and Maria Windell—offered helpful reflections on my first chapter. I thank Laura Winkiel for taking for me; time from her packed schedule to lead this group, which has enhanced the work of junior faculty. As department chairs, William Kuskin secured start-up funding for me; Ruth Ellen Kocher supported my Intellectual Development grant; and David Glimp and Sue Zemka made possible my manuscript workshop— an incredible opportunity.

Thanks to a postdoctoral fellowship at the University of Chicago, I had time to nourish the seedlings of the ideas that would become this book. Ken Warren generously gave of his time as I developed my work on proslavery novels. Reggie Jackson offered impeccable advice at this crucial juncture in my career and is a wonderful friend whose musings strike a chord with me. Later, during my time as a Lapidus Long-Term Fellow at the Schomburg Center at the New York Public Library, Sylvia Chan-Malik, Caree Banton, Jeff Diamant, Tanisha C. Ford, C. Riley Snorton, and Soyica Colbert, under the guidance of Farah Jasmine Griffin, provided helpful feedback on my evolving concept of the book.

Additional funding from the Woodrow Wilson National Fellowship Foundation, the Social Science Research Council, the Folger Library, and the Mellon Foundation was important for my project. Laura Selznick of Stanford's Mellon Mays program was an enthusiastic supporter with boundless energy, as she has been for so many others. Heather Zenone and the University of California, Berkeley, Student Research Opportunity Program offered an incomparable launchpad. John Tofanelli was kind to share his expertise at the Butler Library of Columbia University; and Bebe Chang helped with acquisitions at Norlin Library at the University of Colorado.

At Yale, Christopher R. Miller was among the first to give me detailed and invaluable written feedback on my research. His seminar interpretations always made new poems I thought were familiar. Elliott Visconsi's seminar was a rigorous introduction to thinking about race in the eighteenth century. Ruth Bernard Yeazell guided my larger awareness of novel studies by sending me articles and discussing ideas with me. Stefanie Markovits and Wendy Anne Lee offered thoughtful feedback on my writing. Robert Stepto was a thoughtful interlocuter, and he dispenses apothegms as wise as they are witty. Lawrence Manley helped me develop an understanding of the earlier authors and literary works that shaped the work of eighteenth-century authors. Melissa Ganz offered helpful suggestions for my law and humanities bibliography.

Earlier, at Stanford, Kevin DiPirro sparked my development as a writer by patiently guiding me through the revision process; he also had an unerring instinct for the right book to recommend. John L'Heureux was a stalwart mentor who inspired me not only with his belief in me but also with the joy he found in the life of the mind. Pamela Lee's teaching was bracing in its unabashed assertion of the symbiosis between art and social change. I could not have asked for a better undergraduate thesis adviser than Terry Castle; she always leveled with me, took my questions seriously, and taught me to challenge critical orthodoxies. David Palumbo-Liu drew exhilarating connections among seemingly disparate readings. To this day, I look to Seth Lerer for sage advice; he has the ability to make any text interesting. James Reichert encouraged innovative interpretation and propelled me to engage with an unfamiliar literary tradition. Earlier, Stuart Groningen, Sarah Morrison, Karla Herndon, Alan Miller, Heidi Ramirez-Weber, and Elaine Hall dedicated themselves to helping me and other students hone writing skills and discover unfamiliar literary vistas.

Throughout the years, friends have made treks to visit me, talked with me late into the night, and plied me with dumplings. I particularly thank Meredith Jackrel, Alex May, Jean Otsuki, Jennifer Holtzman, Andy Heisel, Liz Appel, Ramin Setoodeh, Shuang Zhang, Kristin Larson, Jeff Johnson, and Gabriele Hayden.

I am grateful to my family for all of their help. My grandmother, Eugenie Byron, is a tower of courage and strength. I remember with love my paternal grandmother, Mary Claire Wright, an intrepid traveler and nonjudgmental supporter. Owen Wright and Adele Wright cheered me through an intense phase of writing. My godfather, Will White, and Olivia White welcomed me into their home in Ithaca. Matthew Wright inspires me with his integrity, work ethic, and caring nature. I come away from conversations with Davern Wright feeling intellectually refreshed, with a more nuanced perspective on things. Elena Mayville is a sparkling gem of a sister, and she brightens my day with her calls; she and Luke Mayville offered helpful suggestions for my book. I feel blessed to have such excellent parents: Marguerite Alejandro-Wright is a beacon of light to those around her; her love sustains me, and her work as a columnist and author has inspired me from my earliest years. I trust her judgment implicitly. Brian Wright has been a pillar of love and a guiding force; he also instilled my love of reading and motivated my choice of an academic career. I hope all those hours of rereading *King Orville and the Bullfrogs* and tolerating my questions about blue books and academic journals when I tagged along to the office were worth it. Rick Mansfield devoted countless hours to reading my work and discussing it in detail; words convey only a glimmer of my gratitude to and love for him. I delight to spend life with a man of such brilliance and kindness.

Defending Privilege

A Neglected Inheritance

Why study classic novels? An oft-repeated justification has been that reading literary fiction is a means of self-improvement that yields a more empathetic person, one who can relate to those unlike themselves. From its eighteenth-century debut, the literary form that came to be known as the novel was hailed—and sometimes castigated—for bringing into view the lives of the marginalized and lowly or the ordinary and obscure.[1] Arguing for literature as a catalyst for personal growth has led some well-intentioned scholars of eighteenth-century and Romantic-era literature to invest their critical energies disproportionately in the segments of the Western literary legacy that promote democratic values as well as ideas such as the equality of persons. Certainly, humanitarian fiction—including Samuel Richardson's *Pamela* (1740) and *Clarissa* (1747–48)—and "novelistic autobiographies"—such as Olaudah Equiano's *The Interesting Narrative* (1789)—reached a wide audience and altered popular understanding of what types of stories could be told.[2] While a number of critics have questioned this approach by arguing that novel-induced empathy rarely translates into real-world altruistic action,[3] they leave intact the undergirding premise that the lowly and marginalized are the rightful objects of empathy. Consequently, scholars have neglected other novelists' efforts to cultivate empathy to support the privileged.

As the eighteenth century waned, the legal system was a target of complaint not only from those who had never enjoyed its shielding in the first place but also from members of society accustomed to protection by the law and dismayed by the prospect of its loss. Channeling these complaints, and downplaying or neglecting the problems identified by humanitarian fiction, a variety of conservative novels were composed to support the polar opposite ideological objective: safeguarding an establishment whose legal perquisites were threatened, and sometimes felled, as those of lower status made their way up the rungs of the social ladder. Although conservative authors held complex and sometimes self-contradictory political views, they shared interests in defending the preeminence of the civil rights of the privileged and in advocating legal reforms designed to protect traditional social hierarchy.

This study explores the ways in which a series of these novelists, working between 1750 and 1830, struggled to justify traditional social hierarchies despite progressive cultural headwinds. While a number of critics have hailed the rise of the liberal subject as a key factor in expansions of rights for society's lowest-status members, I demonstrate that conservative novelists capitalized on this development to defend the priority long enjoyed by the privileged in the legal system.[4] If "liberalism itself is a fiction of harm" (as Sandra Macpherson puts it),[5] these authors fashioned fictions that used the rhetoric of liberalism to conservative advantage, presenting readers with the plight of impoverished or abandoned descendants of distinguished families brought low by the legal system. They cast the privileged as society's most vulnerable. Although scholars today tend to associate appeals to sympathy with liberatory discourse of the period (such as the writings of protofeminist and black Atlantic authors), conservative authors made their own claims on readers' sympathy, intuitively understanding "this disposition of mankind, to go along with all the passions of the rich and powerful," as Adam Smith stated in *The Theory of Moral Sentiments* (1759).[6] As did their humanitarian counterparts, these authors turned to the novel as a demotic discursive form to amplify their agenda and reach a popular audience beyond like-minded elites.

Humanitarian and conservative novels share at least two prominent elements. First, both categories of novel cast protagonists as victims of undeserved persecution and explicitly express antipathy toward the legal system. Yet humanitarian fictions such as William Godwin's *Caleb Williams* (originally published in 1794) suggest that the institutions that shape social environments—rather than the individual people within them—are terminally damaged, casting aspersions on marriage, government, and the legal system. Conservative novels, by contrast, assert that such failed institutions can be rehabilitated and restored: devoted guardians step in to repair the damage wrought by cruel or absent fathers; kindly aristocrats rescue women from abusive husbands; ethical judges provide counterexamples to self-serving, corrupt magistrates; and laws preserve peace and order when properly enforced.

Second, both types of fiction foreground interactions among different classes that often relate to legal disputes. Some 1790s and early 1800s Jacobin fictions such as Mary Wollstonecraft's *The Wrongs of Woman; or, Maria* (1798) model interclass sympathetic affinity, as when privileged Maria, on entering the asylum to which she has lawfully been relegated by her husband, is befriended by impoverished Jemima. In conservative novels, however, characters of lower status are commended for maintaining their place; these characters show loyalty to their betters and dedicate themselves complacently to physical and emotional toil. Subordinates who violate this norm—duplicitous servants and rebellious slaves—are reviled. Lawyers and judicial authorities who aspire to improve their station and seek to marry into landed families are cast as malevolent usurpers.

In shifting focus from humanitarian fiction to conservative novels, *Defending Privilege* offers new vantage points from which to test various conceptualizations of legal rights and to reevaluate criteria for the legitimacy of legal institutions. While conservatism is associated with the powers that be, or the establishment, writers who held conservative views frequently employed an accusatory rhetoric of unjust deprivation and loss resembling that voiced by their humanitarian counterparts. Scrutiny of literary formulations of conservative ambivalence toward and grievance against the legal system can help us to see how foundational principles of societal obligation took hold in the eighteenth century and became entrenched. This study illuminates a pervasive logic of legal merit, based on victimhood, that has persisted ever since, making strange bedfellows of right and left, down to today's African American reparations-seekers and white "sovereign citizens."[7] As the political scientist Robert Nichols observes: "Since dispossession presupposes prior *possession*, [radical progressive critics'] recourse to it appears conservative and tends to reinforce the very proprietary and commoditized models of social relations that radical critics generally seek to undermine."[8] Because claims involving legal standing and status were (and are) construed as more affecting and morally compelling when victimhood is invoked, it is essential to understand the narrative mechanisms by which particular legal claims were cast as especially poignant and deserving of redress during a foundational historical era.

Legal Agency

The novelists whose works are discussed in this study—Tobias Smollett, Charlotte Turner Smith,[9] anonymous British proslavery authors, and Walter Scott—are not typically grouped together, but they share a track record of attempting to shape mainstream readers' perceptions of who deserved legal agency—a rapidly evolving concept in the late eighteenth and nineteenth centuries.

Although *legal agency* was not a phrase contemporary to eighteenth-century England, it offers critical purchase on social and legal developments with which people throughout the British Empire were reckoning in the second half of the long eighteenth century, which is generally considered to span from the Glorious Revolution of 1688 to the Reform crisis of 1830–32.[10] The term refers broadly to individuals' access to legal fora and processes and the latitude they are granted to take on roles within the legal system that influence the outcome of a case—roles that command a measure of regard and respect. The most obvious meaning of *legal agency* is the ability to act as a party in a lawsuit—to have what is known as standing. Yet the term carries a range of meanings—including the status to assert a claim at all (an option forbidden to wives under coverture and to the enslaved), the ability to raise a claim and obtain a hearing (instead of being treated as a troublemaker or irritant), the ability to act as a witness and provide testimony in court, the ability to retain legal counsel or represent oneself in court, and the ability to have a court take notice of one's efforts as legally valid acts (such as entering into a contract or drawing up a will).[11] Yet, as I contend, legal agency is also manifest in still other, less visible, forms, such as the ability to instruct a lawyer or to obtain and understand legal documents.

While conservative novels depict loss of legal agency, or inability to exercise it, as the regrettable but natural order of things for the lower and middle classes, these same novels aim to persuade readers to regard a privileged person's loss of favored status in the eyes of the law as a catastrophe. Literary representations of legal agency do not simply pertain to an individual human being's access to and autonomy within the legal system's processes and institutions; these depictions also highlight the justice or injustice of the systemic operations of legal institutions and the societal impact of the limits and exclusions imposed by law. As the legal theorist H. L. A. Hart commented: "Justice constitutes one segment of morality primarily concerned not with individual conduct but with the way *classes* of individuals are treated."[12] Legal agency was essential to life that amounted to more than mere subsistence, and it was widely perceived as something that could be won or lost: the spoils of a zero-sum competition. Members of the higher echelons of society carefully monitored indications of impending modifications to their relative allotment of legal agency—an allotment that was increasingly subject to change and diminution. For those who were privileged but downwardly mobile, at stake was nothing less than the power to escape or avoid social ruin.

A Broader View of the Legal Landscape

For decades, critics working in eighteenth- and nineteenth-century studies have devoted considerable attention to the legal, and particularly the penal, systems of the era. A formative influence, of course, has been Foucault's *Surveiller et punir: Naissance de la prison* (1975).[13] It precipitated a concentration in scholarship of the period on criminals and criminality. A notable emphasis within this vein of scholarship has been the figure of the notorious criminal defendant;[14] certainly, early eighteenth-century authors such as Daniel Defoe and John Gay were beguiled by the glamour of the charismatic, larger-than-life criminal icon. Other scholars, such as Jonathan Grossman, Alexander Welsh, and Jan-Melissa Schramm, have examined the trial episodes that pervade the eighteenth-century and Romantic-era literary canon.[15] Still others, including John Bender and John Bugg, have productively delved into the implications of prison tropes and episodes that recur in literature of the period.[16]

Although studies of criminality in fiction have been crucial to our understanding of the era, their predominance in scholarship of the last several decades has distorted twentieth- and twenty-first-century impressions of the legal landscape at the dawn of the modern era of law in the West. Noncriminal contexts have received more thoroughgoing attention in literary and historical scholarship in other periods and fields. While I do engage with some lesser-known aspects of criminal law, such as the long-running battle over slave testimony, I focus extensively on civil legal disputes in order to engage with the kinds of legal matters that had significant potential to impact the ability of the privileged to safeguard their property rights and retain their position in society, including bankruptcy, defamation, naturalization, government seizure of private estates, contestations of wills, and suspensions of *habeas corpus*. Consequently, I consider a wider array of legal players beyond criminal defendants, including plaintiffs, witnesses, and foreign detainees, as well as the legal professionals and authorities with whom they interacted, including lawyers and judges.

Although sometimes derided in its day as mere entertainment, popular literature such as the novel supplements the historical record. Court records and legal treatises do not record certain pivotal but private interactions, such as consultations between lawyers and indigent clients. To a greater degree than other literary forms, novels render visible legal communication that would otherwise remain invisible to the general public and demonstrate how such encounters can bolster or diminish a person's sense of belonging in the legal sphere. As legal historians have shown, even as lawyers took significantly more prominent roles in criminal trials near the end of the long eighteenth century, other legal vistas were extended in realms far afield from the public spectacle of criminal trials—for example, the behind-the-scenes business of conveyancing, a branch of law that particularly interested wealthy and aristocratic clients.[17]

Because the privileged were willing to use any means necessary to retain their power, they exerted their influence wherever they could. Thus, I emphasize that eighteenth-century and Romantic-era notions of legal agency took shape in a wide array of institutional and informal or private spaces. As Joseph Slaughter has noted, the locations in which legal agency can be exercised extend well beyond the formal settings of legal institutions.[18] The novels I discuss venture into judges' chambers in rural England, lawyers' offices in urban Scotland, and legislative debates in the West Indies. When legal institutions fail them, the powerful resort to entirely extralegal settings—where their influence remains intact—to challenge or renegotiate undesirable legal outcomes: private asylums, rural cottages, smuggler's outposts, and hidden repositories in plantation mansions.

The Arc of the Legal Universe: Bending toward Justice?

Looking back from the perspective of the twenty-first century, it may seem inevitable that the privileged would be forced to relinquish some of the favor they enjoyed in the legal system and that marginalized human beings such as women, the enslaved, non-Christians, the poor, and other groups would accumulate regular victories in their attempts to gain legal agency. Yet this impression of linear progression from the early modern era toward a telos of universal enfranchisement is the faulty product of retrospect. Authors working in the eighteenth and early nineteenth century followed in the wake of a period—the Restoration era and the early decades of the eighteenth century—in which major setbacks in regard to legal access and affordability had been dealt to the poor and marginalized. An early modern interval during which underclass legal agency flourished (to a relative extent) was followed by periods in which these gains gradually receded or were abruptly quashed. Given this oscillation, the fate of the distribution of legal agency would have seemed to hang in the balance: conservative authors would have had the impression that by detailing for a popular audience the legal misfortunes of the advantaged, they really could sway public sympathies and alter the course of events.

During the early modern period, the English poor had benefited greatly from access to the Court of Requests, to which they brought many cases. Founded in 1425, and known in the 1500s as the Court of Poor Man's Causes, this was a court of equity, distinct from the common law court system. Judges there ruled based on broad definitions of fairness and used discretion rather than rigidly adhering to the letter of the common law alone. The court earned a reputation for processing cases quickly and with minimal fees. As indicated by its sobriquet, it was supposed to be reserved for the poor and servants of the king: its rules stipulated "That all gentlemen which bring complaintes to the King's Grace [the Court of Requests] . . . or all such other persons that have goods and chattells . . . be remytted to the Common law, and in default of remedy there, to chancerie, considering their suits to be greatly to the hinderaunce of poor men's causes."[19] In addition, those who brought cases were supposed to take an oath that the worth of their land and goods did not exceed a certain given value. Despite these measures, the wealthy made their way into the court in growing numbers, raising the ire of the common law courts that competed with the Court of Requests for business. Those courts, alarmed by what they regarded as usurpation of their jurisdiction, took measures that culminated in the lapse of the Court of Requests during the English Civil War, only a few decades before the beginning of the long eighteenth century. In other words, privileged men disingenuously presenting themselves as in need of the aid of the Court of Requests had sped the demise of a legal institution designed to assist the poor. In subsequent years, justice would be increasingly out of reach for those who lacked the financial means to fund lengthy legal battles that resulted from desultory, inefficient procedures and years-long backlogs of court cases. The demise of the Court of Requests was an instance of a larger trend: across a number of jurisdictions, the rate of civil litigation plummeted.[20]

The next several decades marked a surge in expenses related to civil litigation: Christopher W. Brooks contends that "of all juridical factors so far connected with the drop in the number of civil plaints, increases in court fees and other associated costs of legal services (lawyers' charges) appear to be the most striking."[21] From the late seventeenth century through the mid-eighteenth century, the average costs associated with a lawsuit doubled or tripled, deterring not only the poor but also some of the less exalted echelons of the powerful—the provincial gentry—from litigation.[22] Criminal law saw the opposite trend: in the first half of the century, victims had to fund prosecutions of their cases out of their own pockets, but in the 1750s, statutes introduced state funding for poor people who initiated felony criminal prosecutions, if the prosecution was successful; in 1778, another statute expanded the provision of funding to all such prosecutions, regardless of outcome.[23] Furthermore, zealous law enforcement by John Fielding's protopolice force, the Bow Street Runners, induced a spike in criminal prosecutions in the 1770s.[24] Nevertheless, lower criminal prosecution costs were mitigated by other factors: for one, considerable time was necessary to bring a case, time that poor working people could not easily spare. Data recorded from cases at the Old Bailey show that 10.3 percent of plaintiffs between 1690 and 1800 were in low-status occupations, but working-class or lower-middle-class people constituted the "vast majority" of defendants.[25] Elite defendants hardly ever appeared at the popular venue.[26]

To be sure, London residents could initiate both civil and criminal cases to the summary courts, where fees were low.[27] But even in those courts, the poor did not make up the majority of the constituency: only 17–20 percent of litigants were poor, although "poverty vulnerable" trades were well represented.[28] Most of the poor who sought relief at these courts were the working poor, including servants attempting to recover unpaid wages from employers.[29] In these courts, too, employers had the advantage.

In addition, women's participation in certain sectors of the legal system had declined from an early modern pinnacle: historians have claimed that "one of the central puzzles for students of gender and crime should be the vanishing female participation in the criminal process."[30] A peculiar inverse relationship between marginalized people's visibility in fiction and their real-life legal agency becomes apparent: although marginalized people retreated from the courts as the eighteenth century began,[31] their presence in the legal arena was increasingly depicted in the emerging literary form of the novel.

Yet to highlight only the aforementioned developments is to tell a selective story, one that gives the impression that privileged men of the aristocracy or gentry had little reason to fear that their societal monopoly on legal agency would be imperiled. Some historians have recently argued that in the decades following the Restoration, married women increasingly bypassed or evaded in practice the strictures of coverture regarding credit or property ownership; others have pointed to records indicating that wives were well represented in some courts as sole or coplaintiffs.

Efforts to increase access to the legal system for other marginalized groups beyond women and the poor were resisted by the powerful over the course of the long eighteenth century. Among a number of relevant episodes, two in particular indicate the magnitude of the pushback of the privileged against efforts to expand legal agency. The Yorke-Talbot slavery opinion of 1729 was perceived by slaveholders as upholding the legality of slavery on English soil. And upon receiving news that Parliament had passed the Jewish Nationalization Act of 1753, which granted affluent Jewish émigrés the right to own property, riots and anti-Semitic parodies abounded, and the act was repealed; subsequent bids for Jewish emancipation continued to fail throughout the nineteenth century.

Toward the end of the century, however, there were indications that the tide was beginning to turn once again, betokening better prospects for the marginalized. The 1772 Somerset case delivered a watershed blow against the legality of slavery. The French Revolution notoriously brought to the fore the risks of ignoring the grievances held by those in the lower ranks of society. In 1795, the Poor Removal Act mandated that indigent people could not be forcibly removed from a parish unless they had applied for financial relief.

In the context of such upheaval—with some developments favoring the marginalized, others favoring the privileged—writers from the 1750s onward worked through a period of decades when it was becoming clear that these were not minor fluctuations; the relative allocation of legal agency was poised either to undergo a paradigm shift or revert to the status quo.

The Novel: Conduit of Democratic Ideals or Redoubt of the Privileged?

The standard history of the eighteenth-century novel casts it as a dismantler of traditional hierarchies and associates it with the emergence of the liberal subject.[32] As stated previously, this understanding of the novel's legal and political reach has encompassed the emerging discourse of human rights: a number of critical studies posit the novel's implicit endorsement of human dignity even in the absence of actual legal agency.[33] By bringing to light the interiority of its subjects, so the logic goes, the novel as a literary form created pressure for institutions to validate this worth through the conferral of legal roles and access hitherto withheld.[34]

Yet by noticing which best-selling or widely reviewed novels are omitted or excluded from these valuable and pervasively influential histories, we can begin to discern a parallel sequence to the familiar trajectory of the development of the novel: an array of antidemocratic texts that deploy legal agency not for reformist purposes but rather for reactionary ones. Each author included in this study complicates the standard critical narrative of the valorization of the liberal subject—that "abstract, universal legal subject, formally equal to all others"[35]—whose legal agency was to be respected and guarded. In these novels, the majority of violations of legal rights or deprivations of legal agency are inflicted on wealthy or privileged characters. As did the protagonists of humanitarian fictions, these characters seek to elude, transcend, or counteract the operations of legal authorities. Whereas humanitarian fictions typically sought not to diminish the scope of the law so much as to alter its nature so that all human beings would have the prospect of impartial justice, no matter their status, some conservative fictions sought to decrease this scope, positing that human beings of all stations—including the poor and the enslaved—generally benefited from minimal interference from the law. Other conservative fictions implied—and, at times, openly stated—that the powerful, in particular, should have more latitude to conduct their affairs without interference by the law.

In reading against the grain of models of novelistic liberalism, I work alongside others who have questioned the prevailing framework. Daniel Stout sees Romantic and Victorian novels as sites for "confront[ing] the philosophical difficulty (and maybe the impossibility) of thinking about individual accountability in a collective world."[36] Mark Schoenfeld notes that while Romantic-era literary representations of justice played an essential role in "underpinning the individual as the bearer of rights and property," they also "foreclosed more radical transformations and possibilities."[37] While Schoenfeld attributes this limitation to writers' adherence to formal realism and the standard of the "rational man," the conservative novelists I survey were driven by personal and political objectives incompatible with radical visions of broad-based social reconfiguration that would produce a more equitable future for all. Moreover, it is useful to apply to the history of the novel Peter de Bolla's observation that "rights" remained conceptually vague throughout the eighteenth century.[38] The language of rights was thus liable to be seized upon not only by humanitarian authors but also by conservative ones. Other critics dismiss claims of eighteenth-century origins for human rights: Samuel Moyn argues that human rights emerged as a "strikingly distinct" movement only in the 1970s.[39] These two latter views, however, place significant emphasis on the chronology of the emergence and frequency of specific terms—that is, the "when." While terminology and word frequency are important evidence, this study also considers episodes in which the idea of rights was implicitly evident if not explicitly invoked.

Throughout this study, I focus on novels that belong to or incorporate sub-genres that today are widely ignored or have conventionally been read as hackneyed and derivative (the Gothic novel); obsolescent (the epistolary novel); or politically reactionary and upholding classist, sexist, or racist views now widely rejected (the chivalric romance, the proslavery novel). Until recently, British proslavery novels were largely shunned by academics—perhaps owing to concerns about legitimizing what is today deemed noxious ideology, and giving rise to a literary variation of the "Streisand effect."[40] In other cases, conventional classification of authors according to gender or chronology limits our ability to see them in terms of other literary genealogies or networks: Charlotte Smith tends to be distanced from histories of the novel and relegated to the female-author ghetto of Gothic romance. Walter Scott is hailed as a pivotal influence in some major scholarly accounts of the development of the novel, but he is more often bracketed from the main line of descent (although recognized as a key developer of the historical novel genre), when he is not disparaged or omitted altogether.[41]

I turn to these currently neglected or taboo modes and subgenres because they were taken up by authors to stage conservative views within the form of the novel. It is important not to overlook or attempt to palliate their some-times counterintuitive or even offensive propagandistic constructions of what constitutes oppression and victimhood under the law. Conservative novels are validations of privilege cast in accessible demotic language. Fusing an old-fashioned mode (the romance) with a new form (the novel) enabled some conservative authors to conceal their propagandistic agenda in plain sight, although others (the proslavery novelists) were more blatant in communicating their political motives. The inherent conservatism of the romance has led today's readers to underestimate the full extent of the critique offered by the novels under discussion. Had the championing of the socially advantaged been too explicit, it could have alienated ordinary readers. Yet it did not, because these novels incorporate older subgenres—such as the romance, in which aristocratic heroes were standard—or plot trajectories—such as the belated discovery of aristocratic heritage—that were so timeworn that they did not ring alarm bells of class warfare. The occasional inclusion of passages in which protagonists express compassion for the poor, or where narrators highlight the deficiencies of legal institutions that impeded justice for both the marginalized and the privileged, further occluded the extent to which the novels favor haves over have-nots. These works advocate for perpetuation of, or return to, social hierarchy and brook no question of the scale of redistribution that would have been necessary to alleviate poverty on a systemic level.

The authors under examination represent an especially legally attuned subcategory within a broader reactionary frame: each author in this study was significantly involved in the law and believed that their privilege was degraded through lengthy disputes. Given their lived experience, it is understandable that these authors cast elite members of society as particularly vulnerable to miscarriages of justice. Although some of the authors enjoyed significant proceeds from their literary endeavors, their legal ordeals placed them at high risk of downward mobility. The best-selling authors Tobias Smollett and Charlotte Smith both wrote in prison. Smollett was humiliated during prosecution for his violent assault on an impoverished writer whom he had financially supported. Estranged from her profligate, abusive husband, Smith endured a futile thirty-year Chancery battle to gain access to money guaranteed to her family and elevate them to the genteel lifestyle of her childhood. Walter Scott trained as a professional advocate before turning to literature and worked himself to death to stave off bankruptcy proceedings. Cynric R. Williams and the anonymous British proslavery authors reviled plantation "attorneys" (a term that in the British West Indies referred ambiguously either to privileged legal professionals or to low-born estate managers)[42] for betraying—through misappropriation or poor management—the financial interests of prominent families who entrusted plantations to their care.

Additional connections among these authors are evidenced through their paratextual and allusive nods to one another's work, in particular with regard to their shared interest in the role of law in maintaining or dismantling power structures. Scott opens his edition of Smollett's work by telling how Smollett's grandfather, a consistorial judge and member of Scottish Parliament, "helped dissolve that representative body for ever, being one of the commissioners who framed the union with England."[43] Scott looked to Smith's novelistic accounts of aristocratic families brought low as a template for his own fiction.[44] In the proslavery novels, when unscrupulous administrators seize control of the plantations they manage for remote English owners, they resemble the ambitious Irish underlings who appropriate the estates of absentee Anglo-Irish landlords in the "national tales" of Maria Edgeworth, saluted by Scott as a key influence on his writing.[45]

The firsthand understanding of the law displayed by these authors lent a verisimilitude to their novels. By using an accessible literary form—the novel—to portray legal conflicts, the authors gave readers the impression of an access portal into legal systems that were bewildering and opaque in their complexity. The legal landscape of the British Empire consisted of a complex array of systems. In England, the court system was divided according to various binaries, including urban/rural; criminal law/civil law; year-round/periodic; and fixed/itinerant. There were common law courts, courts of equity, and ecclesiastical, maritime, and military courts. Further complicating matters, the jurisdictions of courts frequently overlapped, and plaintiffs could sometimes choose their venue. Similar complexity held true for legal institutions elsewhere in the empire: from 1661 to the late eighteenth century, the number of court systems in Jamaica doubled from five to ten.[46] Post-union Scotland also had its own separate legal system, comprising five major courts, in addition to so-called sheriffdoms.[47]

Novels provided the illusion of clarifying the operations of this legal archipelago. In vilifying the law for the purpose of defending the privileged, post-1750 conservative novelists also pointed up the inscrutability of legal discourse, an object of vitriol for the high and low alike. Reviving antipathies that can be traced back through Elizabethan England to Imperial Rome, earlier generations of eighteenth-century writers (including the Scriblerians) had criticized scholars of law as "*Quacks* and *Empyricks*" who rendered legal discourse impenetrable.[48] There was no comprehensive and methodical account of English common law until William Blackstone undertook the formidable task of rationalizing it, writing it down in systematic fashion. The English historian Edward Gibbon lauded Blackstone's foundational attempt to clarify English law in his *Commentaries on the Laws of England* (1765–70) for precisely that reason: "Blackstone's *Commentaries* may be considered as a natural system of the English jurisprudence digested into a natural method and cleared of the pedantry, the obscurity, and superfluities, which rendered it the unknown horror of all men of taste."[49]

A number of significant critical studies of legal themes in eighteenth-century and Romantic literature have privileged the influence on the novel of erudite texts (such as legal or philosophical treatises by the likes of Kant and Locke). By "erudite" I mean texts that were not intelligible to people who had not received a classical education, even if general impressions of their major ideas spread to popular audiences throughout Great Britain and Europe. Yet this focus ignores how some authors sympathetic to the elite took an opposite intertextual orientation, folding in allusions to and quotations from nonexpert discourse more familiar and appealing to popular audiences, such as legal dictionaries marketed to laypeople, popular compendia of fictional accounts of legal cases, or epistolary correspondence. Wai Chee Dimock has traced a history of "two languages of justice, law and philosophy."[50] In contrast, I argue that the two primary languages of justice are the expert and the demotic. The novel is of course known for its heteroglossic mélange of languages— that is, its mingling of high and low dialects and terminology from various walks of life—and it is especially associated with registering the speech of ordinary people. It can thus be difficult to distinguish conservative novels from humanitarian novels based on register of language alone because conservative novels are not composed in the haughty, formal, inaccessible register of legal treatises from the period—and this is a feature, not a bug, for the purposes of the conservative novel's mission. Conservative and humanitarian novels alike castigate the opaque language of law and the corruption and arrogance of legal professionals. In my reading, the conservative novel, with its demotic articulation of challenging legal concepts, operated as a Trojan horse: conservative novels were presented to readers as mere entertainment but in fact harbored nostalgic fantasies of a continuation of rigid social hierarchy. Middle-class readers were pressed into the position of hoping that a privileged scion would regain his family's estate or feeling indignation on behalf of an aristocrat compelled to face plaintiffs in court instead of settling matters through combat.

The Paradox of Admonitory Depiction

Despite their efforts to preserve the status quo, some of the most provocative— and, at times, unintentionally forward-thinking—visions of the expansion of legal agency can be found in the unlikely vehicle of the conservative novel. Some conservative novels unwittingly aided certain humanitarian causes, albeit in an incrementalist manner: in portraying legal institutions as mishandling cases involving the privileged, the novels of Smollett and Smith supported the carving out of exceptions that fortified and expanded the rights of certain groups—such as women of the gentry, or wealthy Jewish immigrants—whose marginality in some aspects was tempered by privilege in others. More audaciously, the works of Scott and the proslavery novelists reveal that in order to disparage marginalized figures as unsuited for key roles—impoverished folk as legal clients, animals as plaintiffs, slaves as witnesses—conservative novelists needed to entertain the prospect of such eventualities in the first place. In novels prior to 1750, by comparison, the primary legal role allocated to underclass characters had typically been that of a defendant contesting criminal charges. In another point of contrast, depictions of animals in legal roles in late medieval texts are typically composed as allegorical. Scottish poet Robert Henryson's *Morall Fabillis* (Moral Fables, c. 1480s) features a sheep that loses a lawsuit to a dog, owing to a corrupt ruling by a wolf judge, and must submit to being shorn; the sheep is explicitly identified as a symbol of poor commoners: "This selie scheip may present the figure / Of pure commounis."[51] Centuries later, in the novel *Redgauntlet*, by contrast, a farmer's guest's brief but potent suggestion—that livestock might object to being sentenced to bodily harm—is at once playful and reflective of contemporaneous debates over animal rights. In the course of implementing their literary strategy intended to safeguard privilege, conservative novelists inadvertently envisioned a more radical legal ecosystem than even their most progressive contemporaries could conceive.

The Legacy of the Conservative Novel

This study unites discourses that are typically isolated in distinct subfields: discussions of the legal agency of the enslaved might be addressed primarily in African American studies, while analysis of women's legal struggles is too often limited to gender studies. A continuing theme in scholarship on present-day judicial matters is the consideration of justice in terms of intersectionality or the interplay of socially conferred attributes such as status and gender. In conservative novels of centuries past, I see a prototypical version of an additive approach to identity: just as intersectional theorists see qualities such as indigeneity and poverty compounding each other to exacerbate an individual's exposure to the regulatory force of law, eighteenth-century and Romantic-era conservative novelists figured certain traits associated with disadvantage—such as female gender and downward mobility—as attributes that offset advantage (such as noble heritage or wealthy connections). Privileged protagonists could thus be cast credibly as dispossessed victims.

The invocation of ostensible prior loss or deprivation as a basis for legal redress is manifest today not only in attempts from the left to protect affirmative action and humanitarian asylum but also in calls from the right to reform "predatory" tax assessment[52] and preempt efforts to "penetrate our vulnerable immigration system."[53] Some conservative commentators impugn their right-wing peers' grievance-based rhetoric as an "unmanly" deviation from what they characterize as Ronald Reagan's ethos of empowerment; they repudiate it as a lamentable "mimicking of the [left's] perpetual victimhood" and a tendency developed only in the twenty-first century.[54] Yet recourse to such logic by the right is, in fact, deeply rooted. While today this rhetoric takes newer discursive configurations—ranging from law review articles to the digital ephemera of social media—it can be traced back to the novel's heyday centuries earlier.

To understand how aggrieved victimhood became a primary index of legal merit in the popular imaginary of the West, we need a different history of the novel. While some humanitarian authors wrote fiction for mainstream readers in attempts to generate sympathy for the lowly, conservative authors exploited the novel as a literary vehicle to foster popular favor for special treatment for those to whom most of society's rewards already flowed. This study introduces into the record literary exhibits—drawn from the eighteenth century through the Romantic era—demonstrating that the novel both reflected and attempted to influence the balance of legal power, even as this balance was unsettled by calls for enfranchisement and the expansion of civil rights. Rejecting a simplistic binary between "oppressor" and "oppressed," this study tracks the dynamic movement of authorial personae and characters zipping back and forth across a spectrum that stretches between these poles. Yet this study also reveals the surprising tendency of conservative authors to represent the marginalized as asserting themselves in an entirely new set of legal roles—albeit from an alarmist perspective. We need to see what conservative novels can show us, then and now, about elite anxieties regarding the law in an empire undergoing inexorable demographic change. We need to understand, too, how the terrifying prospect of social usurpation by hostile subordinates compelled elites to join in reshaping the very same literary and legal institutions to whose preservation they were avowedly devoted.

Outline of the Chapters

Chapter 1, "Bad Citizens and Insolent Foreigners: Tobias Smollett's Elite Outsiders and the Suspension of Legal Agency," examines Smollett's treatment of suspensions of legal agency inflicted on privileged outsiders by lower-status legal authorities and other opponents in hostile jurisdictions. Central to the chapter are Smollett's midcareer works composed during his own legal battles: *The Adventures of Ferdinand Count Fathom* (1753); *The Reprisal: or, The Tars of Old England* (1756); and *The Life and Adventures of Sir Launcelot Greaves* (serialized in the *British Magazine; or, Monthly Repository for Gentlemen and Ladies* in 1760–62 and published in two volumes in 1762). Anticipating later developments in international law, Smollett envisioned a model of community that upheld, rather than stymied, the autonomous movement of cosmopolitan elites across local and international jurisdictions.

Chapter 2, "Covert Critique: Genteel Victimhood in Charlotte Smith's Fictions of Dispossession," explores Smith's lengthy sagas of legal vindication for privileged families who manage to retrieve estates of which they have been defrauded: *Emmeline* (1788), *The Old Manor House* (1793), and *Marchmont* (1796). Critics tend to group Smith with other female authors of formula-driven Gothic novels.[55] I identify her, instead, as a key adapter of the French and German *pitaval*, an immensely popular genre of compendia of fiction-alized legal cases in which an array of traditionally marginalized litigants—including women, the enslaved, and orphans—gain justice through the courts. One of Smith's first published works was an English translation of several of these tales. She converted the ideology of the pitavals from progressive to re-actionary by selectively translating tales of female aristocrats or members of the gentry. Carving out exceptional legal status for privileged women, her novels redirect attention from elite patriarchs' mismanagement of financial or legal affairs to the exacerbation of these afflictions by dysfunctional legal institutions and the avaricious social climbers who have supposedly achieved plebeian capture of the legal profession.

Chapter 3, "Letters of the Law: Ambivalent Advocacy and Speaking for the Voiceless in Walter Scott's *Redgauntlet*," treats Walter Scott's 1824 epistolary novel as a reflection on the continuum between advocacy and authoritarian control of those who cannot speak for themselves. Whereas the previous chapters survey elite antipathy to the law from outside the legal profession, this chapter addresses the perspective of the educated men working within it, who see a conflict between the safeguarding of their own privilege and the upholding of their professional responsibilities as advocates for the lowly. Scott's decision to revisit the epistolary mode—by then out of favor with novelists—complemented his shift of focus to intimate communicative mo-ments between lawyers and those whom they represent and away from the spectacular trial scenes that were centerpieces of other legally oriented nov-els of the Romantic era (and, later, the Victorian period).

Chapter 4, "Masters of Passion and Tongue: White Eyewitnesses and Fear of Black Testimony in the Proslavery Novel," demonstrates the attempts of early nineteenth-century British proslavery authors to intervene on behalf of privileged white plantation owners in West Indian legislative debates over whether enslaved blacks should be allowed to serve as witnesses against whites. Although slave narratives and antislavery literature from the mid-nineteenth-century United States have received copious academic and popu-lar attention, early British proslavery fiction—which tended to be published anonymously—has been largely ignored. Scrutiny of this underexamined body of literature casts further doubt on two long-held assumptions: first, that portrayals of displays of pitiable emotions such as sadness and distress are the optimal means of humanizing those unprotected by the law and, second, that humanization necessarily strengthens the case for conferral of legal agency.

The epilogue, "Abiding the Law," considers how twentieth- and twenty-first-century British and American writers and political leaders have styled two competing mythic visions of an idyllic eighteenth-century legal land-scape, one progressive and one reactionary. The reactionary version was de-signed to insinuate a rationale for valuing nationalism and property rights over human rights. It distinguishes patriotic, "law-abiding" property owners as uniquely deserving of legal agency and the law's protection. In considering politicians' speeches, interviews, and comments to the press, I demonstrate that these writers and leaders misrepresent the eighteenth-century literary heritage, misconstrue the era's groundbreaking legal developments, and out-right invent historical bases for changing the law. They scour the eighteenth-century legacy to generate pretexts for supporting authoritarianism.

PART I

DOWNWARD MOBILITY AND
THE SAFETY NET OF THE LAW

CHAPTER ONE

Bad Citizens and Insolent Foreigners

Tobias Smollett's Elite Outsiders and the
Suspension of Legal Agency

The first pages of Tobias Smollett's *The Life and Adventures of Sir Launcelot Greaves* (1760–62) appear to defy the centuries-long literary tradition of castigating a predatory legal profession. Readers are instead presented with a heartwarming portrait of a crusader for the downtrodden. As an odd assortment of strangers takes refuge from inclement weather at a rural English inn, the narrator zooms in for a close-up of a lawyer, Tom Clarke, who is introduced as "a young fellow whose goodness of heart even the exercise of his profession had not been able to corrupt."[1] He is, readers are informed, committed to serving the vulnerable: "Before strangers he never owned himself an attorney, without blushing, though he had no reason to blush for his own practice; for he constantly refused to engage in the cause of any client whose character was equivocal, and was never known to act with such industry as when concerned for the widow and the orphan, or any other object that sued *in forma pauperis*" (3–4).[2] Clarke, in other words, facilitates legal legerdemain: he transforms helpless "objects" into litigants who can assert their rights in a court of law.

Yet by foregrounding Clarke's rigid binary—between deserving seekers of justice and "equivocal" characters—the novel is shadowed from the beginning by the implication that equal access to the law is not among the primary values of even its most conscientious guardian of justice. The term *equivocal* means "doubtful in character or reputation," but it also connotes a quality that is not necessarily pejorative: that of being "ambiguous" and "open to interpretation." The novel thus primes readers to consider Clarke the narrative's ethical reference point, but a problem arises: as additional characters are introduced, it turns out that most of them are seen by others, at least initially, as similarly equivocal; until they prove themselves worthy, they are abandoned by law to fates including wrongful detainment or abuse by others, without recourse. Smollett examines questions that in his time (and for decades to come) catalyzed vehement debates in Parliament and gave rise to nationalist fervor: Are some people—by dint of factors including social position, gender, prior crimes, or place of birth—less deserving of access to justice? How can valid bids for legal remedies be differentiated from meretricious ones?

This theme—the challenge of distinguishing those who deserve legal representation and due process from those who do not—unites the apparently disparate literary experiments that Smollett undertook during the period after he had achieved international fame as one of the century's best-selling authors. He had an abiding interest in the ways people choose to define membership in a polity or society—a problem more recently explored by Seyla Benhabib, Marianne Noble, and Christopher Warren.[3] If, as Benhabib states, the "methodological fiction of a 'unitary community'" is constructed to rationalize divisions between insiders and outsiders, Smollett's works show just how tenuous and pieced-together these fictions are.[4] Smollett does not approach the problem of exclusion from legal protection from the angle of humanitarian literature—that of promoting the "right to have rights" of those deemed abject and socially expendable owing to poverty or low status.[5] He has in mind an entirely different constituency: privileged nonlocals scooped up and detained by authorities indifferent to actual innocence or exculpatory factors and hostile to lofty status.

In this chapter, I demonstrate that Smollett celebrates a flexibility of affinity that overrides both rigidity of jurisdiction and default parochialism to reinforce local connections. He suggests that true justice thrives when the community of the deserving is continually subject to ad hoc redelineation of its boundaries to incorporate individuals who have been excluded and denied legal access. Smollett's method of refashioning community appears to promote evenhanded appraisal while, in fact, bolstering veneration of privilege. I contend that the apparently heartwarming notion of reconfigurable "community" celebrated by Smollett serves as the pretext for, rather than a bulwark against, legally sanctioned violence and the nightmarish suspension or denial of civil rights. Ultimately, this model of justice can endanger the elite as well.

Smollett's triptych of midcareer work overlaps with what some critics have labeled his "journalistic" period.[6] In the span of a decade, he published three literary works that take up the question of what manner of legal agency should be afforded to a privileged foreigner. *The Adventures of Ferdinand Count Fathom* (1753), a widely panned novel, describes a sociopathic grifter's transcontinental campaign of fraud and seduction. *The Reprisal: or, The Tars of Old England* (1757) is an all-but-forgotten two-act comedy of naval rescue and "the law of nations." *The Life and Adventures of Sir Launcelot Greaves* is his least popular novel; it chronicles an aristocrat's attempt to dispense justice throughout the land and is dismissed by some critics as a lackluster imitation of *Don Quixote*. The three vary widely in setting and characterization, but all failed to inspire the lasting affection of Smollett's readers. Relative to *The Adventures of Roderick Random* (1748) and *The Expedition of Humphry Clinker* (1771), these works are neglected by scholars,[7] who generally view this period as the nadir of Smollett's literary career, culminating in failure in the marketplace and humiliation in the courtroom.[8] The modest share of scholarship with more regard for Smollett's midcareer work has focused on themes such as literary mode (satire, the picaresque)[9] or aspects of identity (nationality, gender).[10]

Yet these works deserve more critical attention; they offer an unusual and forceful perspective on the problem of determining who deserves legal agency. In Smollett's era, the size of the category of those deemed outsiders was rapidly expanding, as unprecedented social mobility in England meant that people were moving from place to place at historically atypical rates.[11] Smollett explores the juridical limbo in which travelers, noncitizens, and other outsiders become marooned on entering alien jurisdictions. Abruptly and often arbitrarily inflicted, suspensions of legal agency for outsiders are buttressed by a conception of jurisdiction as subject to continual renegotiation ("a process of legal order rather than a stable fact," as Bradin Cormack terms it).[12] Whenever Clarke and his privileged friends—Sir Launcelot Greaves and Captain Crowe—venture beyond their village, they spend much of their time confronting obstacles that in humanitarian fictions more typically befall "equivocal" figures: arrest without warrant, wrongful imprisonment, suspension of *habeas corpus*, and corrupt judges.[13]

It is no coincidence that Smollett explores these high-stakes concerns in work between 1753 and 1762; this was a time of divisive efforts within Britain to expand the range of civil rights. For T. H. Marshall, the influential British sociologist who identified the eighteenth century as "the formative period of civil rights," the term *civil rights* denotes "the rights necessary for individual freedom: liberty of the person, freedom of speech, thought, and faith, the right to own property and to conclude valid contracts, and the right to justice."[14] Of these, Marshall places particular emphasis on the right to justice: "The last is of a different order from the others, because it is the right to defend and assert all one's rights on terms of equality with others and by due process of law."[15] Smollett considers the problem of legal agency in the context of mobility not from the perspective of the vagrant or the refugee but, instead, from that of privileged travelers or high-born prisoners aghast at the revocation of their liberty.

Terms of Association: *Community* versus *Connexion*

Smollett repeatedly invokes "community" as a touchstone for determining who deserves protection under the law in his nonfiction *Continuation of the Complete History of England* (1760–65),[16] where he comments on legislative and legal controversies ranging from the Jewish Naturalization Act of 1753, to bankruptcy reform petitions of 1757–58, to the Habeas Corpus Act of 1758. According to the political theory of the time, a well-bounded community is necessary to establish grounds for enforcing the social contract, which in turn is the foundation of a stable society.[17] As Amy Buzby has argued, "Lockean liberalism . . . rationalizes exclusion, despite its emancipatory themes and outcomes."[18] The price of security is the sacrifice of the outsider. Although *community* had from the 1600s denoted "the body of people having common or equal rights or rank, as distinguished from the privileged classes; the commons" (*OED*), this definition dwindled in the eighteenth century. Smollett, along with others, rebooted *community* to denote instead a discrete group identified according to status. The newly prevailing usage, first recorded in 1713, corresponds to "a group of people distinguished by shared circumstances of nationality, race, religion, sexuality, etc.; *esp.* such a group living within a larger society from which it is distinct" (*OED*). As revived and articulated by Smollett, the term *community* contrasts with *connexion*, which was preferred by followers of his ideological adversary, the Methodist theologian John Wesley (hailed as "the single most influential Protestant leader of the English-speaking world since the Reformation").[19]

By introducing "connexion" as a new type of social relationship that prioritized shared faith as opposed to nationality, status, or class, the Methodists were in the 1740s countering "the terminology of 'strangers' widely used by contemporaries" to describe the mobile poor who traveled from parish to parish seeking relief from the revised Settlement Act.[20] David Feldman suggests that Methodists "were attracted to the needs of the mobile poor [due], perhaps, [to] their own disregard for parish boundaries."[21] In his sermons, Wesley conceived of adherents to his denomination as a transnational network that transcended all manner of state borders: "Methodists are one people in all the

world," he wrote.[22] Wesley would have approved of Ernest Gellner's suggestion, as paraphrased by Benedict Anderson, that "'true' communities exist
which can be advantageously juxtaposed to nations."[23] Smollett, by contrast,
would have sided with Anderson's rebuttal: "Communities are to be distinguished, not by their falsity/genuineness, but by the style in which they are
imagined."[24] Unlike Wesley, Smollett treated community as inherently exclu-
sionary but open to reconfiguration when strangers demonstrate the manners and sophistication of the elite. As Ratchcali explains in *Ferdinand Count
Fathom*: "Every stranger . . . provided he can talk sensibly, and preserve the
deportment of a sober gentleman . . . will be the more remarkably pleasing, as
it will agreeably disappoint the expectation of the person who had entertained
notions to his prejudice. When a foreigner has once crossed this bar, which
perpetually occurs, he sails without further difficulty into the harbour of . . .
good will. . . . While [a man] despises a people in the lump, an individual of
that very community, may be one of his chief favourites."[25] Although Ratchcali
refers here specifically to the English reception of foreigners, this possibility
of reconfiguration applies for nonlocals across Smollett's novels, including
English elites in foreign custody. At the same time, the case-by-case manner
of granting safe "harbour" ensures that no systemic overhaul takes place.

As invoked by Smollett, community differs considerably not only from
connexion but also from subsequent models of social belonging. His contemporary Adam Smith disparaged as primitive kinship-based neighbor-
hoods, in which extended family banded together for mutual security—what
Ferdinand Tönnies termed *Gemeinschaft* in the late nineteenth century.[26]
Smith applauded dissolution of these protective associations and societal
gravitations toward the rule of law: "In commercial countries, where the authority of law, is always perfectly sufficient to protect the meanest [that is,
most impoverished] man in the state, the descendants of the same family, having no such motive for keeping together, naturally separate and disperse."[27]
Smollett, too, saw dispersion as a positive development. In contrast with some
humanitarian novelists, he would not gauge civilization's advancement according to whether the poor are level with the high-born in the eyes of the
law, although he shared their skepticism of legal institutions but not of law
monolithically. Instead, his version of community accommodates the caprice
of privilege, as high-status foreigners establish homophily selectively with
native-born peers whom they encounter by chance.

Smollett's novels demonstrate how, in a context in which regulation of
the community depends on gatekeepers who define its boundaries and

membership, privileged outsiders can be reframed as insiders based on emotional emphasis of similarities rather than differences. Yet these works inadvertently unveil the problems that occur when the protections of citizenship (in *Fathom* and *Greaves*) or the law of nations (in *The Reprisal*) are supplanted by dispensations of justice arbitrarily granted in response to appeals to homophily and "community." Authorities legal (in *Fathom* and *Greaves*) and military (in *The Reprisal*) are given excessive discretion to determine who deserves access to justice. Yet Smollett's proposed resolution is inadequate. His works inadvertently show that when the boundary between those deserving and undeserving of justice—those "inside" and "outside" the law—can be arbitrarily defined, everyone is at risk.

A different potential solution to this problem involves extending legal representation and due process indiscriminately to nonlocals, foreigners, and others who do not belong to the jurisdiction in question.[28] Smollett rejects this solution: these benefits, in Smollett's ideal system, are not givens: they must be *deserved*. Smollett held that one merits legal agency not based on community membership or citizenship status alone but also through the ability to contribute to a community, which, for Smollett, correlates with social status.[29] If, as Derrida claims, polities are vulnerable to "an autoimmunitary process," wherein the system mistakenly "works to destroy its own,"[30] Smollett's privileged outsiders deliberately induce this process, managing to persuade members of communities they enter that they are similar in kind and thus wrongly targeted for attack; the outsiders redirect the aggression aimed at them toward their attackers, who are recast as the actual foreign bodies. Whereas Derrida saw this process as catastrophic, Smollett portrays it as a salvific act that not only restores to their rightful place characters wrongfully deprived of their rights but also reinvigorates moribund localities.

By emphasizing the compassion that some of the privileged characters show for the plight of the less fortunate, Smollett palliates a reboot of a status-based hierarchy. Evincing little concern for the average person wrongly caught up in the net of justice, Smollett is far more alarmed that persons of high status are vulnerable to jurisdictional boundaries that reduce them to legal nonentities. This prioritization of status over nationality helps resolve the puzzle of Smollett's midcareer hiatus from promoting what Charlotte Sussman calls his "vision of the dangerous consequences of cross-cultural contact."[31] Ian Campbell Ross has speculated about "the reason for unwonted tolerance from an author whose insularity often verges on xenophobia."[32] As noted by Ross, there are several "virtuous" foreigners in *Count Fathom*, the first work of this new era, but he does not address the other key attributes they share: all are very wealthy, and some are even nobility. Vehemently criticizing John Wesley for advocating class-leveling practices such as literacy for all,[33] Smollett instead prioritizes the rights of an exclusive group: a prototypical version of the "man or woman of transnational affairs" who zipped across borders in the 1990s. Marking the rise of this "denationalized global elite," Richard Falk warned that it is "an elite that shares interests and experiences, [and] comes to have more in common with each other than . . . with the more rooted, ethnically distinct members of its own particular civil society."[34] Smollett reveals, I argue, the extent to which the championing of due process, fair sentencing, and humane confinement is not necessarily an egalitarian project that upends the status quo; instead, it can be a reactionary maneuver that upholds it. Preservation of class hierarchy is facilitated via high-minded defense of civil liberties, couched in the language of universal extension of legal agency.

The preoccupation with community that pervades Smollett's midcareer works registers still more vividly through comparison to the output of canonical predecessors and foremost novelists of his era. The term *community* occurs many times in each of Smollett's novels, but it is absent from Defoe's major novels of 1719 through the 1720s and from Richardson's *Pamela* (1740) and *Clarissa* (1747–48), although it appears four times in *Sir Charles Grandison* (1753). The word appears once in Fielding's novels (in *Amelia*, published in 1751). For the two latter authors, the term shows up only in their final novels, perhaps registering a more general shift toward the "social problem" novel. Public, nondomestic contestations of social and legal power are not a main concern in Richardson's novels. His characters are restricted to increasingly hermetic household environments: Pamela moves from one country estate to another, where she tries and fails to escape; Clarissa is confined first to the family home, then her bedroom, and, eventually, to lodging-house rooms as Lovelace's captive. The heroines interact primarily with a small group of recurrent characters and have few opportunities to encounter strangers.

While Fielding's characters do move around—the protagonists of *Joseph Andrews* (1742) and *Tom Jones* (1749) are constantly in transit—their primary identities are ultimately construed in terms of familial ties rather than community relationships and interactions. The culmination of their adventures is reinstatement in socially prominent families. Smollett shared with Fielding and Richardson an interest in the legal consequences of the severing of familial bonds (whether by abandonment or estrangement).[35] By contrast to Fielding's heroes, the protagonists of Smollett's midcareer works do not find eventual safe harbor with blood relations: their relatives are deceased (the protagonists' parents in *Fathom* and *Greaves*), unmentioned (*The Reprisal*), or diabolical (the heroine's uncle in *Greaves*).[36]

The legal complaints of Smollett's characters serve a considerably different agenda than do the travesties of justice depicted in canonical humanitarian novels of later generations. William Godwin's *Things as They Are; or, The Adventures of Caleb Williams* (1794) and Charles Dickens's *Bleak House* (1852–53) endorse progressive reform of the judiciary through portrayals of aristocrats' stranglehold over judicial outcomes, in the former case, and the sclerotic processing of legal claims, in the latter. By contrast, Smollett's critique is geared toward rehabilitating for a new generation of global elites the remedy of the courts that had protected the old order of privilege.

Ultimately, Smollett's novels expose the collateral damage that results from arbitrary determination of who deserves inclusion within the community of the justice-deserving. Aileen Douglas has observed that "despite all its affirmations of community, of warmth . . . *Greaves* becomes a meditation on the institutional and public uses of terror."[37] This is on target, but Douglas and others see this juxtaposition as a contradiction in terms rather than what it actually is: symbiosis. There is a fluid reciprocity between, on the one hand, Smollett's protagonists' convivial gatherings and, on the other hand, their nightmarish sojourns in prisons and brawls with envious farmers and irate merchants—adventures that terminate in destruction of property, dissolution of marriages, and, in one unfortunate servant's case, lifelong paralysis. I argue that Smollett's work shows that there is no conflict between community building and "institutional and public uses of terror"; on the contrary, the terror and oppression wrought through the law depend on conceptualizations of community that rationalize the exclusion of equivocal characters.

Smollett's Convictions: From Acclaimed Author to Community Menace

Smollett modeled *Sir Launcelot Greaves* on *Don Quixote*, a novel whose composition was directly informed by the author's firsthand encounters with the law.[38] As Susan Byrne observes, "Cervantes's intimate experiences with law, and the polemical legal situation in [his nation], place *Don Quixote*'s author at the center of [a] maelstrom of literary-legal-historical developments."[39] Smollett was likewise brought into personal contact with the law as he was composing and publishing his works. A number of critics (most notably Walter

Scott in the nineteenth century) have argued that Smollett wrote part of *Greaves* while serving his sentence of three months in prison, although others have minimized this claim.[40] Just as Smollett's characters are falsely vilified in court as outsiders who endanger upstanding citizens, Smollett himself found that his public image was distorted, and he was refigured as a threat to the community.

In 1753, immediately after he published *Count Fathom*, Smollett was accused of assaulting Peter Gordon, a poet manqué who had borrowed substantial sums from him. Gordon was one of several struggling writers to whom Smollett offered financial relief; he decamped to the London "verge" (a district where debtors could not be arrested) and mocked his benefactor, even as he continued to list Smollett as guarantor on promissory notes. After several months of legal efforts to obtain payment, Smollett tracked down Gordon and attacked him and his landlord with a cane. Gordon had Smollett arrested for assault.

During the ensuing trial, which took place six days after *Count Fathom* was published, Smollett was incensed by the actions of the opposing counsel, whom he perceived as violating a sacred duty to honor their shared status in the ranks of the privileged. Instead, the eminent barrister Alexander Hume Campbell attempted to convert Smollett's literary renown into a liability. During cross-examination, Campbell mockingly asked the witness whether he knew that Smollett was an "Author."[41] From advance proofs of *Count Fathom* that he had somehow obtained without authorization, Campbell read aloud to the jury passages detailing the protagonist's sociopathic exploits. Smollett provided ongoing service to the community as a generous benefactor who kept needy writers afloat with financial infusions; yet Campbell characterized him as a violent menace. In an aggrieved letter that he never sent (although it was widely reprinted by Scott and others), Smollett rebuked Campbell: "Sir, this was a pitiful personality, calculated to depreciate the character of a gentleman to whom you was a stranger. . . . You was hardy enough to represent me as a person devoid of all humanity and remorse, as a barbarous ruffian" (22). Smollett stated that Campbell, rather than prosecuting him, should have represented him; he implied that he deserved Campbell's support (as "an injured person who, as well as yourself, is a gentleman by birth, education, and profession" [23]) because they shared membership in a community to which Campbell's client, the low-born, undereducated, and penniless Gordon, could never belong. Smollett was mystified as to why Campbell chose, instead, to take up the cause of a man from an entirely different social world:

"I could not divine the mysterious bond of union that attached you to Peter Gordon, Esq." (24–25).

Smollett declared that Campbell was a symptom of the English courts' decline: "You . . . give the world a handle to believe that our Courts of Justice stand greatly in need of reformation. Indeed, the petulance, license and buffoonery of some Lawyers in the exercise of their function is a reproach upon decency, and a scandal to the nation."[42] He disparaged Campbell as a mercenary who designated wrongdoer and victim according to who was first in line to pay a retainer to secure legal services. Ultimately convicted of assault, Smollett was forced to pay heavy fines to the man who had defrauded him.

A few years later, in 1759, these same adversaries tangled anew. Campbell signed on again as prosecutor against Smollett, who was indicted for libel after he criticized the military strategy of an admiral whose bad judgment had resulted in a British defeat by the French. Under English libel law of the period, the verdict was not based on the validity of Smollett's statement; rather, the key question was whether there was damage to the admiral's reputation.[43] Once more, Campbell prevailed. Instead of being commended as a patriot who shed light on dereliction of duty, Smollett was punished for sullying the good name of an esteemed military commander. Time and again, despite his stature as a nationally renowned public figure, Smollett was recast by Campbell as a predator whose liberty must be curtailed.

Smollett's personal experience reinforced his concerns, expressed in earlier works, regarding legal institutions' disregard of due process and fair treatment. In *The Adventures of Peregrine Pickle* (first published in 1751), the eponymous protagonist and an acquaintance, Pallet, are arrested at a masquerade and detained in the Bastille without being charged. Notified of the incarceration, their friend predicts that the pair will "fall a sacrifice to the tyranny of lawless power."[44] Unconcerned, Pickle tells his lawyer—who weeps in an effort to persuade him to formally apologize to the prince—that "he would stoop to no such condescension, because he had committed no crime, but would leave his case to the cognisance and exertion of the British court, whose duty it was to do justice to its own subjects" (225). Pickle's faith in due process is naive: the British ambassador manages to secure his and Pallet's release only by threatening to retaliate by seizing innocent Frenchmen living in London and detaining them in the Tower. Smollett's novels offer naturalistic, unsanitized accounts of how the judiciary and the penal system fail to sort innocents from malefactors. It is when "arbitrary power" jeopardizes "gentlemen," however, that Smollett indicates its threat to be most dire.

Bad Citizens versus Insolent Foreigners in
Ferdinand Count Fathom

In *Ferdinand Count Fathom*, Smollett challenges the notion that nationality should be the basis of legal agency. He explores the perspective of an impecunious man who from birth is subjected to marginalization in the legal system and ridicule in society because he is perceived as a foreigner. The sham "Count" Fathom, however, is not the type of blameless, wretched figure who is easy to condole in humanitarian fictions: an innocent brought low through the machinations of the cruel. On the contrary, he is a cold-hearted fraudster who exploits all who help him. Contemporary readers found the character odious, and the novel was a rare commercial misstep for Smollett. Lewis M. Knapp hypothesized that *Ferdinand Count Fathom* alienated audiences because the protagonist was "too complete a monster."[45] To satisfy his lustful, avaricious appetites as he travels through Europe and back to England, Fathom consigns business partners to financial ruin, destroys the livelihoods and reputations of his closest friends, and sows discord within families, until he suddenly repents at the end of the novel. Precisely because he is not a sympathetic character, Fathom is an especially intriguing case study for exploring the extent to which outsiders, even the most repugnant, deserve equitable treatment at the hands of the law.[46]

From the beginning, Fathom is marked as an outsider who defies categorization within a specific jurisdiction. He was born to an unmarried Englishwoman as she traversed the border from Holland to Flanders; because his father's nationality is anyone's guess, he is not a British subject but an alien.[47] As an adult traveling to England for the first time, "he found himself a monument of that disregard and contempt, which a stranger never fails to meet with from the inhabitants of this island" (131). This unshakable aura of strangerhood enables Fathom to perpetrate his schemes, but it also exposes him to xenophobia.

Traveling in a stagecoach entering London, "he resolved to pass himself upon his fellow travellers, for a French gentleman, equally a stranger to the language and country of England" (128). Another passenger, an English wine merchant, addresses Fathom in broken French with "a series of interrogations, concerning the place of Ferdinand's abode in that city, and his business in England, so that he was fain to practise the science of defence, and answered with such ambiguity, as aroused [the merchant's] suspicion" (132). When they alight in London, the merchant hauls Fathom before a magistrate, declaring,

"I have brought this foreigner before you, on violent suspicion of his being a proclaimed outlaw" (133). In the courtroom, the merchant startles the audience by identifying Fathom as Prince Charles Edward Stuart, Italian-born claimant to the English throne, who attempted to overthrow the government in 1745. The arrested man's actual English ancestry and fluency go entirely unsuspected.[48] Fathom's plight illustrates the potential futility of attempting to manage strangers' impressions of one's belonging and rights, particularly in an increasingly urban Britain where the dynamic mobility of the industrial age had unsettled the agrarian era's stable communities of long-term neighbors familiar with one another.

Fathom is at a significant disadvantage in the courtroom; nobody in the audience except the merchant knows French—the language Fathom is bound to speak to maintain his assumed identity. Despite a clear conflict of interest, his adversary steps in to serve as his interpreter (eighteenth-century historical records show similar real-life cases in which foreign defendants in London trials had to rely on adversaries for interpretation or were otherwise disadvantaged by inadequate provision of interpretive resources).[49] Because Fathom does not want to admit that his original cover story was false, he cannot challenge the merchant's misrepresentations:

> The [merchant], instead of acting the part of a faithful interpreter, [mistranslated Ferdinand's answers] . . . Ferdinand now began to repent of having pretended ignorance of the English language, as he found himself at the mercy of a rascal, who put a false gloss upon all his words; and addressed himself to the audience successively in French, High-Dutch, Italian, and Hungarian Latin, desiring to know if any person present understood any of these tongues, that his answers might be honestly explained to the bench. But, he might have accosted them in Chinese with the same success: there was not one person present tolerably versed in his mother-tongue, much less acquainted with any foreign language, except the wine-merchant. (135–36)

Fathom's desperate—and ludicrous—multilingual efforts to outwit his interpreter attest to the vulnerability of foreigners making their way through unfamiliar jurisdictions. For centuries following the Norman Conquest, so-called "Law French" had been the standard language for English court proceedings, and statutes were primarily composed in Latin; but a few decades before Smollett's heyday, a major change was implemented. Parliament approved the Proceedings in Courts of Justice Act 1730, which mandated that "all proceedings . . . be in the *English* tongue and language only, and not in *Latin* or

French, or any other tongue or language whatsoever."[50] The novel thus indicates nostalgia for a time when courts accommodated elite mobility through a shared language of law, a language that required a rarefied level of education. At the same time, it denigrates the monolingual provincialism of the ordinary English folk who sit in judgment of a "gentleman."

Fortuitously, an English nobleman who happens to speak French arrives late to watch the trial, and he soon rises to contest the charges against Fathom by assuring the judge that he has seen Prince Charles Edward Stuart several times in Paris, and Fathom bears no resemblance to him. After Fathom is exonerated, his servant unmasks the merchant as a smuggler, and the magistrate orders the merchant's arrest. The accuser is himself revealed to be a "pretender"; the "merchant" is symbolically vanquished by the "gentleman."

The episode illustrates Smollett's anxious acknowledgment of the downside of the age of unprecedented global mobility that he otherwise welcomes: at a time of high geographic mobility and frequent interaction between men of different station, high status could more easily be feigned, endangering its viability as a basis for legal agency abroad. More generally, in a transnational context when so much else in society was changing—entire populations were shifting from rural to urban, from agricultural to industrial—the nobility also faced the broader challenge of rationalizing their exalted societal position despite the upheaval. Casting Fathom as an imposter, however, also enables Smollett to avoid showing an actual nobleman engaging in disreputable acts.

In what turns out to be a repeated pattern in the lengthy novel, British strivers accuse foreigners of the same transgressions that they themselves attempt: insinuation into a realm of power. When the accusers' efforts are neutralized, an exclusive bond is forged between the British upper-class savior and the foreign accused. In many such episodes across his midcareer works, Smollett implies that ad hoc formation of a new community is a solution to the legal no-man's-land in which outsiders are stranded. Whereas the basis of the community in which Fathom is accused is assumed to be natural-born British subjecthood, Fathom ingratiates himself with the nobleman by establishing their similitude of status—claiming that he is in fact a German nobleman traveling abroad under an assumed identity to avoid an arranged marriage.

Another episode of misbegotten allegations further illuminates the vulnerability of foreign elites forced to defend themselves in unfamiliar jurisdictions. Still passing himself off as a Continental nobleman, Fathom is embroiled in an extortion scheme devised by "an old citizen of London" (169) and his young wife. The husband is repeatedly referred to as "the citizen," as well as by his given name, Trapwell (a generic "speaking name"). At the time, and in Smollett's usage, *citizen* meant something quite different from what it does today; it was a pejorative designation of class status, meaning "an ordinary (city- or town-dwelling) person as opposed to a member of the landed nobility or gentry" (*OED*). During a tryst between Fathom and the wife, the citizen and two of his associates spring out of hiding and confront Fathom. Because Fathom has presented himself as a count, the couple believes that he is wealthy, and they demand a large sum from him as recompense. Fathom, knowing he cannot meet their demand, reluctantly opts to go to trial instead: "The plaintiff, far from seeking to cover, affected to complain loudly of his misfortune, that he might interest his neighbours in his behalf, and raise a spirit of rancour and animosity, to influence the jury against this insolent foreigner, who had come over into England to debauch our wives and deflower our daughters" (172). The citizen, who has retained "a formidable band of lawyers" (172), presents Fathom not simply as an intruder on his marital turf but as a threat to national security. Although aristocratic men had greater resources for protecting their legal agency relative to others, the trial scene illustrates their additional vulnerability in legal matters: they were more likely than men of lower status to be targets of extortion. Smollett is preoccupied with the consequences of abridged legal agency for the elite traveler, not the likes of the lowly immigrant. While *Ferdinand Count Fathom*'s debt to the picaresque tradition is evident, here can be seen how the novel reverses picaresque values. Whereas "in its basic conception the picaresque is the rancorous, embittered view of the underdog contemplating those more fortunate than he" (as José Ortega y Gasset argued in his influential overview of the genre),[51] *Ferdinand Count Fathom* disparages the envious citizen for resenting and bringing to law the foreign aristocrat (actually, of course, an imposter) enjoying the customary perquisites of privilege.

To mount his defense, Fathom hires a lawyer recommended by one of his few acquaintances in the area. That lawyer exploits him financially: after losing his case and paying damages to the citizen, Fathom receives an exorbitant invoice for the solicitor's services: time billed includes happenstance encounters "in the park, the coffee-house or the street. . . . [Fathom] had great reason to believe the sollicitor had often thrown himself in his way, with a view to swell this item of his account" (175). The novel thus acknowledges the extent to which the social is imbricated with the legal: foreigners not embedded in local social networks can lack access to circuits of legal expertise and competent, trustworthy practitioners.

While Fathom seeks exalted status in foreign lands by attempting to pass himself off as nobility, other episodes in the novel show Smollett's endorsement of an alternative path to the kind of social approbation that facilitates the acquisition of legal agency within an inhospitable community: a foreigner can make substantial contributions to the well-being of the local residents. This route to inclusion is evidenced by his elevation of a character belonging to a group identified with extremely low status in England at the time: "a rich Jew, whose wealth they considered as proof of his rapaciousness" (225). Fathom and his friend (and sometime victim) Renaldo, Count de Melvile, reluctantly visit the moneylender in an effort to borrow money for Melvile to litigate the theft of his inheritance in his homeland of Hungary. Introduced as a "usurer" with stereotypical ethnic features, the man's exclusion from the British community is geographically evidenced by his location in a separate "quarter" removed from the community of the Christian moneylenders who rejected the group. Yet he proves far more generous than his gentile peers, telling the men he will lend them the money without interest. Having demonstrated his community mindedness, the man is formally reintroduced in the novel's final chapter as "Mr. Joshua Manasseh, merchant in London" (347). (Manasseh ben Israel was a widely respected Jewish leader who in 1655 visited England to meet with Oliver Cromwell in an attempt to convince him to authorize the entry into England of Jewish refugees;[52] Smollett's character may be his namesake.)[53] He proves to be a stalwart supporter: throughout the characters' various legal ordeals, he lends his coach to them for travel to appointments, connects them with noblemen and diplomats who can advocate for their cases, lends them money at no interest, receives mail for them, and hosts them at his home. If, as J. Hillis Miller argues, novels in general are "models of community" that both reflect reality and project a vision of ideal behavior,[54] Manasseh establishes himself within the novel's community by coming to the aid of other characters of foreign descent. When Fathom's friend Don Diego views him with suspicion upon meeting him, Manasseh calms him by responding in fluent Castilian, Diego's native language; he informs Diego that he has heard about his legal troubles and has drawn on connections to help him retrieve his estate (which the Spanish government seized, when Diego was accused of treason, and awarded to his accuser). Notably, Manasseh's contributions generally consist of safeguarding or rehabilitating the legal agency of noblemen.

While Manasseh does not become a litigant himself, the character appeared at a pivotal historical moment. Jewishness was on trial in England,

and the relationship between the Jewish character and the national community was central to the debate; the legal status of many members of England's Jewish population hung in the balance. In 1747 and 1751—that is, during the half-decade immediately before Smollett published *Ferdinand Count Fathom*— Parliament considered, but did not pass, the general naturalization bill, which would have naturalized foreign Protestants without the piecemeal passage of private acts.[55] Undaunted by these failures, in 1753—the year the novel was published—the Jewish community rallied behind the Jewish Naturalization Act, which would have naturalized some foreign-born Jews. The legislation has been perceived as a means of showing gratitude to the Jewish denizens who helped protect and stabilize England in the unrest of the 1745 uprising through financial and military support. The act was passed but was soon rescinded owing to the demands of a hostile public.

Against such a background, the prominent depiction of a "high-minded, saint-like Jew" (as one early twentieth-century critic described him)[56] who tirelessly contributes to the legal defense of strangers was no small literary innovation. It was a striking departure both from anti-Semitic portrayals that were standard for the day and from Smollett's own earlier portrayals of Jewish characters. Throughout the twentieth century, a number of scholars hailed Smollett as the first English novelist to cast Jewish characters in a positive light.[57] Jews had been expelled from England in 1290, but they returned after informal readmission in the 1650s.[58] By Smollett's heyday, they had resided in the country in significant numbers for little more than a century. Foreign-born Jews were not allowed to own property beyond the house in which they lived or leave property to heirs. Even if naturalized, they would have remained second-class citizens along with native-born members of their faith. Because neither Cromwell nor Charles II had formally readmitted Jews into England, "legal lacunae existed around Jews' status, and the intent of the limits posed upon them was ambiguous. . . . Jews . . . lacked certain civic rights."[59]

Discarding its earlier governing binary (formulated by the Swiss chevalier and Fathom) of good citizen versus bad citizen, the novel proposes a new model of belonging through its Manasseh episodes: an international community of men privileged by dint of birth or wealth, who are connected to each other and protect their rights through deploying commercial and social power across borders. Half a century earlier, the eventual transition of Jews from figures of suspicion to fellow members of the community had been adumbrated by the counsel's argument in *Wells v. Williams*, a case in the Court of Common Pleas that in 1697 reaffirmed the right of Jews to initiate lawsuits:

"A Jew may sue at this day, but heretofore he could not, for then they were looked upon as enemies. But now commerce has taught the world more humanity."[60]

Smollett's discussion of the Jewish Naturalization Act in *Continuation of the Complete History of England* reflects dueling visions of the permeability and changeability of "community," suggesting that the proposed legislation was supported by governmental ministers who welcomed the prospect of blurring boundaries between native-born Britons and Jewish émigrés. Those politicians, he wrote, envisioned "a considerable increase of their own influence among the individuals of that community" and hoped "that it would encourage persons of wealth to remove with their effects from foreign parts into Great Britain."[61] By contrast, Smollett wrote, the act's detractors stoked fear by imagining an amalgamation so thoroughgoing that Jewish people would take precedence in society: "The adversaries of the bill affirmed . . . that such an adoption of vagrant Jews into the community, from all parts of the world, would rob the real subjects of their birthright . . . and endanger the constitution both in church and state."[62] Specifically, "Jews would multiply in such number, engross such wealth, and acquire so great power and influence in Great Britain that their persons would be revered, their customs imitated, and Judaism become the fashionable religion of the English."[63] Bearing out Smollett's account of the conflict, some contemporary pamphleteers warned explicitly that Jews would commandeer the legal system and deprive England's Protestant natives of legal agency. "Archaicus" prognosticated, "They will be admitted as Witnesses and empannell'd on Juries, by all our Courts; by which means, they will, as allow'd by their *Talmud*, Right or Wrong, cast and condemn any Christian, as they please."[64] "Britannia" asked, "Would not a *Christian* be overawed frequently by a *Jew* Justice of the Peace?"[65] Smollett dismissed such concerns as "frivolous and chimerical, being industriously circulated among the vulgar."[66] Notably, in keeping with his protective attitude toward the elite, Smollett here chiefly attributes anti-Semitic bias to the English lower classes (a view shared by eighteenth-century supporters of the act and twentieth-century historians).

Smollett's account was a postmortem; in the months after his novel was published, the bill was introduced and passed but was repealed as a result of public outcry.[67] Public resentment was so adamant that no further measures for expansion of Jewish civil rights were introduced for seventy years. Bowing to popular opinion, Smollett would later exhibit a disappointing reversion to the vicious stereotypes he spread through his early career work: Squire

Matthew Bramble, the gruff yet esteemed protagonist of Smollett's final novel, *The Expedition of Humphry Clinker*, comments that if one accepts the mistaken proposition that riches are proof of merit, "there are Jews and others in Amsterdam and London, enriched by usury, peculation, and different species of fraud and extortion, who are more estimable than the most virtuous and illustrious members of the community. An absurdity which no man in his senses will offer to maintain."[68] *Ferdinand Count Fathom* had introduced into English literature a Jewish character whose financial expertise has a beneficial social impact, helping members of the Continental elite assert their rights and reclaim their property. In *Humphry Clinker*, the same actions are depicted not simply as predatory but as criminal; the recasting of Jews from restorers of legal agency to malefactors only reinforces Smollett's dynamic model of community formation, in which all manner of persons remain constantly under threat of vilification.

Drifting Allegiances: The Rights of Foreign Captives in *The Reprisal*
In the seven-year interval between *Ferdinand Count Fathom* and *Sir Launcelot Greaves*, Smollett continued to reflect on the extent to which privileged foreigners deserved equal justice under the law. *The Reprisal: or, The Tars of Old England* (1757), the successful comic drama that Smollett brought to the stage with the star power of David Garrick (the most famous English actor of his day, who served as the play's producer[69]), is entirely devoted to the subject. On its debut, it garnered reviews of only a few lines despite its positive reception,[70] and to this day, the play has a minimal presence in Smollett criticism. A representative criticism is Paul-Gabriel Boucé's dismissal: "The only literary interest of this play . . . is the doggedness of the sailor characters and the constant linguistic jokes."[71] Yet the play merits a closer look, for here the curtailment of legal agency is rendered with a more clear-cut sense of injustice. Whereas Fathom committed some of the deeds for which he is charged, the foreigners taken prisoner in *The Reprisal* are wrongly accused of breaking the law. Fathom is regularly afforded the opportunity to contest the charges against him in court (albeit in circumstances that favor his accusers). By contrast, the prisoners of *The Reprisal* are deprived of any opportunity for a trial.

The play depicts a standoff that brings to the fore contrasting strategies for outsiders who seek justice in a jurisdiction to which they do not belong. With England and France on the brink of war, an English pleasure boat accidentally drifts into French waters and is captured by a French military vessel. Smollett's play explicitly refers to legal scholarship that influenced how educated Britons perceived legal standing at sea. In the decades that preceded Smollett's heyday, publishers had issued new English translations of the works of the Dutch jurist Hugo Grotius and the German legal theorist Samuel Pufendorf, who were key to the modern development of international law. Both authorities are cited explicitly and by name in the dialogue of *The Reprisal*, as well as elsewhere in Smollett's works.[72] In *Mare liberum* (*The Free Sea*, first published in 1609), Grotius argued that the sea was a territory more akin to air than land and should be open to all.[73] In a series of treatises in the 1670s and 1680s that focused on the rights of foreigners, Pufendorf upheld the rights of foreigners as they moved through others' jurisdiction. In his writings, he addresses the legal scenario portrayed in *The Reprisal*: "There scarce appears any probable color on which we should deny unarmed vessels the liberty of the open sea."[74] The play concisely depicts the paradoxical role of ideas derived from foreign legal authorities to consolidate affiliation among two initially distinct groups of British subjects divided by status. Improbably, the underclass sailors discuss legal theory in deciding whether to take up the legal cause of a "lady" and "gentleman" on holiday, Heartly and Harriet (she is the sole female passenger, and they are betrothed).

After the English passengers have boarded the ship, Champignon—the zealous French captain—and his crew restrain them as captives and seize their valuables. The passengers protest their captivity, to no avail. After Champignon isolates Harriet from the group and threatens to sexually assault her, she defiantly lectures him in an attempt to persuade him to release the group: "Nothing can be more disgraceful than what you have done. . . . You have carried off an unarmed boat contrary to the law of nations; and rifled the passengers in opposition to the dictates of justice and humanity."[75] When Champignon leaves to confer with a servant, Heartly manages to slip into the area where Harriet is sequestered. Expressing his naive belief that they will eventually receive due process from the French legal system, he reassures Harriet, "Champignon has certainly exceeded his orders, and we shall be released as soon as a representation can be made to the French court" (1.5.187). Harriet prefers an alternative to law: "I should be loth to trouble the court of France with matters of so little consequence. Don't you think it practicable to persuade the captain to set us at liberty?" (1.5.187). She suggests that the prisoners can win their case if they choose the right "figure in rhetoric" (1.5.187) to advocate for themselves. Her double entendre foreshadows the failure of this strategy; her expatiations on law do not convince Champignon but, instead, stoke his sexual desire for her; another passenger reports over-hearing that he has threatened to "confine her for life" (1.8.192).

It is not until the two sailors, the Scottish Maclaymore and the Irish Oclabber, break away from the French crew and align with the passengers that the English begin to escape their plight. The two are self-exiled from Britain for undisclosed reasons and joined the French crew for pay. On their first appearance, they are regaling each other with wistful stories of how they wish they could return to their families and hometowns. These wistful expatriates are prime targets for conscription into a coalition of their countrymen. While Oclabber politely greets Heartly, he initially seems inclined to uphold Champignon's orders regarding the prisoners, but Heartly reminds him that they met previously in England through mutual friends. Oclabber begins addressing him as "friend" and eventually agrees to join forces with him against Champignon to "defend her [Harriet] from the maggots of this daft Frenchman" (2.3.199). Puzzlingly, given their status, the sailors extensively quote the ideas of Continental legal theorists. Together, the Englishmen stage a fake attack that scatters the French crew; serendipitously, an English military commander appears with his crew; he arranges a détente between the French and the English.

Unmoored from the physical territory of Britain, the prisoners and expatriates form a coalition devoted to a notional British community united by a shared language, while they neglect competing affiliations that threaten their emerging cohesion: Oclabber and Maclaymore are never shown as speaking with their colleagues, the rank-and-file French sailors—who are given no lines and only appear in the plot scrambling in a panic to escape the fake attack. The French monitors of jurisdiction are recast as the actual lawbreakers: Oclabber likens his French shipmates to "pyrates and privateers" (1.2.179) and worthy of execution, although Smollett indicates that Champignon truly believes he is simply following government orders. The emerging reconceptualization of community downplays specific provenance (Scottish, Irish, English) in favor of shared British identity.[76] Indeed, the power of community comes into greater relief precisely because it unites characters from such varied local contexts who speak a range of dialects.

Compared to the novels, the play proves to be a limited vehicle for presenting the types of legal context that trigger realignments of community affiliation. The characters are static and unidimensional; they regurgitate snippets from legal texts, but their banter lacks the sardonic undertone of some of the dialogue in the novels, in which certain characters convey more nuanced recognition of the high stakes of jurisdictional ordeals. For his next literary project, Smollett would return to the novel.

"Injured" Elites and Litigious Commoners in *The Life and Adventures of Sir Launcelot Greaves*

The episodes highlighted in *Ferdinand Count Fathom* and *The Reprisal* revolve around vulnerable foreigners who are forced to self-advocate when their legal agency is hampered through conditions ranging from denial of due process to indefinite detention without trial. Smollett's next literary work, *The Life and Adventures of Sir Launcelot Greaves*, narrows the critical aperture to focus on legal conflicts within England; the novel's conflicts between elites and commoners exemplify the real-life problems that arose, as Smollett perceived them, when intranational jurisdictional boundaries and plebeian legal self-assertion imperiled the prerogatives of status. *Sir Launcelot Greaves* suggests that the forces of rising geographic and class mobility were compounded by the judicial initiative of members of the lower classes: litigiousness and demands for equitable treatment in the legal system. Members of the elite, the novel warns, can no longer assume they will automatically receive preferential treatment before the law. Differentiating legitimate legal grievances of the elite from the groundless complaints of upwardly mobile commoners, the novel features conspicuous episodes responding to major progressive legislative efforts, including the 1758 Habeas Corpus Bill and the 1759 Act for Relief of Debtors with Respect to the Imprisonment of Their Persons. The novel illustrates how, in legal contexts, seemingly egalitarian avowals of concern for the many against the interests of the few can be invoked to support elite preeminence.

Three years before publishing *Sir Launcelot Greaves*, Smollett made a case, not yet couched in illusive tributes to egalitarianism, for preferential judicial treatment of the elite. In his *Continuation of the Complete History of England*, he proposed a two-tier system of legal consequences according to social status. Acknowledging that a nobleman who in 1760 had been executed for treason deserved his fate, Smollett nonetheless argued that in other cases members of the nobility should be treated leniently relative to commoners:

> As the nobility of England are raised by many illustrious distinctions above the level of plebeians, and as they are eminently distinguished from them in suffering punishment for high treason, which the law considers as the most atrocious crime that can be committed, it might not be unworthy of the notice of the legislature to deliberate whether some such pre-eminence ought not to be

extended to noblemen convicted of other crimes, in order to alleviate as much as possible the disgrace of noble families which have deserved well of their country; to avoid any circumstance that may tend to diminish the lustre of the English nobility in the eyes of foreign nations; or to bring it in contempt with the common people of our own, already too licentious, and prone to abolish those distinctions, which serve as the basis of decorum, order, and subordination.[77]

Here Smollett argues that shielding the nobility from punishment is a matter of national security and international reputation. His argument anticipates the rhetoric of later eras.

From its outset, the novel similarly—but less provocatively—foregrounds the conflation of the upholding of justice and the preservation of community security. The young, lovelorn, and slightly deranged aristocrat Sir Launcelot Greaves appoints himself as "coadjutor to the law." (17)[78] He dons his grandfather's armor and sets forth to traverse the countryside, trailed by a lawyer friend (the aforementioned Tom Clarke) and Clarke's ungainly cousin, Captain Crowe, who emulates Greaves in aspiring to knight errantry. Although Greaves renounces another character's comparison of him to Don Quixote, he is clearly patterned on that character (Smollett's translation of Cervantes's novel was published in 1755, almost a decade before the publication of *Sir Launcelot Greaves*).[79] The novel chronicles Greaves's path to wed his beloved Aurelia, but the book's amorous scenes are listless, and the dialogue between the lovers smacks of obligatory adherence to a standard-issue romance plot trajectory; Greaves is at his most passionate when agitating for justice. He proclaims that his mission is to "redress injuries, chastise oppression, protect the helpless and forlorn, relieve the indigent, exert my best endeavours in the cause of innocence,"[80] and "even to remedy evils which the law cannot reach."[81] Although, at this early moment, the aristocracy is firmly in control—Sir Launcelot designates himself as an arbiter of justice—the emphasis on "oppression" and "the helpless" appears to shift the primary locus of concern from the elites to the lowly. The quest, that staple of the romance, serves as a plot device to dislodge the characters from their local context and propel them into unfamiliar jurisdictions where they no longer enjoy the advantage that accrues in legal contexts to those whose high status is common knowledge in the surrounding area.

In the handful of scholarly works that substantively consider *Sir Launcelot Greaves* in the context of law, most critics have accepted the novel's initial framing, in which the primary function of members of the elite is to control adherence to the law. For the most part, the debate is restricted to argument over the extent to which Greaves supports or circumvents the legal system. Robert Folkenflik characterizes Greaves as ultimately embodying "the modern English gentleman" who resorts to "the law, not the lance."[82] Others cast him as eschewing the legal system: Alice Parker contends that "for justice [Smollett] turns to the benevolent aristocrat, who usually acts in a private capacity, avoiding recourse to the law."[83] Peter Wagner, Ronald Paulson, and Robin Fabel[84] each contend that the novel upholds the rule of law, as opposed to vigilantism, as the proper solution to conflict. The critics offer two incompatible interpretations: either Smollett considers the legal domain as the proper venue for resolving conflicts, or he rejects it as a corrupt realm that invalidates the rightful privileges of the aristocracy.

Yet on examination, the novel takes a third approach that again casts elites not primarily as enforcers of the law so much as victims of it. There are occasional brief references to the legally condoned suffering of the poor at the hands of the wealthy (as when Clarke states that Greaves "supported divers poor tenants against the extortion of the landlords" [40]), but in the cases to which the novel devotes major episodes, the offenders are not the elite but, instead, common folk who use jurisdictional advantages to abuse the legal system and torment those of superior status with arrest, lawsuits, or false allegations. As Greaves proclaims his mission to "act as a coadjutor to law" (17), the misanthropic attorney Ferret interjects with a mordant warning that "some determined constable ... will seize your worship as a vagrant, according to the statute" if Greaves strays from his native jurisdiction (16). Here, again, is raised the problem of sorting those who belong within the legal sphere from undeserving outsiders whose rights should be abridged (with a similar awareness of status: constables tended to be poor or old men and were at the bottom of the legal hierarchy).[85] From its earliest pages, the novel advocates for better accommodation of elite mobility across jurisdictional boundaries.

One of the novel's early episodes fosters skepticism concerning requests from humbler folk for extrication from legal predicaments related to jurisdiction. This instance of a bad-faith plea for legal assistance occurs when the novel's resident malcontent, the misanthropic attorney Ferret, is arrested for unauthorized peddling after he makes a speech to a crowd to market some questionable wares:

> Mr. Ferret would not have stood so long in his rostrum unmolested, had not he
> cunningly chosen his station immediately without the jurisdiction of the town,

whose magistrates therefore could not take cognizance of his conduct; but, application was made to the constable of the other parish, while our nostrum-monger proceeded in his speech. . . . He had just stepped down from his stool, when the constable, with his staff, arrived, and took him under his guidance. Mr. Ferret, on this occasion, attempted to interest the people in [*sic*] his behalf, by exhorting them to vindicate the liberty of the subject, against such an act of oppression; but finding them deaf to the tropes and figures of his elocution, he addressed himself to our knight, reminding him of his duty to protect the helpless and the injured, and earnestly soliciting his interposition. (79)

Ferret has literally rendered himself an outsider, but he presents himself as a victim of others. In describing Ferret as "earnestly" seeking help, Smollett's narrator challenges the reader's credulity: the enterprising Ferret, who turns his legal education to his advantage and throughout the novel can talk his way out of any scrape, would hardly seem to deserve protection as one of the "helpless and injured." Mere minutes after he denounces credulity in legal matters—mocking "ideots" (77) who sustain a "kingdom full . . . of . . . quacks in law" (77) and provide a ready audience for public presentations by "wretches who perjure themselves in false affidavits of cures that were never performed" (78)—Ferret makes his own attempt at legal subterfuge: he mockingly voices the same rhetoric of legal crisis found in appeals for relief elsewhere in the novel. In those episodes (including the two mentioned above), phrasing centering on "liberty" and "oppression" of "the helpless" is invoked, without satire, by the most admired members of the community—including the lawyer Clarke and "coadjutor to the law" Greaves.

Writing in the 1960s, Philip Stevick disparaged Smollett as "among the least careful of novelists . . . among the least philosophical of novelists," and stated, "Normally . . . Smollett's style is a vehicle for the presentation of a series of fairly uncomplicated events and unidimensional emotional states."[86] Yet Stevick was intrigued by a particular element of Smollett's "stylistic energy" that, he admitted, resisted easy interpretation: Smollett's use of hyperbole. On one hand, noted Stevick, "The hyperboles are often ironic. The reader is invited to question the sincerity of the response of a character, for example, and thus the hyperbole becomes a kind of shorthand for rendering hypocrisy." On the other hand, he contended, "Quite frequently . . . the hyperbolic style of Smollett exists not as an ironic ploy, not as an eccentric extravagance, but as direct description, as highly charged as it is because that is the manner in which experience is seen, as shocking, grotesque, and absurd."[87] Stevick did not apply his insight to the proliferation of legal concerns in the novel (in particular, he dismissed Smollett's profusion of legalese as trivial stylistic embellishment rather than substantive statements to be parsed). Yet when it infuses appeals to legal authority, this type of hyperbole conveys both the urgency and the potential spuriousness of characters' demands for legal agency; Ferret's manipulative description of himself as "helpless" in the face of arrest is one conspicuous instance. In vetting the novel's instances of hyperbolic declarations of legal exigency, the reader is drawn into the tricky business of distinguishing valid appeals to reclaim legal agency from meretricious ones.

In a later, similarly charged episode, the novel makes clear which side deserves to prevail. Greaves and Crowe are attacked without provocation by strangers while traveling on the highway (accompanied by their companions Crabshaw and Clarke) and are subsequently indicted and brought to trial on charges of assault. Immediately before the trial, all but one of their attackers—all of whom are local farmers—decide to drop their case against the travelers because, they admit, they initiated the affray. The sole holdout is Prickle, "the most quarrelsome fellow in the whole county; and so litigious, that he had maintained above thirty law-suits" (133). In arguing his case before the court, Greaves converts Prickle's home-turf advantage—his identity as a local resident—into a liability. All members of the community transfer their support to the outsiders when Greaves recasts Prickle from native son to a drain on community resources who has abused his power and brought groundless yet costly lawsuits against others in the town. Smollett's view of Prickle anticipates twenty-first-century right-wing characterizations of litigiousness as "symptomatic of . . . the breakdown of communal cohesion" rather than as conducive to "empower[ing] the weak and disadvantaged."[88] Judge Elmy reprimands Prickle for his failures as a community member: "Farmer Prickle, I am both sorry and ashamed to see a man of your years and circumstances so little respected, that you cannot find sufficient bail for forty pounds; a sure testimony that you have neither cultivated the friendship, nor deserved the goodwill of your neighbours. I have heard of your quarrels and your riots, your insolence, and litigious disposition, and often wished for an opportunity of giving you a proper taste of the law's correction" (137). Elmy, generally hailed by critics as a model of an impartial judge, attributes Prickle's failure to garner support to his decisions to operate in ways that harm the community. Abandoned by the other plaintiffs, and unsupported by the community, Prickle drops his case.

Elmy's apparently unobjectionable emphasis on social contribution runs parallel with his more controversial suggestion that status is an appropriate heuristic for sorting those deserving of legal agency from those who are abusing the system. Elmy castigates Prickle for "abuse against me . . . [as] a gentleman" (137) and, in private conversation with Greaves, speaks disdainfully of the farmers as "a set of people naturally boorish" (133). The narrator renders this status-based bias still more explicit when he derides Prickle for attempting to educate himself on legal matters and for leveraging this knowledge: "This peasant had purchased a few law-terms at a considerable expence, and he thought he had a right to turn his knowledge to the annoyance of all his neighbours" (135). The notion that legal knowledge ought to be the exclusive province of the elites was earlier supported by the lawyer Clarke's father, who advised Sir Everhard Greaves before he died regarding young Launcelot's proclivity for "squandering away his time among the dregs of the people" (24). The youth was known to avoid "any of his relations, except when he was in some manner forced to appear at table" (22). Clarke describes the planned solution, which involved the Temple, the central institution of English legal education: "My father counseled him to send the young gentleman up to London, to be entered as a student in the Temple, and recommended to the superintendence of some person who knew the town, and might engage him insensibly in such amusements, and connexions, as would soon lift his ideas above the humble objects on which they had been hitherto employed" (25). Although Sir Launcelot eventually forsakes his legal studies, by this earlier point in the novel, Smollett has established a view of the legal sphere as properly a bastion of privilege.

As the novel continues, other episodes similarly recast the legal advantages enjoyed by the privileged as promoting the well-being of society as a whole, while complicating and sometimes contradicting Smollett's suggestion that aristocrats alone should enjoy special treatment in the sight of the law.

Sorting Community Debtors from Selfish Spenders

In an additional instance of his interventions in contemporary debates regarding legal agency, Smollett (following in the footsteps of Daniel Defoe) used his writings as a platform for critiquing what he saw as the antisocial impact of English bankruptcy laws on debtors and their social networks. Economic historians have traced a paradigm shift in thinking on bankruptcy law: following seventeenth-century debates on whether to impose more lenient sanctions on debtors whose bankruptcy did not result from profligacy or inordinately risky investments, the eighteenth century ushered in significant changes in bankruptcy law. Ann M. Carlos and Jennifer Lamping have found that 1706 marked the first time that "misfortune" is mentioned in a British bankruptcy statute.[89] As Ian P. H. Duffy observes, "Bankruptcy thus came to be viewed as an act of mercy for innocent victims of the uncontrollable workings of the economy."[90] At the beginning of the eighteenth century, English law thus came to formally acknowledge that bankruptcy was not inherent proof of attempts to defraud but could happen to honest men, as well.

In 1758–59, a few years before *Greaves* was published, a parliamentary committee reviewed petitions to reform the bankruptcy laws. Influenced by a pamphlet detailing the misfortunes of the righteous debtor Captain George Walker, presented as evidence for the committee, Smollett lambasted the re-vamped law for creating new inequities: a single creditor could withhold the "certificate of conformity" needed to exempt the debtor from imprisonment and absolve him of his debts. Moreover, he complained, the arbitrary £100 debt limit, beyond which debtors did not qualify for relief, resulted in the unjust confinement of many who had not intended to defraud their creditors. As Earl Briden has noted, the novel tracks with his political commentary on the legislation.[91] In the *Continuation*, Smollett insisted that there was no essential correlation between amount of debt and moral fault.

Late in the novel, Greaves tours King's Bench Prison in London, where he hears multiple sad tales of bankruptcy that, more often than not, result from attempts to rescue others in need; it is the legal system that punishes community-minded financial decisions by failing to differentiate between honest and dishonest debtors. Rather than framing bankruptcy as a hostile act aimed at a community of interdependent financial actors—a calculated betrayal that flouts responsibility to uphold one's obligations to others and erodes trust within that community—Smollett depicts it as a lamentable out-come of futile but commendable efforts to support others in need and bolster the social safety net. Greaves's friend Felton regales him with a lengthy ac-count of the woes of a prisoner, Captain Clewlin, as they pass him. Before he was incarcerated, Clewlin "was commander of a sloop of war, and bore the reputation of a gallant officer," but he goes broke after "he unwarily involved himself as security for a man to whom he had lain under obligations" (159). When the man reneges on his debt, Clewlin is on the hook for "a considerable sum," and his "sole creditor" turns out to be none other than his vengeful father-in-law, a wealthy merchant who aims to punish Clewlin for marrying his daughter without his knowledge (159). The father arranges for Clewlin to be arrested in a humiliating public scene. The couple appeals to the father, but he is unforgiving; once the family is incarcerated, the couple's son dies, and they turn their hostility on each other, engaging in bloody boxing matches before raucous crowds of fellow prisoners. Clewlin's generous provision of a social safety net for someone to whom he is unrelated but involved in mutual obligation is contrasted with the unnatural (but, in Smollett's oeuvre, all too frequent) action of a father who condemns his child to penury.

As fictional exemplars of the community-minded—and thus exculpated— bankrupt, Clewlin and Felton are juxtaposed with an undeserving bankrupt, a "fine lady" (163) who fritters away the donations she receives from charitable visitors on exorbitant petty luxuries: "About a fortnight ago she received a supply of twenty guineas; when, instead of paying her little gaol-debts, . . . she laid out the whole sum in a fashionable suit and laces" (164). According to the narrator of *Greaves*, the lady "seems to think her rank in life intitles her to this kind of assistance" and is deprecated as a drain on the community: "She talks very pompously of her family and connexions, by whom, however, she has been long renounced. She has no sympathy nor compassion for the distresses of her fellow-creatures" (164).

In the *Continuation of the Complete History of England,* Smollett had criticized a proposed debt relief act for setting limits on the amount of debt that could be forgiven, thus, to his mind, discriminating against men of means who undertook financial risks that benefited society at large: "A man, who through unavoidable misfortunes, hath sunk from affluence to misery and indigence, is generally a greater object of compassion than those who never knew the delicacies of life, nor ever enjoyed credit sufficient to contract debts to any considerable amount."[92] At the same time, the passage makes clear that Smollett's compassion is limited to those whose spending he believes generates prosperity for the larger community. Smollett underscored the ramifications of the punishment not only for the debtor but also for the general public: "Wherefore many valuable individuals should, for no guilt of their own, be not only ruined to themselves, but lost to the community?"[93]

In the case of Coleby, another hapless figure whose troubles are recounted for Sir Launcelot during his tour of the prison, the narrator emphasizes the reputation formerly enjoyed by the bankrupt man: a "person of unblemished character" and a "reputable tradesman," Coleby had "failed through inevitable losses"—that is, through no fault of his own (165). As in Felton's case, debt relief is stymied by a single creditor: all of the tradesman's creditors sign Coleby's certificate, except for one, "a quaker," who is unnamed by the narrator. When Coleby's wife visits the creditor's house to appeal to him and "kneeled before him with her five lovely children, imploring mercy with tears and exclamations," the man "stood this scene unmoved, and even seemed to enjoy the prospect" (165). The "quaker" is singled out as an alien presence within the community, oddly immune to the natural sympathies that govern normal people. As with the "fine lady," a caricature of ruinously materialistic femininity, Smollett contrasts an honest debtor's public track record of recognized civic virtue with the self-interested intransigence of a member of a widely stigmatized identity group. Similar characterization of members of the Society of Friends as threatening the fabric of the community are found in contemporary writings, even ones that found some aspects of Quaker life admirable. Notably, in *The History of England*, published a year prior to *Sir Launcelot Greaves*, David Hume had portrayed the Quakers as a sect that deliberately disengaged from the rest of the nation's subjects: "They never made such a figure in public transactions as to enter into any part of our narrative"; in following a founder who "broke off all connexions with his friends and family" to follow his calling, society adherents renounced social hierarchy.[94] Presenting a vignette that surely was not representative of the situation of most debtors, the novel scapegoats a religious minority and demurs from critique of the mainstream men of capital who were more typically creditors.

Detaining the Elite

In contrast to *The Reprisal*, which from its opening focused on wrongful detainment of the elite, *Sir Launcelot Greaves* gradually escalates the severity of violations from commoners verbally mocking the protagonist, to attempted assaults by highwaymen, to imprisonment without trial. Written in the shadow of the failed 1758 Habeas Corpus Act, the novel repeatedly underscores the gravity of violations of due process, featuring several vignettes involving elite detainees. The act would have expanded the legal protections of *habeas corpus* to protect from illegal imprisonment not only those accused in criminal cases but also those charged in civil matters. Whig legislators introduced the act in the midst of an abrupt surge in *habeas corpus* petitions caused by the Seven Years' War (1756–63), as men forced into service as sailors sought to be released.[95] Most men abducted by the state for "impressment" were from the lower classes. Yet the 1758 reform had originated with the plight of an elite man, and this anomaly captured Smollett's attention, as reflected in the *Continuation*:

> The occasion that produced the . . . bill . . . [was] an incident equally extraordinary and interesting. . . . During the recess of parliament, a gentleman having

been impressed by the commissioners, and confined in the Savoy, his friends made application for a habeas corpus, which produced some hesitation, and indeed an insurmountable difficulty: for, according to the writ of habeas corpus, passed in the reign of the second Charles, this privilege relates only to persons committed for criminal, or supposed criminal matters, and the gentleman did not stand in that predicament. Before the question could be determined he was discharged, in consequence of an application to the secretary of war; but the nature of the case plainly pointed out a defect in the act, seemingly of the most dangerous consequence to the liberty of the subject.[96]

The gentleman's predicament motivates Smollett's critique of the defects in the law. Although the chief beneficiaries of the act, had it passed, would have been low-status men who lacked the financial resources and powerful friends that supported "the gentleman" at the center of the episode (William Hamilton, a prosperous wine merchant), Smollett's commentary does not reflect any urgent concern for their distress under the law. He is instead disturbed by the indignity suffered by the privileged subject who was the impetus for changing the law. Smollett had portrayed impressment in his earlier novel *Roderick Random* (1748), where the protagonist, the son of a wealthy gentleman, is set apart from the other men forced to work as sailors, who are depicted as loutish and undisciplined. Although in the *Continuation* Smollett concludes the section on the 1758 habeas measures with a general encomium to liberty, his focus on the plight of the gentlemen mistakenly caught up in impressment reflects the same class bias expressed by the author of a 1777 pamphlet, *An Essay on the Legality of Impressing Seamen*, who wrote, "In the distribution of the duties of society, those which are the offensive and disagreeable public duties . . . must fall to the lot of that part of mankind which fills the lower ranks of life. . . . This mode of distribution, howsoever hard or unjust it may appear to the human eye, is necessarily incident to society."[97]

The novel's depictions of *habeas* cases present the elite complainants as uniquely deserving of a legal remedy: unquestionably innocent and highly informed as to their rights. Midway through the novel, Greaves attempts to extricate Clarke and Crowe (who have been wrongfully arrested on charges of assaulting a group of belligerent peasants) from prison, only to find himself locked into their cell by a jailor who believes a false claim by the novel's aforementioned agent of discord, Ferret, who implicated Greaves as a fugitive in exchange for avoiding arrest. In step-by-step detail (the procedural formal realism of which is at odds with the conventions of the chivalric romance tradition in which the novel is steeped), the narrator documents for readers the practical hurdles to seeking release through the writ:

> He entered into consultation with Mr. Thomas Clarke concerning the steps he should take, first for their deliverance, and then for prosecuting and punishing the justice. In result of this conference, the knight called aloud for the jaylor [*sic*], and demanded to see a copy of his commitment, that he might know the cause of his imprisonment, and offer bail; or, in case that should be refused, move for a writ of Habeas Corpus. The jaylor told him the copy of the writ should be forthcoming; but after he had waited some time, and repeated the demand before witnesses, it was not yet produced. (88)

Greaves demonstrates here the legal acumen of a model English subject exercising legal agency: deliberative, knowledgeable of the law, patient, and trusting to law rather than to violence. Yet he is trapped in an area beyond his own community, where others refuse to recognize his rights. Even after the jailer realizes the mistake—Ferret gave false information to escape imprisonment—the trio of prisoners are nonetheless compelled to appear before the corrupt Judge Gobble, whose wife mistakes Greaves for a person of low status and belittles him accordingly: "Can you deny that you are a vagram [vagrant], and a dilatory sort of person?" (90). Her hostile line of questioning fulfills the prediction by Ferret at the outset of Greaves's quest that, if he moves beyond his own jurisdiction, officers of the law will seize the opportunity to take a high-status man into custody as a "vagrant." The couple's malapropism-laden speech marks them as arrivistes; Gobble is a low-born ignoramus who ascended to the bench when he married the widow of a justice of the peace. Mrs. Gobble's mistaken impression is corrected when a prosperous surgeon, Dr. Fillet, comes to Gobble's chambers to visit the trio. Seeing Fillet address Greaves in terms befitting his status as an aristocrat, the judge immediately agrees to release him. Gobble is reprimanded and forced to relinquish his judgeship, following a pattern in Smollett's novels where unworthy (because low-born) agents of the law are challenged and expelled from the legal arena. While Greaves is alarmed by his wrongful imprisonment, he is extricated from the situation with his faith in law intact.

The stakes are yet higher in the penultimate chapter of the novel: Greaves is abducted and transferred to a holding cell by ruffians hired by Philip Sycamore, his rival for Aurelia's hand. Whereas previous imprisonments lasted a few hours, his captivity here is lengthy. The episode is thus a more rigorous test of the hero's naive trust in law's capacity to safeguard his right to due process:

> The knight, being thus abandoned . . . began to ruminate. . . . What made the strongest impression upon his mind, was a notion that he was apprehended on suspicion of treasonable practices, by a warrant from the secretary of state, in consequence of some false malicious information; and that his prison was no other than the house of a messenger, set apart for the accommodation of suspected persons. In this opinion he comforted himself by recollecting his own conscious innocence, and reflecting that he should be entitled to the privilege of *habeas corpus,* as the act including that inestimable jewel, was happily not suspended at this juncture. (175)

The description of *habeas corpus*—hailed as the "inestimable jewel" of British law—is at once ironic (the phrasing is another instance of the equivocally hyperbolic statements of legal exigency that proliferate among Smollett's characters) and in earnest. The historian Paul Halliday observes, "As an instrument of jurisdictional management, *habeas corpus* covered a wider space and a wider range of people than we often appreciate, pulling many who were not the king's 'natural' subjects into the benefits of subjecthood."[98] Yet Smollett's narrator reminds us that this protection could vanish at the whims of state: "happily not suspended at this time" sardonically registers the historical reality that *habeas corpus* had been suspended in 1689, 1696, 1708, 1715, 1722, and 1745.[99] The protections it offered were fragile, if not illusory.[100]

A more immediate reason, though, that Greaves is wrong to find comfort in law is that he has been conveyed not to a government jail but to a private asylum, where his rights as a British subject and his elite prerogative alike mean nothing. Similar to Agamben's "state of exception," Sycamore's asylum is an "anomic space."[101] As opposed to the state of exception, though, which instantiates a devolution from democracy to totalitarianism, Sycamore's jail is in some ways oddly democratic. It pays no respect to distinctions of rank: "How little reason . . . have we to boast of the blessings enjoyed by the British subject, if he holds them on such a precarious tenure: if a man of rank and property may be thus kidnapped!" Greaves exclaims to himself (179). He elaborates: "In England, the most innocent person on earth is liable to be . . . sequestered from his wife, children, and friends . . . and subjected to the most brutal treatment from a low-bred barbarian, who . . . may, during his whole life, practise this horrid oppression without question or controul" (180). His description of the asylum as "brutal" does not match his treatment, which is humane but not deferential: his shackles are removed on request, and he can roam through the place. Whereas Greaves was comforted by his initial belief that he had been arrested for treason—a charge that recognizes a person as a full-fledged member of the national community, albeit one who has betrayed it—he is incensed by his actual fate: unheroic existence in a place where fellow prisoners from a variety of social ranks talk and write, freely expressing themselves; where jailers refuse to converse with him, and nobody shows much deference to an aristocrat.

Greaves is eventually freed after his friends announce a reward for information leading to his recovery. After prosecuting his captors, he returns to marry his beloved Aurelia in the midst of a crowd of cheering peasants; but his firsthand, experiential realization—that a pillar of the community can morph into an isolated nobody with the stroke of a legislator's pen or the crossing of a jurisdictional boundary—shadows the novel's joyous resolution. Greaves has, with each episode of wrongful incarceration in unfamiliar jurisdictions, glimpsed what it is like to operate in the world as do ordinary folk bereft of the privileges he enjoys—what it is like to lose that sense of boundless freedom and movement without consequences. Unalloyed by the condescension that runs through the scenes of Greaves's prison tour, with its tableaux of "everyman" prisoners duped by predators and deprived of their freedom, episodes of Greaves's experiences of "oppression" convey the indignation of the loss of legal agency with a particularly galvanizing heatedness. Unexpectedly, it is focalization through an aristocratic character that conveys some measure of the types of ignominy endured by those deemed "equivocal characters."

⌒

Composed in the midst of his own courtroom battles, which compounded his long-standing disenchantment with the legal system, Smollett's midcareer literary works cast doubt on the belief that we can reliably differentiate between those who deserve access to the legal system and those who deserve—whether by dint of their moral failings, place of origin, or innate inferiority—to be deprived of due process and consideration. Taken together, Smollett's midcareer novels and play suggest that access to due process must accommodate elite mobility across jurisdictions. All three works neglect to muster similar rancor for violations of the legal agency of the poor; in a similar vein, efforts of the upwardly mobile to assert their power as officers of the law are mocked and reviled.

The violations of due process experienced by Greaves, the self-appointed guardian of his land, could simply be taken as an illustration of Derrida's notion of "disastrous autoimmunity," in which the community's security measures malfunction and begin attacking its own, mistaking its constituents for invaders. Such an eventuality, J. Hillis Miller asserts, is "an absolutely universal condition of any political order or community."[102] Yet Greaves is more properly considered an outsider in the context of the small rural communities he visits: he represents the type of elite travelers who chafe at jurisdictional restrictions on their autonomy. Such problems are resolved when the upwardly mobile (emphatically nonelite) officers of the law—justices of the peace and jailers—who present themselves as providing security for the community find their authority assailed when community members question the basis of their shared ties. For Greaves and the so-called global citizens who would arrive centuries later, the "autoimmunity" of a community—and its shifting loyalties and susceptibility to reorganization around new values—is not an indicator of social dysfunction, but rather a beneficial corrective force: it facilitates the transfer of control to the elites.

The view that the novel was an innovative form particularly suited to facilitating empathy by conveying to readers the perspective of those marginalized by the legal system is now a critical commonplace. Smollett's midcareer works imagine "oppression" from the point of view of elite persons—aristocrats, the gentry, or the wealthy—who are assaulted on the highways or assailed in the legal system by those below them on the social hierarchy, who are invariably disgruntled or envious. The legal critique embedded in Smollett's work cannot be described as reactionary, for it demonstrates the need for reform. Yet the changes they support are geared toward further entrenching the long-standing social hierarchy. To those who believe in the salvific power of the ideology of rights and due process, Smollett's work provides a cautionary example of the extent to which claims of "oppression" in legal contexts, along with demands for rights, can be mobilized to protect those who were best equipped to wield power over the human quarries of their choice.

CHAPTER TWO

Covert Critique

Genteel Victimhood in Charlotte Smith's
Fictions of Dispossession

How can victims of a broken justice system convince a cynical public of the need for legal reform—especially when the people in need are those of privilege? The spirited and still underappreciated novels of Charlotte Turner Smith are devoted to this formidable undertaking. The protagonists of Smith's novels, which she began writing in the late 1780s to support her beleaguered family, tend to be seekers of justice whose profiles mirror her own: cultured, intellectually curious, and on the cusp of poverty owing to the decisions of morally compromised patriarchs who have failed to safeguard the family wealth. In her works, Smith launched fierce attacks on the legal institutions that blighted her life; people of status, she implied, had the most to lose. At a time when women had minimal legal agency, this chapter shows, Smith built a popular audience for her grievances because her novels were packaged as innocuous sentimental romances appropriate for female readers: her tales of bereft orphans and far-flung lovers served as crowd-pleasing, socially condoned vectors for disseminating legal critique and reflections on civil liberties. Yet Smith encouraged even middle-class readers to care about a select demographic with whom most had little in common: downwardly mobile members of once-wealthy landed families. Smith lambastes the English legal system for imposing barriers to access and resolution—barriers that had become increasingly difficult to surmount for cash-poor gentry who sought to claim and protect their ancestral property.[1]

Even scholars who admire her work often categorize Smith as either a derivative practitioner of the sentimental novel that had peaked in the mid-eighteenth century or an unpolished adopter of the Gothic tradition that originated in the 1760s and flowered in the 1790s.[2] Others regard her as an informed discussant of the ideas of prominent male philosophers such as

William Godwin[3] or as an inferior though influential predecessor of geniuses such as Jane Austen and William Wordsworth.[4] Yet the groundbreaking nature of Smith's novels becomes clear if she is properly recognized as the first English female author to adopt a thriving Continental tradition of legal discourse for laypeople. She converted her victimhood at the hands of the law from shameful imbroglio to a foundation for epistemological authority on legal matters, and her early translations of French legal texts known as *pitavals* empowered her to compose novels of unusually specific detail. With keen commercial acumen, she discerned that there could be demand for such work; with few exceptions, earlier eighteenth-century British writers of lay legal guides had not tailored their work to address a mixed-gender audience. Even guides designed for middle-class men were typically little more than glorified legal dictionaries.

By examining Smith's translation of French legal cases, *The Romance of Real Life* (1787), as well as her novels *Emmeline, the Orphan of the Castle* (1788), *The Old Manor House* (1793), and *Marchmont* (1796), I will show that Smith conveyed knowledge of the law to readers with scant personal legal agency or knowledge of legal discourse by smuggling in didactic primers in the guise of sentimental romances—one of the only genres seen as acceptable (even if only marginally) for women writers. From the beginning of the century, women who dared to bring their literary work to market were chastised for self-exposure: one of the century's most famous English poets, Alexander Pope, in his mock-epic masterpiece *The Dunciad* (1728–43), had notoriously represented the author Eliza Haywood as a sexually available woman whose "cow-like udders" are her most conspicuous characteristic; in his poem, she stands in public to be ogled by men who vie to win her as a prize in a urination contest. Smith preempted such objections by styling her self-promotion in the marketplace of print as a task reluctantly taken on to feed her nine children, who were "starved" by a father who had abdicated his role as provider. Similarly, her characters' attempts at self-assertion in legal matters are contextualized as efforts to defend their families, who have been targeted by predatory aristocrats or self-serving, upwardly mobile lawyers.

Smith's critique of the law was rooted in personal experience. By the late 1780s, as her career ascended to new heights, Smith was both a prolific author and a single mother on the brink of poverty, and she broadcast her plight to her readers while writing hundreds of letters to lawyers and trustees involved in her family's ongoing legal ordeal. Her children, she claimed, had been deprived of an inheritance explicitly bequeathed to them by their paternal grandfather, who had devised his will to ensure that his wealth would not go to his abusive, spendthrift son—Smith's estranged husband, Benjamin Smith. Yet because the will was made without the assistance of a lawyer, it lacked the necessary legal verbiage and was contested. In the meantime, Benjamin further imperiled the family by pocketing his wife's literary earnings and refusing to provide financial support for the nine children he left in Charlotte's care. The legal battle raged in and out of Chancery for three decades and was resolved only after the estranged pair died; by then, the once sizable fortune had been consumed by legal fees.[5]

Some Romantic-era readers objected that Smith publicized her troubles in a manner too self-indulgent even for the intensely emotional genres in which she specialized: lyric poetry and sentimental romance. These genres more readily accommodated female authorship because of their supposed compatibility with feminine sensibility and subject matter. Yet Smith was rebuked for emphasizing the challenges she faced as a privileged woman over the sufferings of those in more desperate straits: "The pity we should naturally feel for [emigrants'] overwhelming and uncommon distresses, is lessened by their being brought into parallel with [Smith's own] inconveniences of a narrow income or a protracted lawsuit," one reviewer tartly commented.[6] This criticism of her work persisted centuries later: the author of a 1941 critical study of Smith's work described her style as usually "plaintive or querulous."[7] Even Smith's twenty-first-century boosters expect that today's readers, too, may dismiss Smith as a navel-gazing harpy: the editor of the author's hundreds of letters to patrons, lawyers, and publishers anticipated that readers would view Smith as "obsessed with the inheritance, ever ready to insult the trustees of the estate, sinking into despair, or, less acceptably, self-pity over her lot in life."[8] Others follow Smith's own lead in describing her as an "exile" from the centers of power.[9]

Her self-positioning as a victim was strategic and prone to selective emphasis: Smith cast herself as an indigent single mother and downplayed the advantages she enjoyed as a best-selling author with a substantial public platform.[10] Her affluent upbringing had afforded her the extensive reading knowledge and social connections to exert herself to become informed about her legal case. She also benefited from an unusually high level of personal energy and a fierce work ethic.

Smith was uniquely positioned to educate female readers, not only because she wrote in stereotypically feminine genres but also because her leading role in her family's drawn-out legal battles gave her rare insight into what it was like to navigate the legal system as a woman. The philosopher François

Laruelle has encouraged scholars to reject long-standing cultural tendencies to define victims primarily in terms of their suffering.[11] I extend his idea to suggest that the victim can be construed not simply as an object of knowledge or figure of sentiment but as an epistemological agent who acquires knowledge through dire experience. The victimhood Smith claimed was not only a means of seeking pity; she also strategically cultivated it as grounds for claiming legal standing and bolstering the credibility of the legal information she featured in her novels. As Smith's protagonists undergo a course of learning by experience similar to that which she endured, she reframes their ordeal of loss of privilege as part of their claim to moral clarity and legal acumen.

Male novelists had previously ventured into this terrain, but their conceptualization of victimhood tended to be less innovative. Although Godwin's 1832 reflection on his novel *Caleb Williams* (1794) associates victimhood with epistemological agency—"the innocent victim should be impelled by an unconquerable spirit of curiosity"[12]—the thirty instances in which the term *victim* appears in the main text of the novel connote a passive, helpless target of physical brutality as opposed to a bearer of hard-won knowledge. The eighteenth-century novel tended to dwell on the legal calamities of charismatic criminals or tableaux of helpless innocents rather than the efforts of ladies to empower themselves with legal knowledge; nor was demystifying the realm of law a primary objective of eighteenth-century fiction in the first place. Popular novels, particularly those aimed at female readers, rarely featured scenes detailing the mundane indignities and financial struggles of legal conflict. Women were perceived as especially impressionable (and thus in need of protection from immoral content) as well as neither intellectually capable of, nor interested in, understanding the intricacies of law.[13]

Smith's pathbreaking novels slipped under the radar of cultural censors because her writing appeared to uphold gender norms regarding legal expertise. Although several of her protagonists are female, it is Smith's male characters who serve as mouthpieces for her ambition to popularize legal discourse and demystify legal practices for readers unfamiliar with the law. Tim Period—the impecunious law-student-turned-author in her play *What Is She?* (1799)—disparages the "out of fashion" works of Hale, Bacon, Littleton, and Coke, and proposes to restyle "dry—dry [and] dull" legal discourse for readers through literary legerdemain: "I'll so reform the dissonant language of the law—then you shall see reports measured into blank verse—Briefs like the descriptions of the moon in modern romance, and chancery suits in the style of Gibbon."[14] Period's status-preoccupied uncle, Ap-Griffin, is aghast, and he chastises Period as "profane" and "unnatural" for having the temerity "to violate the venerable obscurity of the law." Yet Period suggests that there is a conduit between lawyerdom and authorship: "Don't the lawyers write plays and pamphlets till they get briefs?"[15]

Fulfilling Period's aspirations, in her novels and published translations of French law cases, Smith makes the legal process relatable, in the sense both of "narratable," rendering complex legal conflicts intelligible through narrative, and of "familiar," tethering those conflicts to the standard plot trajectory of a young person's misadventures en route to marriage. From covert representations of defiance toward legal authority in *Emmeline* to explicit condemnation half a decade later in *The Old Manor House*, Smith gradually amplified her characterization of law as a battleground that pitted dispossessed youths of status and merit against ineffectual or abusive patriarchs and scheming legal professionals. The sections that follow show, first, how Smith modified French source texts to highlight the legal ordeals faced by privileged women and, second, how several of her novels depict her protagonists advancing from resentful compliance with the legal system to acquisition of skills that allow them to bypass the predatory officials and professionals who control it to envisioning its destruction.

Skirting the Law: Critical Misperceptions of Smith's Intervention

Surprisingly, it was Smith's adherence to popular expectations of what constituted work typical of female authors, not her defection from such protocol, that was most apt to rouse her detractors: although her lengthy complaints in her prefaces, replications of standard romance plot templates, and hyperbolically emotive characters were frequent targets of critical derision, no eighteenth-century reviews object to Smith's incorporation of legal themes or her lambasting of the legal status quo as subject matter unbefitting a female novelist. The derivative surface elements of Smith's novels may have distracted critics from objecting to the innovative legal critique embedded within her derivative plots of love and vicissitude. Strikingly forthright and protonaturalistic passages of legal critique are enveloped in the sheer frothiness of her plots, in which improbable coincidences and hackneyed proclamations of love and suffering abound.

When critics do discuss the role of legal conflict in Smith's novels, they do so in service of the type of biographically oriented readings of female novelists that have remained predominant long after the second-wave feminist reclamation of eighteenth- and nineteenth-century female authors. Such readings imply that law figured in Smith's life simply as a catalyst for her interminable personal crises rather than as an intellectual concern—a sympathetic characterization that hardly seems to advance the objective of raising Smith's profile and ushering her beyond the feminized genre backwater of pseudo-autobiographical transcription.[16]

Smith's political themes (especially in her 1792 novel *Desmond*, which focused on the French Revolution) have garnered more interest over the past few decades.[17] The debate over Smith's politics continues to focus on the extent to which she either repudiated or continued to adhere to her early support of the revolutionary cause, an emphasis that goes back at least to Katharine M. Rogers's recovery work in the 1970s.[18] Smith's legal critique is more innovative and original than her political writings, because she was directly involved in legal concerns but far removed from the political halls of power. Whereas Smith was an also-ran among the phalanx of British Romantic writers who initially supported the precepts motivating the French Revolution, her novelistic accounts of members of once-affluent families who endure near-constant legal intimidation and humiliation have few counterparts in late eighteenth-century prose. Smith limns in painstaking detail the legal processes and terminology germane to these experiences. In her novels, Smith offered what amounted to a trove of edifying scripts for legal predicaments ranging from refusing a request for a warrantless search of one's home to negotiating the fees of legal counsel.

By contrast, her more famous contemporary, Mary Wollstonecraft, glosses over the technical details of the legal predicaments of her heroines, dedicating more attention to the emotional strain they suffer. Wollstonecraft's unfinished novel *The Wrongs of Woman; or, Maria* (published posthumously in 1798), for example, features a righteous speech by the heroine at trial but provides the barest outline of the proceedings.[19] Later women novelists showed female characters capably discussing law with male practitioners, but they did not go as far as Smith had earlier. In *The Wanderer; or, Female Difficulties* (1814), for instance, Frances Burney's antiheroine Elinor Joddrel helps prepare her fiancé for his cases by serving as his sparring partner in mock trials ("I always took the opposite side to that which he was employed to plead, in order to try his powers, and prove my own").[20] While Burney may have chosen Elinor's surname to call to mind a prominent legal family,[21] Elinor is limited to playacting legal cases, and the activity is summarized in two sentences. Smith's female protagonists, by contrast, intervene in actual legal conflicts with large sums and precious lives at stake.

In her correspondence, Smith explicitly yearned for more; she desired the legal autonomy that men enjoyed. When in 1801 her brother, Nicholas Turner, declined to take steps that would advance her case—legal measures of which she could not avail herself because she was a woman—she vented her anger in a letter: "Mr Turner talk'd (& *ought to do* it) of fyling a bill agst M^r B Smith to compel him to fulfill *his* agreement in regard to the marriage Articles. I know this might be done, & who but my Brother is there to defend me from the injustice I sustain? Would to God *I* had been the brother—I think no sister of mine should have been oppressed as I have been by such a biped as that wretched Madman."[22]

In a similar vein, recalling praise from Lord Egremont (the trustee who was assisting her case), Smith wrote in an 1802 letter, "His Lordship . . . has often *ordered* me to write & explain this or that thing [concerning the legal case]—He has often said, no one understood the business, but me; & as often commended my activity—He once, in 1800 said of Mr. Turner [Nicholas]—'If *he* had half your activity & perseverance there would be some chance of saving him from ruin.'"[23] Through her fiction, Smith envisioned a British society in which active involvement in legal concerns was no longer the exclusive province of powerful men.

A Departure from Earlier Legal Guides for the Masses

The 1700s were characterized by one commentator as "the century of popularization of legal lore."[24] Increasing literacy rates and cheaper production methods brought a wave of new customers for all types of literature,[25] especially lay legal discourse. To grasp the magnitude of Smith's innovation, it helps to contrast her work with the English-language legal guides as well as the Continental texts that directly inspired her.

Of the British texts, Giles Jacob's works had the greatest longevity, with new editions issued well into the nineteenth century.[26] His works were peddled as affordable digests of legal concepts for readers who were flummoxed by the vast and nonsystematized array of legal texts. In *The Student's Companion, or The Reasons of the Law of England* (1725), he declared:

> I could instance Bracton, and Britton, Littleton, Lord Coke, Plowden, Wingate, and others, whom I have Read and Studied. . . . And I hope I may have the Liberty of saying, that in all their Elaborate Treatises, the Reader, for want of a due Method and by their overgrown Prolixity, is generally in a Wilderness, and like a Traveller in a Wood without a Guide, who, when once he is got in, is sure

to be lost, and not to find his Way out. . . . It hath been my principal Care to trace and lay open a Path that is *New* . . . For Students of all Kinds, whether in the Profession of the Law, or Gentlemen out of it, this Book is universally adapted.[27]

In his final work, the best-selling *Every Man His Own Lawyer* (1736), Jacob again stated that he aimed to palliate "obscure" laws by elucidating legal information in "plain Language," as he termed it: "What I shall now attempt, is to introduce an Instructive Treatise, writ in the easiest Method, and adapted to any Capacity, whereby the Unskilful, and those who are Ignorant in the Practice of the Law, may in some Measure be their own Advisers."[28] Yet Jacob's tracts are themselves written in dense, jargon-heavy prose (several passages were quoted verbatim and mocked by Smollett in *Sir Launcelot Greaves* as verbose and pretentious). They are also unengaging: instead of clarifying terms through illustrative case studies—as did later guides—*Every Man His Own Lawyer* merely offers definitions occasionally interspersed with templates for standard legal documents.

Appearing a couple of years earlier, *A Treatise of Feme Coverts, or, The Lady's Law* (1732) presented a similar bait and switch. The anonymous author promises empowerment: "The fair Sex are here informed, how to preserve their Land, Goods, and most valuable Effects, from the incroachments [*sic*] of any one; to defend themselves and their Reputations against all unlawful Attacks of Mankind, and to maintain Actions, and to carry on Prosecutions in cases of Violation of their Person to the Death of a daring Offender."[29] Yet the book consists mainly of descriptions of legal actions in which women cannot participate without the aid of husbands. At one point, the author remarks, "A Feme Covert [married woman], in our Books, is often compared to an Infant, both being Persons disabled in the Law; but they differ very much: an Infant is capable of doing any Act for his own Advantage, not so a Feme Covert."[30] This state of affairs is not explicitly lamented, nor are remedies proposed. Thus, the self-help legal publications of the era—packaged as keys to disrupting a bewildering legal system—provide little in the way of substantive guidance.

The Lady's Law did feature two promising innovations: first, it catered to a neglected female audience. By contrast, at the beginning of *Every Man His Own Lawyer*, Jacob proclaims that he will demystify the law for "all Manner of Persons,"[31] but he defines "persons" as male; he mentions women only occasionally, in the context of what law-related roles they are prohibited from holding (for example, constable). Second, *The Lady's Law* intermingled practical information on topics such as real estate and inheritance law with lively fictional anecdotes: "Some Things of Entertainment . . . are mix'd with the Law. And our old Laws and Customs relating to Women, are many of them very merry, though the Makers of them might possibly be grave Men."[32] Although *The Lady's Law* was not as successful as Jacob's guides, it anticipated the popular nonfiction-fiction hybrids that appeared in France a few years later—works whose authors welcomed female readers and most directly inspired Smith's early forays into publication.

After an early tangle with the law, in which her translation of a French novel was foiled by legal threats,[33] Smith published *The Romance of Real Life*. *The Romance* is a translation of select episodes from two compendia of French legal cases: François Gayot de Pitaval's eighteen-volume series *Les causes célèbres et intéressantes* (1734–41) and François Richer's twenty-two volume expanded edition of the series (1772–88). A transnational, primarily male-authored tradition, *pitavals* came to be known as an eponymous genre of texts based on real-life court cases.

For the century following the enthusiastic reception of Gayot de Pitaval's collection, pitavals flourished in France and Germany, where they were used to educate law students and cited in jurisprudence; Susanne Kord asserts that in Germany, such texts were "an integral part of the legal curriculum."[34] Difficult to imagine today, when literary fiction is clearly set apart from law journal articles, the pitaval's boundary-straddling between edifying legal discourse and entertaining fiction was perceived as an asset in German legal education, where students were taught that the "relation" of a criminal case "had to incorporate both juridical and poetical rules."[35]

Gayot de Pitaval envisioned a wide audience for his work that included both men of law and women traditionally marginalized from the legal sphere: in a prefatory letter defending his project in one of the subsequent volumes, he wrote, "J'ai voulu mettre mon livre entre les mains des gens du Barreau, des gens du monde, & même des Dames"[36] (I wanted to get my work into the hands of members of the bar, members of society, and even the ladies). Yet the price of the collections meant that only affluent consumers ("professional jurists and members of the social elite," as Sarah Maza notes)[37] could afford to own it. Decades later, in the expanded series, Richer similarly asserted that his paramount objective was to reach a vast readership; he proclaimed that succeeding in this objective was more important than convincing readers to agree with his legal views.[38]

Smith stated that she did not expect to make her literary name through the project: "I am aware indeed that it is a kind of work from which little fame can arise to its author" (*RRL* v); but in selecting the pitaval as an entry point into the publishing market, Smith was making a shrewd commercial decision: the genre was popular on the Continent, but curiously underexploited in Britain. As did earlier authors, she capitalized on the eighteenth-century British legal trend toward Anglicizing legal texts: a 1731 act of Parliament had abolished the usage of law Latin, the language preferred by barristers, in published court proceedings.[39] Explaining her plan to bring the pitavals to a wider English audience, Smith attests to the significance of the achievements of Gayot de Pitaval and Richer but contends that despite her predecessors' explicitly stated intentions to reach a wide audience, "The style of the original is frequently obscure. . . . The attention is bewildered and the interest weakened."[40] She declared that she was rescuing the earlier work for a new generation of readers who otherwise would not bother "wading thro' the obscurities and extraneous matter of M. de Pitaval" (*RRL* iv).

The *Romance* remains underexamined; as Angela Wright notes, "Critics thus far—with the recent exception of Michael Gamer—have tended to overlook the import of [Smith's] second translation venture."[41] Gamer finds that the *Romance* is "usually dismissed as hackwork," if it is mentioned by critics at all.[42] Earlier readers were condescending even in praising the work. One of London's leading periodicals, the *Monthly Review*, applauded Smith for removing the "judicial" substance of the cases—that is, the details of the legal procedures that had been included in the French originals—and compressing the multivolume works of legal reportage into sentimental fiction: "On looking into the original work, which consists of upwards of twenty volumes, we find that many of these 'stories,' as the translator calls them, are *Trials* and *Cases in law*, and consequently they are not the objects of criticism. The few which are here selected, however, being stripped of the judicial forms of proceedings, will no doubt meet with the approbation of those persons who are fond of tracing the errors and wanderings of the human heart."[43]

The publishers of Smith's work welcomed this assessment; in fact, they used the passage from the *Monthly Review* as a blurb on the first page of subsequent editions. It was apt to reassure a certain sector of Smith's prospective readership. The reviewer's term *stripped*, implies a view of acceptable women's fiction as the refined result of literary processing, in which the raw material of legal reportage—all that judicial fiber too tough for ladies' rumination—is sloughed away. This wholesome version of "stripping" justifies female writers' audacious presence in the literary marketplace, counteracting the allegations of whorish self-exposure so memorably prosecuted by Pope and his fellow literary grandees. The review is emblematic of critics' tendency to bypass or miss altogether the legal commentary latent in Smith's work.

The reviewer's assessment is puzzling, for it does not accurately describe Smith's translations. Angela Wright finds that while Smith "truncates pages of Gayot's legally precise account of the proceedings," it is also the case that "his narratives of the events leading up to the trials that he witnesses are less speculative and more economic than Smith's rendition." Wright is correct in noting that Smith adds "more emotive and descriptive" content to the *Causes célèbres*.[44] Wright's account of Smith's work contributes to the efforts over the past several decades of a number of scholars who consider Smith part of the Gothic literary tradition and have characterized her work in terms of emotion, a primary aspect of that mode. To do so, however, runs the risk of downplaying the legal substance of Smith's novels, particularly the later ones.[45] As will become clear in the following sections, as her literary career continued Smith provided increasingly granular accounts of the mundane transactions involved in legal processes, with a special emphasis on characters' interactions with legal professionals outside the public spectacle of the trial.

Smith's principle of selection indicates her agenda of legal critique. She chose stories of victims whose suffering mirrors her own: they are cast out by their wealthy parents or mistreated by vengeful husbands. As arranged, her tales are intended to elicit sympathy for a specific type of victim: a woman in genteel poverty, entrapped by the law. She elected not to translate cases that featured other categories of litigants, including one involving a Caribbean-born black enslaved man who struggles to gain freedom, whose story and associated legal documents consume more than one hundred pages of one of Gayot de Pitaval's installments.[46] Of the fourteen tales included in the three volumes of *The Romance of Real Life*, only one does not feature an inheritance case in which a female member of the gentry or aristocracy is threatened with the loss of wealth or barred from recognition as an heir in the first place (usually because of the machinations of relatives competing for the fortune, as in Smith's experience). By comparison, in a sample volume of Gayot de Pitaval's *Causes célèbres*, only one case out of forty-five involves inheritance; that topic is outnumbered considerably by accounts based on Scripture or early modern ecclesiastical controversies.[47] German adaptations of the pitavals also do not place particular emphasis on inheritance: in *Merkwürdige Rechtsfälle*

(1792–95—published only five years after Smith's collection), only 15 percent of the cases involve inheritance, while in *Der neue Pitaval* (1842–90) only 2.3 percent do,[48] compared to 92 percent in Smith's version.

Smith emphasizes and supplements the female self-empowerment aspects of Pitaval's originals: when women are barred from official legal roles, they seek other means of influencing legal decisions. In one tale, a wealthy mother campaigns to annul her son's marriage, which has been finalized without her consent: "Madame de Villiers, the mother of the Chevalier, despairing to succeed in her suit by the direct means of equity and justice, was known to have solicited the judges, and to have exerted undue influence to obtain their suffrage" (*RRL* 103). Smith adds the following footnote, not present in the original source: "In the towns in France, where parliaments are held, it is very usual to see the judges walking to the courts with ladies related to the persons whose causes are coming on, or who are interested in the decisions, attending them on each side full dressed" (*RRL* 103). This interpolated commentary undercuts conventional wisdom about legal history, according to which unyielding male oppressors uniformly exiled women from judicial centers of power. Seeing an opportunity for proximity to legal authority, Madame de Villiers takes the initiative. She does so, however, not to effect female liberation but to preserve her own privilege: to engineer the ruin of the lowborn young woman who has charmed her son into marriage. While the pitaval certainly reflects Smith's bitterness toward her own stepmother, her translations show a more general pattern in which women readily forgo gender solidarity to protect or restore their social status.

In the cases that Smith chose to translate, some women find a winning strategy when they summon the nerve to travel far from their local jurisdiction to appeal to higher courts and testify in front of strangers. The key to success is a direct appeal to judicial authorities, unaided by legal professionals. One female protagonist, wrongly accused by the townspeople of arranging her husband's murder, travels from her home region to seek a fair trial in a new district: "Madame de la Pivardi[è]re then went to Paris, where she laid before a superior court, an account of the prosecution that had been commenced against her, and desired . . . its being referred to an officer of the law more impartial than him who had instituted the process. Her request was granted, and the judge of Remorentin was directed to investigate the whole" (164). Smith is describing a distaff variation on what the historian Martin Dinges terms *Justiznutzung*[49] (use of justice),[50] an activity known to be practiced in the early modern period by another group who endured restricted legal agency:

Jewish minorities who sought jurisdictions that would be receptive to their claims. The heroines of the pitavals translated by Smith typically travel alone to seek justice, unaccompanied by male chaperones; more often than not, rather than serving as traditional protectors, male relatives exacerbate the women's social vulnerability and legal troubles. Unlike in a standard-issue sentimental romance, Smith's chosen pitaval episodes rarely culminate in the bliss of conjugal love or the harmony of family life: husbands are murdered or murderous, and lost sons remain missing.

As she made her own way through the "Wilderness" of law, Smith tried to educate herself by reading legal texts and corresponding with lawyers, an assiduous feat of legal autodidacticism that realized the spirit of Jacob's book title. In a letter to her publisher, Smith reported that she spent "more than a week" on "some never ending law business . . . answering and copying Legal papers." Hundreds of letters make up her personal correspondence with the lawyers managing the estate of her deceased father-in-law in her failed quest to restore her children's inheritance. Compared with the nonfiction law guides of an earlier generation, her translations, and particularly her subsequent novels, provide more in-depth details on tactics for navigating a hostile legal system—tailored for those who strived to regain their birthright status.

Feminine Diffidence as Legal Self-Assertion: *Emmeline* (1788)

The litigants featured in the pitavals that Smith translated do not make it easy for the average reader to relate to them. Their royal connections and the notoriety of their lurid cases make them too singular to serve as aspirational models for developing legal agency. Smith's protagonists, by contrast, seem emphatically ordinary at the beginning of her novels. They remain obscure throughout childhood; the years-long legal combat in which they engage garners little public attention, and they undergo a wide variety of sufferings, both acute and banal, that parallel those of regular folk in the real world. Yet as they reach maturity, her heroines invariably enter realms of privilege with which few readers had experience.

Emmeline is the tale of an orphan who rises from obscurity and dependence on others' largesse to claim her ancestral estate. Neglected by her uncle, Lord Montreville, who has dispatched the supposedly illegitimate daughter of his deceased brother to a dilapidated estate where she is under minimal supervision, Emmeline spends hours educating herself by reading all she can in a crumbling library. No books by female authors can be found in the library of the uncle, who trained as a lawyer, and many of the volumes in the collection are ruined by neglect; the roof of the library has caved in. In particular, all of the tomes in "black letter"—a style in which law books were printed through the eighteenth century—have been destroyed by nesting birds and are "so injured by time, that the most indefatigable antiquary could have made nothing of them."[51] This image of a decrepit discursive tradition evokes the extent to which the old ways of disseminating legal knowledge among the scribal elite were inaccessible to the more diverse demographic of later eighteenth-century readers. Emmeline leaves the black letter volumes to perish in a literary semblance of mass graves, "piles . . . tumbled in heaps on the floor, [or] promiscuously placed on the shelves" (47). She prefers to salvage canonical literary texts: the works of Addison and Steele, Shakespeare, Spenser, Milton, and Pope.

For all her hours spent in the library, Emmeline is not a sufficiently circumspect reader. She avoids examining documents that prove to be essential to establishing her birthright: letters from Emmeline's mother to Emmeline's paternal grandmother (who despised her son's chosen bride of humble birth), which include evidence that Emmeline was not born out of wedlock. This information is verified by two separate marriage licenses (one French and one English) for her parents, with dates preceding her birth, that Emmeline has the possession of throughout the book. She keeps the sheaf of papers for years but cannot bring herself to go through it because she fears that accounts of discord among her family members would upset her. Fortunately, when Emmeline was born, her elderly female caregiver astutely rejected demands from the Crofts, Lord Montreville's evil lawyers (a father-son duo), to take possession of the documents, and instead concealed them for Emmeline to find eventually.

Within an ultraformulaic plot, Smith thus embeds anomalies: she shows disempowered female characters—the teenage Emmeline and her illiterate female servant—refusing to comply with the dictates of legal professionals. Even as they defy the law, though, the women comply with conventional expectations of feminine self-conduct. Out of duty to the child in her care, the nurse circumvents the demands of the lawyers while avoiding overt conflict. She hides the papers in a place she believes men will overlook: a container for hair ornaments. Years later, Emmeline, now an adolescent, continues this strategy of seeking legal agency under the cover of adhering to gender norms. She gains legal representation not through strident demands but, instead, through the affective ties that she has nourished: Lord Westhaven, the husband of a female friend, funds her legal representation. Having discovered the hidden papers, Emmeline correctly anticipates that the Crofts will try to seize her copies of the documents if they find out that the papers are in her possession, so she entrusts them to Lord Westhaven rather than to his attorney or the Crofts. Emmeline's social rise depends on her cultivation of male protectors and nurturing of friendship with members of the aristocracy.

By contrast, the interclass male friendships made possible by the remarkable social mobility within the eighteenth-century legal profession are vectors of treachery. When Lord Montreville and the villainous Richard Croft meet while studying to become lawyers, they hail from very different social strata: Richard Croft's "immediate predecessors were known to be indigent and obscure" (116). Nevertheless, "Lord Montreville, during the short time he studied at the Temple, became acquainted with Sir Richard . . . who, tho' there was a great difference in their rank, had contrived to gain the regard and esteem of his Lordship" (116). Bearing a surname meaning "crypt," the Crofts are dead-souled, money-hungry social climbers who manipulate their aristocratic clients into doing their bidding. Following in his father's footsteps, Croft junior—who plays a large role in the plot but is never referred to by his given name—insinuates himself into Lord Montreville's family by marrying the uncle's prideful daughter, Augusta. The Crofts alienate Emmeline from her uncle and suppress Montreville's copies of the documents attesting to the legitimacy of Emmeline's birth because they hope to gain his wealth for themselves; according to the rules of coverture, Croft junior will control his wife's eventual inheritance.

The disdain with which the lawyers address the heroine and their antipathy toward her efforts at self-assertion are not incidental details. Indeed, the lawyers put Emmeline under surveillance in the hopes of catching her in compromising acts and further diminishing her claim to the estate. This tension is emphasized throughout the novel and is emblematic of real-world social dynamics evident in Smith's epistolary correspondence with the legal team of the estate of her father-in-law. Nevertheless, through her connection with the powerful Lord Westhaven, Emmeline manages to protect herself after she flees the Montreville estate.

The emergence of a socially respected aristocrat as a legal ally is a fairy-tale resolution, but Emmeline's choices are what set in motion her legal salvation. As a seemingly assetless female relative whose ability to survive depends in part on her ability to placidly weather even pointed insults, Emmeline has learned to anticipate and minimize conflict. She combines the apparent tractability that is expected of women with an emotional distance that is not typically associated with Romantic-era protagonists: "Emmeline cared nothing about Richard Crofts, and could not enter into . . . bitterness of resentment towards him. . . . The ruder passions of anger and resentment had no influence over her mind" (170). A hybrid of sentimental heroine and savvy legal strategist, Emmeline does not let her emotions imperil her strategy for achieving her legal objectives. At the same time, she is keenly aware of how others' feelings can lead them to make impulsive decisions that may imperil her legal quest, and she uses her insight in planning her maneuvers: "She would not even allow Mr. Newton, the lawyer to whom Lord Westhaven had recommended her, and in whose hands her papers were safely deposited, to write officially to Lord Montreville; but determined to wait quietly the return of Lord Westhaven, on whom she knew neither the anger of Lord Montreville or the artifices of Sir Richard would make any impression" (401).

Emmeline presents her refusal as a means of deferring to the will of Lord Westhaven, but she is making a strategic decision; she uses sentimental fealty to male authority as a pretext to buy time. As a young female ward who is relying on a wealthy man's sponsorship to fund her legal case, she is seemingly devoid of authority, but she has the confidence to veto the requests of male legal professionals. She also carefully chooses whom she will allow to serve as an advocate on her behalf: she rejects the offer of Godolphin, her suitor, to remonstrate with Lord Montreville regarding her legal case, because she wants her case to be assessed on its merits and not perceived as tinctured by Godolphin's ulterior motive of winning her affections. Her strategy succeeds: after the documents are safely conveyed for evaluation, the estate once owned by her parents is transferred to her ownership. Leaning on her adherence to feminine protocol to defuse confrontations with male legal authority, Emmeline demonstrates how the marginalized position of women could be used in the legal realm to reclaim social privilege.

The Price of Representation: Struggling to Find Legal Counsel in *The Old Manor House* (1793)

In contrast to Emmeline's tacit circumvention of legal authorities, in *The Old Manor House* the headstrong protagonist, Orlando Somerive, freely expresses his disdain for the lawyers who thwart his bids for legal agency. The scion of an esteemed family reduced to poverty—his father was disinherited for marrying a low-born woman—Orlando spends years cultivating the favor of his unmarried great aunt, Mrs. Rayland, who hints that she will leave him her estate in her will; in the meantime, he endures the hostility of Mrs. Lennard, her favorite servant. Similar to Smith's other male protagonists, Orlando is properly viewed as providing an occasion for Smith to "reevaluate the naturalization of 'feminine' helplessness," as Derek T. Leuenberger argues.[52] Rather than bending others to his will, Orlando is impoverished, reduced to hiding and pleading, and is even taken captive; this male protagonist is thus an extension of, rather than an exception to, Smith's critique of the law's failure to protect vulnerable people of status.

After Mrs. Rayland passes away, Orlando is chagrined to learn that she has left her entire estate to Mrs. Lennard. A fortune-hunting lawyer, Roker, courts Mrs. Lennard and quickly marries her. Not long after their nuptials, he imprisons her in their bedroom and forbids visitors from calling on her, falsely warning them that she is *"non compos mentis."*[53] Meanwhile, he supports a lavish lifestyle with her wealth. Orlando suspects that the will was forged; despairing of appealing to the Rokers, he plans to sue Dr. Hollybourn, who purchased the property from Mrs. Lennard, and force him to relinquish the property. Daunted by the prospect of contesting ownership, Orlando sets out to find legal representation.

Smith uses this plot development to demystify the process of hiring a lawyer—a topic curiously neglected by earlier French pitavals and English legal guides. She lays out the steps of the process, and the attendant social indignities, in all their cumbersome detail. As a man, Orlando is not hamstrung by the prohibitions that law places in the way of female would-be litigants. Yet owing to his financial difficulties, he is in a similarly disadvantaged position. When Orlando announces his plans to hire a friend, Carr, to represent him, his mother urges him instead to retain Darby, the son-in-law of her wealthy brother, whose favor she cultivates in hopes that he will help support the family. The conversation between Orlando and his mother suggests that finding a lawyer was not only a matter of having sufficient funds; it entailed drawing on social networks and calling in favors from friends or family connections.

The novel draws attention to a crisis of spiraling costs that not only put legal services beyond the reach of the most indigent but also threatened the ability of the genteel poor to engage in legal conflict. Earlier in the eighteenth century, rates of civil litigation had declined precipitously for those of lesser means, due in large part to rising legal fees.[54] In the waning years of the eighteenth century, lawyers were so well-paid that the top echelon commanded "aristocratic" incomes.[55] Another factor in the decline was the significant restriction of the practice of extending legal services on credit.[56]

When Orlando visits Darby, the lawyer demurs from bringing a case against the wealthy Dr. Hollybourn, the man who purchased the estate from Mr. Roker, stating that he "could not think that—hum, a—the doctor, so worthy a man as he was, would be accessary in—hum a, injuring any one, or keeping the right heir out of his estate; but, hum a—hum a—there must be some misrepresentation" (492). The lawyer is more interested in Orlando's account of Hollybourn's riches than in discussing the background of the property dispute. Abandoning Orlando after their initial consultation, Darby immediately approaches Dr. Hollybourn and defects to his legal team, proposing to fight any legal action that Orlando plans to initiate. Darby's actions have a basis in reality. As David Lemmings has shown, late eighteenth-century English lawyers tended to gravitate toward and protect the interests of wealthy men of property.[57] Given this profit motive, impecunious clients were at risk of losing representation if their lawyers were hired away by those with deeper pockets. Rather than exhibiting the failure of the legal system to generate just outcomes, *The Old Manor House* reveals the obstacles to initiating the judicial process in the first place. Legal aid was available only to those in dire poverty: public whipping was often the punishment for those found to have received legal assistance based on false reporting of one's income.[58]

"Would your profession were annihilated!" Orlando vents to Carr after his frustrating meeting with Darby (493). Carr's response is a prime example of Smith's periodic abrupt insertions into her novels of protonaturalistic depictions of social injustice, further eroding the atmosphere of sentimental romance established early in the novel:

> Why, I do not believe . . . that the world would be much the worse if it were; but, my friend, not to be too hard upon *us*, do reflect on the practices of other professions. . . . The merchant, who sits down in his compting-house, and writes to his correspondent at Jamaica, that his ship, the Good Intent of Liverpool, is consigned to him at Port-Royal with a cargo of slaves from the coast of Guinea, calculates the profits of a fortunate adventure, but never considers the tears and blood with which this money is to be raised. He hears not the groans of an hundred human creatures confined together in the hold of a small merchantman. (493)

Growing more agitated, Orlando interrupts: "Do . . . dear Carr, finish your catalogue of human crimes, unless you have a mind to make me go home and hang myself" (493; notably, Smith herself was a slaveholder who in her letters coolly estimated the profit to be made by selling slaves in Barbados to fund her family's needs[59]). Orlando sees only a stark choice between two options: "annihilate" either the legal system or himself. Although Orlando's exclamations are not serious proposals, they speak to his lack of coping skills for moving forward when stymied by the law's obstacles. His directly expressed hostility is less effective than the circumvention and feigned compliance to male authority practiced by Emmeline and her female allies. His maturation will involve learning to work his way into the system rather than calling for its demise.

Carr is the rare lawyer in Smith's novels who does not fit into her rogues' gallery of legal professionals: he is unrelentingly forthright. Yet while he can recite in detail the evils of the institution of slavery, he does not seek to alter the status quo. Orlando, he suggests, is railing against a similarly large-scale problem—the venal legal profession—that a single aggrieved man cannot change on his own. Carr recommends quietism and resignation to institutional realities.

Orlando's prospects improve when he ceases lamenting his plight and channels his energy into moving his case forward without professional legal assistance. This would seem, of course, to be an approach likely effective only for those of means who are also well-spoken and assertive. Growing more certain of his suspicion that the will was forged, he determines that the key to validating his claim to the family property involves eliciting proof that he is the rightful beneficiary. With legal representation beyond his means, he decides to try developing an emotional connection with those who are in a position to provide him with information. As such, he writes a letter of inquiry to Mrs. Roker, although she was invariably cold to him when they were both living with Mrs. Rayland. After ignoring several of his letters, Mrs. Roker replies, admitting to her falsification of the will; her newfound willingness to correspond stems from her loneliness. Because Orlando patiently cultivates this connection, he gains access to the documents that he needs. As Cheryl Nixon points out, "The novel imagines a moral ending in which a woman comes forward to help secure Orlando's estate, overtly stating that she does so 'for the sake of justice.'"[60] Orlando does not automatically gain this female assistance, though; to obtain it, he must adopt a feminized, domestically oriented method of addressing his legal problems. Orlando's legal turmoil is successfully resolved when he shifts to the strategy, earlier used by Emmeline, of developing affective bonds and finding workarounds to bypass legal authority.

A Practical Guide to Law's Labyrinth: *Marchmont* (1796)

With her next published work, *Marchmont*, Smith grew bolder still: she launched a direct assault—in her own voice—on the legal system. The novel recounts the struggle of young Edward-Armyn Marchmont to recover his ancestral estate. After refusing to settle debts spuriously ascribed to his deceased father, Edward is stalked for years by a predatory lawyer, Vampyre, and compelled to go into hiding. Before ushering readers into the fictional conflict, though, Smith devotes much of her preface to vilifying the legal profession:

> It has been observed to me, that such an obscure wretch as an attorney, remarkable only for his skill in saving the ears he has so often deserved to lose, is too contemptible for satire. As an individual he is; but as a specimen of a genus extremely poisonous and noxious he becomes an object to be held up to detestation; and I have figured him here as, in drawings to illustrate natural history, I would delineate the scorpion, whose touch is mortal, or give a figure of the upas-tree—perhaps I should rather say of the strychnos (*nux vomica*), or some more familiar poison—for the deadly upas (if it be not a fable) exists singly: but the destructive monster, armed with the power of doing mischief, and of robbing legally—the wretch without feeling or principle, without honesty or pity—is a nuisance widely diffused, and spreading frequent desolation.[61]

Smith identifies lawyers with nonhuman exotic menaces: the vampire is a creature of Eastern Europe; the scorpion is found in Babylonian, Egyptian, and Persian lore; and the "bohun-upas" tree was fabled to grow in the East Indies.[62] Similar representations are found in a later chapter where saucy young belles malign the "men of law" seated near them at a dinner party as "Hottentots, Vandals, and Caribs" (69). Her seeming xenophobia here may seem at odds with her other writings, such as her long poem *The Emigrants* (1793), which defends political refugees entering England from nativist hostility. Yet each portrayal is consistent with her antipathy to disruptions of social hierarchy. Smith's allochthonous iconography in *Marchmont* conveys her concerns regarding the economic elevation of class interlopers. She was predisposed to sympathize with the French emigrants, who were typically high-status families fleeing the republican regime. Echoing Smollett's comments on wealthy debtors, her poem asserted that the sufferings of the powerful deserved more compassion because they were less inured to hardship than were poor people.[63] By contrast, she expressed hostility toward the legal profession whose apparent democratization invited misperceptions that it had been "invaded by the poor," as the historian Albert J. Schmidt commented.[64] By likening this expanding and increasingly powerful vocational body to invasive species, Smith cast lawyers as unnatural engraftments onto the homegrown common law system on which England prided itself.[65] Smith's condemnation appeared at the tail end of a century when civil lawyers had absorbed a wider array of roles and had become indispensable to propertied families,[66] while criminal lawyers were gaining far more prominence in legal proceedings and assuming responsibilities previously reserved for judges and other authorities.[67]

Marchmont features several episodes that illustrate how to ward off the predations of this hostile force. In a pivotal scene early in the second part of the four-volume novel, Vampyre arrives in the dead of night at the estate formerly owned by the Marchmont family to seek Edward, who is hiding in an unoccupied wing of the mansion. The place is now rented to absentee residents: a pair of elderly caretakers, the Wansfords, and the teenage Althea are the only current inhabitants. The young woman has been marooned in the remote mansion by her father, who pushed her out of the family home at the request of her new stepmother. (Althea is a surrogate for Smith, as indicated by their mirror-image personal history.) A commotion awakens Althea; Wansford explains what is happening:

> He insists, Miss, upon being allowed to search this house. I have refused him;
> for why?—I'm sure by his looks he don't seem an honester man than they he
> pretends to search after—and what if he was?—He has got no right to search
> here—or if he has, why don't he shew it me?—why doesn't he shew his
> warrant?—But instead of that, he won't even tell me who he looks after!—Come,
> come, Mr. What's-your-name, come out of my young lady's room, or I'll shew
> you that, lame as I am, I'll not let any such fellows fright her. (128)

Wansford's bravado is straight out of the fantasies of the privileged: the servant who is willing to risk his life to protect his master's property. While the wealthy, strapping young male aristocrats of Smith's novels usually fail to pass muster as proper heroes, here a disabled and indigent old man steps up to defend the estate of a wealthy proprietor. Despite being roused from bed in the middle of the night, this uneducated man has the quick thinking to ask savvy questions and cite legal stipulations in denying the claims of an intimidating lawyer. The depiction falls into a pattern of Smith's encomiums to faithful servants who support the interests of their high-status employers.[68]

At the same time, Smith's passage furnishes a script for how to resist authorities' demands to search a home. The law was more unsettled than Wansford's unequivocal charge indicates. Over the preceding decades, the rights of property owners had undergone substantial changes. As the historian Leonard W. Levy and the legal scholar Simon Stern have each shown, legal thought on searches of private residences was in flux during the eighteenth century.[69] Jurists since the 1500s had disagreed over what the common law allowed; only in the 1760s did Lord Mansfield rule against a warrantless search in one case, while stating that the common law did allow warrantless searches under different conditions.[70] Wansford exemplifies Levy's notion that nonspecialists contributed to the late eighteenth-century mythmaking of rights, offering interpretations that established a baseline for future legislation, as what people thought the law said became as important as what it actually stated.[71]

For her part, Althea does not display the fear and passivity that was customary for female protagonists. "Collecting all her courage," she confronts Vampyre herself: "Who are you, Sir, that takes the liberty of thus intruding?" (128). She orders the lawyer to leave: "I will not hold any converse with you. I am perfectly convinced that a person of *your* appearance can have no business in this house, and I must insist upon your leaving it" (129). The absence of male relatives occasions Althea's self-assertion; it also enables Smith to sidestep what feminist critics have claimed to be incompatibility between the "liberal ideal of nonintervention of the state into family life" and the best interests of women, who in that framework were beholden to male heads of households.[72] Writing in a literary era when proper heroines fainted over minor breaches of social decorum, most of which fell far short of home invasions on the emotional Richter scale, Smith reimagines the kind of behavior that befits a sentimental heroine.

Althea's evolution is startling. As a teenage girl who is shy even in conversations with her own father, she initially falls within the traditional standards of female modesty and reserve—but she then veers from gendered conventions, developing into a woman who willingly risks physical assault to advocate for her endangered household. Althea shows that speaking based on knowledge of the law is not the exclusive privilege of male professionals. During the attack, she turns legal theorist: "She knew not, in the confusion of her thoughts, whether she feared these people as common robbers, or as ruffians authorised by law to hunt some unhappy person to destruction. The latter, though she knew not whom they sought, seemed to her more detestable than the former" (129). Althea's reflections range beyond her own immediate danger to posit value judgments of relative social harm. In repudiating the devaluation of rights by legal authorities, Althea expresses a perspective similar to that observed by a twenty-first-century anthropologist in his survey of indigent people who fear and avoid police and thus leave even brutal crimes unreported: a pervasive "sense of the law as worse than crime, as the ultimate injustice."[73]

Some readers bristled at Smith's critique. One reviewer ascribed Smith's vilification of lawyers to personal animus stemming from "her own misfortunes":

> We are prepared by the Preface (in which the author introduces the story of her own misfortunes) to expect the appearance of the attorney to whose agency she attributes much of the calamity she has experienced. Mrs. Smith should have done well to have considered that to draw the character of the enemy by whom we consider ourselves injured, requires a degree of coolness and candour, that falls to the lot of few. Instead of suffering the character of Vampyre to be developed by his actions, it is given in epithets which sufficiently evince the irritable feelings of the writer's mind. *"That fiend in the shape of an attorney"*—*"that miscreant, for it debases the species to call him man"*—*"the malignant reptile"*—*"a monster, who disgracing the name of man, seemed to be some subaltern agent of Mammon and of Moloch, let loose to blast all on whom his evil eyes were turned"*—are the most favourable terms in which this gentleman is introduced.[74]

The reviewer presents the motivation for Smith's novel as simple self-interest. In similar vein, another reviewer wrote: "Neither Mohun, nor Vampyre, give you that horror at their crimes which the Authoress labours to excite:—they do not do *enough* to merit the bitterness with which she writes; and, for that reason, we are apt to imagine, she is *in them* aiming at personality."[75] In this context, *personality* meant "personal attack"; by minimizing Smith's lampoon as the petty vituperation of a "bitter" female litigant, rather than considering it as a more general critique of law, the reviewer reaffirms his era's tiresome insistence on relegating women's writing to the zone of the apolitical and autobiographical. Equally important, the reviewer's claim that Vampyre does not "do *enough* to merit bitterness" is surprising, even disturbing, given that the lawyer and his henchmen stalk an innocent private citizen and break into and illegally search a residence in spite of the inhabitants' objections. Such commentary is symptomatic of a social milieu in which even fictional depictions of exertions of legal agency by women were deemed impermissible.

While Althea and Wansford are restricted to the domestic realm as they combat legal authorities, Edward Marchmont's quest for a legal adviser draws him from the refuge of his home into disorienting legal spaces. More than half a century ahead of Charles Dickens's *Bleak House* (1852–53), with its interminable, ruinous lawsuits, Smith conveys in fine detail the glacial pace of legal processes that paralyzed the lives of ordinary people.[76] A friend of Edward advises him of the challenges to expect:

> "It is an affair which from the very nature of it can only be settled by Chancery," says my Counsellor: "you must apply to that court undoubtedly; yet I own I can hardly advise it, for the costs and time will be immense."—"Calculate," say I, "the costs, and the time."—"Why," returns my friend, "as to the costs, it is not easy to say what *they* may amount to among so many parties: and then, as for the *time*, it will be at least *three* terms, but more likely *six*, nine, twelve, or fifteen, before your adversaries will put in their answers; and if they are hostile, why it may be *three or four years*; and then your bill must be amended perhaps: and then, if any of the parties die among the three-and-twenty individuals whom you must make parties (people of all ages, from the old man of seventy-five to an infant born last week), why in that case, you know, you will have all the business to begin over again." (291–92; emphasis in original)

This description of a case's progress through court, which closely resembles Smith's own legal battle,[77] dwells on quantification: it lists the number of persons involved and their ages, segments time in "terms," and underscores the "years" needed for the case to unfurl. According to Ian Watt, one of the characteristics of formal realism is "the modern sense of time . . . a sense of duration which was minutely . . . discriminated."[78] It is in depicting processes such as legal negotiations that Smith's novels adhere most closely to the tenets of formal realism. Yet the seeming transparency of the quantification is illusory: although specific numbers are cited, the vague ranges given underscore the mystery of the legal process rather than clarifying it. As *Marchmont* pulls away from the conventions of sentimental romance, it demonstrates the evasive answers and opacity of pricing that would-be litigants could expect to face when they attempted to recover money or property owed to them.

As Edward is drawn into the legal web, Smith offers a virtual reality tour of the legal process. In an explanatory manner reminiscent of Jacob's lexicons, she conveys the neophyte's bewilderment, glossing the legal titles, terms, and conventions he is attempting to learn: "Not knowing, however, what else to do, after every other attempt fails which I have made to accommodate the affair,

I venture into this labyrinth, and I engage a man who calls himself a *Solicitor in Chancery*, to draw up my bill; and a learned Chancery Lawyer (a Special Pleader, I believe), *to settle it.* This done, and a heavy charge incurred, I desire in all humility to read it. . . . The composition appears to me to be absolutely nonsense" (292).

Edward counters the lawyer's obscurantist jabber with his own straightforward, linear epistolary narrative that vividly renders his journey through the legal labyrinth. His first-person, present-tense narration is a rare exception to the third-person-omniscient perspective and past tense used for most of the hundreds of pages of *Marchmont*. His narrative has an immediacy and level of procedural detail that is scarce in eighteenth-century and Romantic-era accounts of nonspecialists' encounters with the law. Compare this passage to the exploits of Daniel Defoe's Moll Flanders and Henry Fielding's Jonathan Wild, at one end of the eighteenth century, and to the persecution of William Godwin's Caleb Williams at the other; in those novels, crimes, imprisonment, and executions are described at length, but fine-grained descriptions of interaction with legal counsel are all but absent. *Marchmont's* account of Edward's legal odyssey furnishes the "plain" treatment of the legal process that early eighteenth-century legal guide writers such as Jacob promised but did not deliver.

Edward's attempt to secure legal representation comes to a dismal end. Unmollified by his lawyer's assurance that the nonsensical brief is standard courtroom fare, Edward terminates the case:

> I desire to stay proceedings. My learned Chancery Lawyer allows me to do so, because he begins to suspect that my money and my patience may equally be at an end. . . . But he sends me in his bill . . . with a charge of *only* seventy pounds. It is impossible for me to pay it—and he detains all the papers he had got into his hands on pretence of seeking redress for me—it being, it seems, a rule for lawyers never to restore papers till they are paid, though they have volunteered in the cause, and though the very detention of these documents may be in itself a greater evil than they undertook to cure, and may prevent its ever being cured at all. (292)

Here again, Smith offers details that might otherwise seem minor or inconsequential, including the exact amounts of money involved. The legal guides by Jacob, by comparison, include no information on the costs of legal action. These substantive details add remarkable texture to Smith's narration of lawyer-client interactions. Smith bleakly suggests that terminating legal services was one of the few means by which those lacking funds could exercise authority in the Romantic-era legal arena.

Yet this assertion of minor power further endangered those in financial difficulties: Edward's fictional plight mirrored reality, for when clients could not afford to pay their legal fees, lawyers were entitled to withhold documents related to the case until the debt was paid.[79] This prerogative, known as a "retaining lien," was yet another impediment to justice for those whose finances were uncertain. It was in the eighteenth century that use of this device became widespread.[80] Deprived of the papers that prove his claim, Edward is worse off than when he began his legal consultations. He eventually prevails in his effort to regain his family estate, but years elapse before victory. By detailing in her sentimental "fiction" the measures through which legal representation further drained the funds of the downwardly-mobile privileged, Smith made visible to a massive audience the grim logistics of the interrelationship between dispossession and barriers to justice.

What Smith produced was a field guide to an exploitative legal system in the guise of derivative tales of treacherous relatives and thwarted love. She so deftly wove legal critique into her novels that it eluded the notice not only of her many critics but also of her champions. When her novels are deemed worthy of closer analysis, they have been dismissed as the thinly disguised memoirs of a jaded grumbler. In comparing the expertise claimed by legal professionals with the type of experiential knowledge marked as feminine, however, Smith revised standard expectations of the extent to which legal pedagogy could be transmitted or undertaken by so-called low and derivative forms of cultural production. That she managed to do so without raising the objections of cultural censors speaks to the finesse with which she naturalized the hybridization of legal discourse with popular entertainment. As Smith's commentary on the legal process drew closely on her personal experience, she offered readers a singular perspective unavailable in tomes written by legal authorities or professional guides. All the while, though, Smith was melding the two modes of discourse with a view to promoting not general expansion of legal agency but increased autonomy and power for a select group: the distressed descendants of genteel families reduced from the heights of bygone days.

PART II

THE PEN AS A WEAPON AGAINST
REFORM OF THE LAW

CHAPTER THREE

Letters of the Law

Ambivalent Advocacy and Speaking for the Voiceless in Walter Scott's *Redgauntlet*

In the spring of 1824, while Walter Scott was writing *Redgauntlet*—his most autobiographical novel[1]—he hosted the French luminary Nicolas Marie Alexandre Vattemare.[2] At the close of the visit, Scott presented his guest with an epigram entitled "Lines, Addressed to Monsieur Alexandre, the Celebrated Ventriloquist":

> Of yore, in Old England, it was not thought good
> To carry two visages under one hood;
> What should folks say to you? who have faces such plenty,
> That from under one hood, you last night show'd us twenty!
> Stand forth, arch-deceiver, and tell us in truth,
> Are you handsome or ugly, in age or in youth?
> Man, woman, or child?—a dog or a mouse?
> Or are you, at once, each live thing in the house?
> Each live thing, did I ask?—each dead implement, too,
> A work-shop in your person—saw, chisel, and screw!
> Above all, are you one individual? I know
> You must be at least Alexandre and Co.
> But I think you're a troop—an assemblage—a mob,
> And that I, as the Sheriff, should take up the job;
> And instead of rehearsing your wonders in verse,
> Must read you the Riot-Act, and bid you disperse.[3]

As the virtuosic performance is reenacted through the words of the poet, Scott sends Vattemare down Hobbes's "Great Chain of Being": the illusionist morphs from "man" to "woman," "child," "dog," "mouse," and finally "dead implement," eventually endowing the humblest entities with expressive capacity.

Although composed in jaunty light verse, the poem conveys a soupçon of alarm at the prospect of the rise of potentially ungovernable forces, as all manner of "live things" and inanimate objects emerge from obscurity to appear on the public stage.[4] It touches on an impasse to which Scott had devoted considerable thought ever since the Peterloo Massacre of 1819: how to balance his interest in preserving the social hierarchy against his moral inclination to give some measure of voice to the restive sectors of the disenfranchised. The valedictory decision of Scott's poetic persona to "read you the Riot-Act and bid you disperse" echoes a precipitating event of the massacre: in 1817, twenty-five thousand people flocked to St. Peter's Field in Manchester, where protestors prepared to march to London to appeal directly to the Crown. They sought aid for textile workers and reinstatement of habeas corpus, which had been suspended following unrest stemming from the failure of a reform bill for universal suffrage. The uprising was scuttled when the crowd was read the Riot Act by magistrates and dispersed by the royal cavalry.[5] Ultimately, pressures came to a head two years later in the same field, where a larger protest—of at least fifty thousand people—was attacked by a full cavalry charge, leaving seventeen dead and many hundreds injured.[6]

By examining Scott's journal entries and letters, his political satire *The Visionary* (1819), and *Redgauntlet*, I aim to illuminate Scott's proposed solution to the impasse: the voices of those whom he termed the "lower orders" may be brought into the political system—and the legal arena—only via the filtering medium of privileged advocates.[7] I argue that Scott's resuscitation in *Redgauntlet* of the epistolary novel (once popular but in decline by the 1820s) furnishes a literary analogue to his legal and political solution: the voices of the lowly ought to be embedded in, and contained by, the authorized expression of the educated. Rather than depicting unruly masses of protestors agitating for political representation, Scott contracts the diegetic frame to focus on tense private encounters between the marginalized and those who purport to represent them. This solution enables occasional acknowledgment by the privileged of the needs of individual persons lacking resources, without opening an avenue for systemic change. Moreover, by pitting privileged men against menacing outcasts—and emphasizing the intimidation or physical threat presented by the lowly—these scenes cast the privileged as the vulnerable ones.

As does *The Visionary*, *Redgauntlet* indicates that legal institutions are crucial to shielding the privileged from the discontent of the lowly. While Judith Wilt sees *Redgauntlet* as contemplating various iterations of "brotherhood,"

Ian Duncan contends that the novel's primary relationships involve either "friendship" or "paternal authority," which he claims Scott sets in "schematic opposition" as "the modern (horizontal) and traditional (vertical) axes" of the novel's "core ethical value of *pietas* or loyalty."[8] I propose, instead, that the novel considers advocacy as an alternative relational mode, more transactional and distanced and thus less susceptible to the moral compromises borne of loyalty, even as this mode of relation gives rise to complications of its own. Whereas Andrew Lincoln sees in *Redgauntlet* what he describes as Scott's characteristic "bifurcated narrative" sustaining both a "sentimental reading" and a "skeptical reading"—balancing the two, rather than ultimately upholding one—I consider two of the novel's primary narratives as involving, first, marginalized grievance and, second, privileged fear.[9] There can be no balance between these narratives; the second can acknowledge the first, but it must contain it.

Throughout the novel, conflicts of interest arise between privileged advocates and their lowly clients or subordinates, both in episodes of formal legal proceedings and more generally in the novel's narration and dialogue. I bring to light the promise and limitations of Scott's proposed solution. The epistolary first section of *Redgauntlet* models the use of advocacy by the educated to control the expression of the marginalized. By *advocacy* I mean both the work of the professional lawyer to represent a client and informal efforts to speak on behalf of others. This method of representation would seem to offer a net benefit to the lowly, providing them with some measure of voice, even if they remain subordinate. In the later segments of the novel, after the epistolary mode is abandoned, it becomes apparent that in the absence of a legitimate legal system that can both provide a forum for resolution of grievances and enforce social containment, men of property and the educated are also at risk.

A hallmark of Scott's career as a best-selling author was rigorous engagement with the difficult questions of justice and legal disparities that underclass demands forced on a rapidly modernizing society. Although certain prominent nineteenth-century authors and thinkers belittled Scott's work as pure entertainment,[10] today's Scott scholars recognize that he was deeply invested in sorting through complex matters of British identity, globalization, the construction of history, and other concerns.[11] Yet Scott's attention to law, and to legal representation and advocacy in particular, remains underexamined. In the quarter century since Bruce Beiderwell published his useful study of Scott, power, and justice, no additional monographs have been devoted to the topic. The novel's portrayal of legal matters is more often than not treated as allegorical—a means of approaching questions of cultural memory or national unity. I, instead, see the account of law in Scott's literary and political writings as reflecting contemporary pressures that would soon yield substantial changes to legal proceedings, such as the expanded role of professional counsel.

While humanitarian authors and activists of the era called for reform that would put the marginalized at less of a disadvantage in the legal and penal systems, Scott questioned the notion that law should "create among individuals a moral, and, in a sense, artificial equality to offset the inequalities of nature," as H. L. A. Hart characterized the relationship between justice and law.[12] Scott's conception of justice was shaded by his steadfast belief in these "inequalities of nature." In a letter to Maria Edgeworth, he wrote, "The state of high civilisation to which we have arrived is perhaps scarcely a national blessing since while the *few* are improved to the highest point, the *many* are in proportion tantalized and degraded, and the same nation displays at the same time the very highest and very lowest state in which the human race can exist in point of intellect."[13] *The Visionary* and *Redgauntlet* evaluate means of insulating the upper and middle classes from the threat posed by the "lower orders." Scott's fictional scenarios of advocacy imposed on the less powerful, purportedly for their benefit—a prosperous architect negotiating on behalf of rioters who disavow his efforts, a lawyer who takes on the case of an impoverished man set on representing himself, a bandit who claims to "answer for" a privileged man under his power—indicate conflicting notions of advocacy as virtuous rectification of injustice, professional duty, or power play.

Reforming Justice: An Urgent Impossibility?

Scott continually elaborated on his paternalist anxieties regarding tensions between the ranks of the propertied and the "lower orders" who clamored for legal and political reform. For years after Peterloo, he evaluated advocacy as a prospective means of addressing the interclass rift. His constructions of advocacy for the marginalized take forms ranging from the work of professional lawyers, to efforts to speak for the lowly in more casual legally inflected contexts, to the rendering of underclass voices in literary forms ranging from poetry to the novel. Although Scott found his vocation as an author, his early training rooted him in the legal system, and he remained tethered to it throughout his life. As a young man, he was educated as a lawyer, and he later held for two decades the position of sheriff deputy of Selkirk (a role winkingly referenced in the lines addressed to Vattemare). He could thus draw on his legal expertise to evaluate a range of options for addressing the grievances of those marginalized by the legal system.

In his personal journal, a year after publishing *Redgauntlet*, Scott expressed ambivalence regarding impoverished people's access to legal representation: "There is something sickening in seeing poor devils drawn into great expence about trifles by interested attorneys. But too cheap access to litigation has its evils on the other hand, for the proneness of the lower class to gratify spite and revenge in this way would be a dreadful evil were they able to endure the expence. Very few cases come before the Sheriff Court of Selkirkshire that ought to come anywhere.... I try to check it as well as I can; 'But so 'twill be when I am gone.'"[14] Scott short-circuits his sympathetic reaction by recalling the need for systemic fortification against the vengeance of the envious lower orders. What Andrew Lincoln describes as the author's "growing concerns about the effects of modernization upon the higher and middling ranks of society" clearly never receded from view in Scott's deliberations over questions of justice.[15]

In his ambivalence regarding the mediation of underclass interests by privileged proxies, Scott anticipated complications that would arise a little over a decade later owing to two major developments in legal systems beyond Scotland. The first was the passage in England of the Prisoner's Counsel Act of 1836, which cleared the way for counsel to present the cases of accused felons in court. Previously, such defendants had to speak for themselves in court. Under the new law, however, a lawyer could present a case only under the condition that the defendant did not testify, as Jan-Melissa Schramm discusses: in Charles Dickens's *Bleak House* (1852–53), a character avers that any lawyer he hires will "shut my mouth up" and deliver a distorted version of his story rather than the plain truth.[16] The change in law stemmed from what Alexander Welsh has described as a shift in emphasis to circumstantial evidence and a suspicion of direct testimony.[17]

A second watershed legal development, also in 1836, occurred across the Atlantic; the verdict in *Commonwealth* [of Massachusetts] *v. Aves* stated that the status of an enslaved person, once brought by his or her master into a free state, could be determined according to the laws of the new location. Following the decision, a number of petitions prepared by white activists through the 1840s requested the liberation of slaves brought north by owners; problems emerged in court when some slaves requested to remain enslaved. Just as under the Counsel Act prisoners were supposed in the eyes of the law to have chosen to remain silent, slaves who ostensibly chose to remain with their masters were (in Edlie Wong's description) "represented in the liberal tradition as . . . social agent[s] free of coercive restraints."[18] The changes in law pertaining to advocacy raised questions that were not readily resolved: how can it be verified that an advocate's attestations reflect the preferences of the person for whom they speak rather than their own interests? Can a marginalized person really be said to *choose* to relinquish their only opportunity to speak for themselves, given the pressures they may face within an institutional context from authorities or prospective advocates? When a lowly person contradicts the narrative given by an advocate, who should be believed? The legal conflicts that ensued from these developments revealed that under the conditions in place, changes in legal representation hailed as liberatory reforms could in practice be paternalism in another guise.

A potential alternative to advocacy involved returning to an older judicial framework, in which landowners themselves administered justice for their tenants. This role is exemplified in Henry Fielding's *Amelia* (1751) by the benevolent Dr. Harrison, who makes home visits to resolve conflicts for his tenants. Scott pointed out the flaws of this model in his early novel *Guy Mannering; or, The Astrologer* (1815), wherein the Laird of Ellangowan, a justice of the peace, moves (as David Marshall observes) "from his previous tolerance to active persecution of every undesirable character in the neighborhood":[19]

> He detected poachers, black-fishers, orchard-breakers, and pigeon-shooters. . . . All this good had its rateable proportion of evil. . . . The zeal of our worthy friend now involved in great distress sundry personages, whose idle and mendicant habits his own *lachesse* had contributed to foster until these habits became irreclaimable, or whose real incapacity of exertion rendered them fit objects, in their own phrase, for the charity of all well-disposed Christians. The "long-remembered beggar," who for twenty years had made his regular round within the neighbourhood, received rather as a humble friend than as an object of charity, was sent to the neighbouring workhouse. . . . The "daft Jock," who, half-knave, half-idiot, had been the sport of each succeeding race of village children for a good part of a century, was remitted to the county bridewell, where, secluded from free air and sunshine, the only advantages he was capable of enjoying, he pined and died in the course of six months. The old sailor, who had so long rejoiced the smoky rafters of every kitchen in the country by singing . . . , was banished from the county for no better reason than that he was supposed to speak with a strong Irish accent.[20]

The passage invites pity for Ellangowan's lowly victims, who, helpless to contest the legal judgments against them, invariably meet sad ends. Scott's own status as Laird of Abbotsford did not preclude his understanding that in a system where there is no provision of legal aid and no forum for appeal, those who are not competent or equipped to defend themselves are completely at the mercy of the landowners who govern them. An early observer[21] remarked that the laird's actions resemble the "power[s] to punish" accorded to justices of the peace by Sir George Mackenzie in his landmark work *The Lawes and Customes of Scotland in Matters Criminal* (1678), the first Scottish criminal law textbook, which was used by generations of students into the later eighteenth century.[22] The allusion is sinister: as Lord Advocate—the chief criminal prosecutor in Scotland—Mackenzie was a proponent of torture; Scott refers to him in *The Heart of Mid-Lothian* (1818) as "Bluidy [Bloody] Mackenzie."[23] Mackenzie was notorious for imprisoning without trial more than one thousand rebel Covenanters in the 1679 Battle of Bothwell Bridge in central Scotland. A number of the prisoners were summarily executed; others were transported to the West Indies and forced into hard labor.[24] Ellangowan similarly condemns without trial; although he abides by the letter of the law, he abuses his authority, unchecked by regulatory forces. Older paternalist dispensations that give the poor no forum for contesting their treatment, Scott suggests, tend to inflict rather than resolve injustice.

Scott considers a still more drastic solution—abandoning legal institutions altogether—in *The Visionary*, his epistolary political satire published in 1819 in the wake of Peterloo. In the first of three dream visions—each of which considers a different aspect of proposed constitutional reform—a landowner struggles to fend off a throng of radicals who gather to raze his estate. Among their targets for destruction is "a confounded place called a court-room, where honest men were put to great trouble" (*Visionary* 24). Prior to the attack, the landowner had worried about how to "put a bridle on the jaws of the Leviathan multitude, and check their fury" (19). As sheriff of Selkirkshire, presiding over his own courtroom, Scott himself later faced the challenge of quelling unrest that had a basis in underclass antipathy to the legal process: "Went up to Selkirk to try a fellow for an assault," he wrote in his journal. "The people there get rather riotous. This is a turbulent fierce fellow. . . . The trial . . . dissipated my attention for the rest of the day."[25]

In the midst of the storming of the estate described in *The Visionary*, the landlord's new architect—Vitruvius Whigham—attempts to take charge. Somnambulus, the narrator, is both exasperated and riveted by Whigham's representational dexterity and derides him as "Orator Puff": Whigham plays both sides, purporting to speak on behalf of the rabble, while surreptitiously promising the landowner, "You shall see how I'll manage them" (28). Similar to Vattemare, Whigham is representing the speech of others but also revising and qualifying it. "Orator Puff, Orator Puff / One voice for one Orator's surely enough" (29), Somnambulus hums in response. The dream vision cultivates skepticism for educated professionals who claim to speak for the lowly. Yet Somnambulus proposes no alternative measures; indeed, his name bespeaks not only his role as the dreamer of the visions but also his political quietism, as he defends the status quo and seems content to let things lie.

The second dream vision imagines the aftermath of the successful over-throw of the propertied class: an etiolated landscape in which the rule of law has been abolished. Somnambulus finds himself walking through tracts of subsistence agriculture, where he is approached by Tom Ten-acres, whose name derives from the portion of land allotted to each resident. As the two men talk, it becomes clear that no legal institutions remain in place. "You have no laws whatsoever?" Somnambulus asks incredulously. Tom replies: "No, my friend: they are the most ready engines by which the rich subjected the poor" (39). Explaining why the radicals gave up on their plans for universal suffrage, Tom states, "What signifies a representation to us? . . . People . . . care very little for other folks' tongues." He declares: "We are every one for ourselves, and God (that is to say *nobody*) for us all" (39). The first dream vision demonstrates that advocacy for the lowly goes wrong when not carried out in good faith, as with the self-serving Whigham. This second vision implies that when the lower orders believe that nobody in power represents their interests, they may resort to destroying the institutions that fail them.

A menacing presence, Tom evinces no sense of stewardship for the land under his care; nor does he exhibit any concern for other human beings. When Somnambulus follows up with another question—"Of course . . . you have no execution of justice?"—Tom proclaims that he lives by "radical justice," whereby might makes right (39). Brandishing a massive tree limb, he demands that the visitor relinquish all personal effects. As the weapon swings toward him, Somnambulus awakens. In retrospect, the complete absence of other people, and the "sterile" and "barren" (33) appearance of their tracts, suggests that Tom, who assumes the role of spokesman for his fellow radicals, may have meted out the same "justice" to them.

In presenting the inherent flaws or undesirable consequences of each of these alternatives—reducing the price of legal representation, relying on landowners to administer justice, or abolishing the law altogether—Scott points to the broader social impact of the ways in which conflicts were resolved. In doing so, he considers the needs of both the propertied and the underclass. While "too cheap" access to legal representation could clog the justice system and expose landowners to underclass vengeance, other models for resolving conflicts would leave the marginalized bereft of any bulwark against draconian punishment or—in the extreme scenario of *The Visionary*'s rearticulation of Hobbes's state of nature—anarchic violence. In *Redgauntlet*, Scott promotes an alternative solution: educated members of the more stable and established ranks of society should act as advocates for the disenfranchised within the legal system.

As *Redgauntlet* shows, however, this solution generated complications as well. Addressing what she terms "the problem of speaking for others," Linda Martin Alcoff cautions that when well-intentioned people of privilege refrain from speaking on behalf of marginalized communities for fear of misrepresenting them, they abdicate their social responsibility.[26] Scott's privileged advocates, by contrast, have no reservations about speaking for the lowly. Yet they do so in a way that reinforces their own power and social standing and does little to effect systemic change. Scott views advocacy by the privileged on behalf of the lowly as a panacea for underclass discontent precisely because it offers some channel for redressing individual grievances without threatening the traditional social hierarchy. This strategy of apparent accommodation reflects Scott's interest in "consolidating economic and social power in middle-class hands," which Miranda Burgess notes is a recurring theme of his later novels.[27]

Enveloping Others' Speech: Scott's Revival of Epistolarity

Scott was intrigued by the capacity of literature to convey what seemed to be the authentic voices of the lowly but were in fact third-party fabrications. His early work openly embraced misdirection and outright deception regarding attribution of speech. This same fascination with mediation of the voices of others would later be reflected in his turn to the epistolary novel in *Redgauntlet*. In his 1802 collection *Minstrelsy of the Scottish Border*, Scott presented what he claimed were transcripts of folk ballads, and he was lauded for his "fidelity" to the originals.[28] In fact, the verse compendium was heavily embellished with his own interpolations, as Andrew Lang carefully documented after investigating complaints by nineteenth-century critics. Lang observes that Scott "spoke very leniently of imitations passed off as authentic"[29] in the

1830 "Essay on Imitations of the Ancient Ballad," in which Scott claimed, "The public is surely more enriched by the contribution than injured by the deception."[30] Some critics concurred with his argument that, through his editorial interventions, he was truer to the ballads' original spirit than if he had not altered them.[31] Such appraisals are based on a logic similar to that of arguments presented later in the 1830s during the controversy over the Prisoner's Counsel Act: as Jonathan H. Grossman notes, professional advocates were said to be more capable of telling defendants' stories than the defendants themselves.[32]

Just as Scott sought to pass off his own compositions as a miscellany of poems by a variety of obscure voices, he went to great lengths to conceal his identity when he shifted to writing novels. He published his novels anonymously until 1827, three years after the publication of *Redgauntlet*. As Kathryn Sutherland notes, Scott developed a system of transcription to shield his identity such that no manuscript in his handwriting was used to set copy.[33] Thus originated Scott's sobriquet, "The Great Unknown."[34] There is an analogy between Scott's cloaking himself in anonymity and the role of the professional advocate. Scott insisted on concealing his authorship, but some scholars claim that his identity was no secret. He was, in fact, an international celebrity who has been cited as an exemplar of the consummate "authorial narrator" whose style is immediately recognizable.[35] Similarly, advocates at law speak for others, not for themselves, but it is their own physical and vocal performance that becomes the center of the audience's attention. In both cases, the enunciator flickers between absence and conspicuous presence.

A similar dynamic can be seen in novels structured around letters, particularly when letter writers are reporting the speech of others. Among dozens of novels by Scott, *Redgauntlet* is a rare sustained foray into the epistolary mode.[36] Scott would have been well aware that, by the time he was writing *Redgauntlet*, the epistolary novel was regarded as démodé.[37] In his prefaces for the Ballantyne's Novelist's Library series (1821–24), Scott demonstrates his command of literary history and of trends in novelistic discourse in particular. Alexander Welsh avers, "Though his informality belies it, [Scott] is as much a theorist of the novel as Fielding and generally stands with his predecessor against the epistolary mode of writing."[38] Scott knew well the trajectory of the epistolary novel, which, following its Continental beginnings, had flourished from the early works of Aphra Behn to the mid-eighteenth-century heyday of Samuel Richardson and into later decades. *Frankenstein* had, of course, received popular acclaim on its publication in 1818, but Mary Shelley had taken on epistolarity in spite of its decline; as Mary A. Favret notes, the epistolary novel was by then considered "stagnant."[39]

Some scholars have claimed that the epistolary mode, in its reliance on the first person, was a hurdle to the eighteenth-century development of the novel as a literary form. Customarily in epistolary novels, each letter is attributed to one specific character, even in the case of dictated, translated, fragmented, or anonymous letters. Reflecting views expressed by other twentieth-century commentators, English Showalter wrote, "The [epistolary] novel was a blind alley in the eighteenth century, as far as technique was concerned. Until the writer was freed from the bondage of the first person, the genre was unable to move forward."[40]

Under such circumstances, what drew Scott to this mode of writing several years later, in the 1820s? Amid an array of possible answers, one rationale is especially salient for the novel's perspective on law. As Scott considered legal and political systems in which practices of representation were on the verge of historic change, the epistolary novel's supposed defects became virtues. Epistolarity occasions scrutiny of claims that one is speaking for others—and thus sheds light on the operations of advocacy. In choosing to revive the epistolary novel, Scott revives in a new generational context the evergreen problem of the "bondage of the first person": can authors ever truly extricate themselves from their own perspective to relay accurately the beliefs and needs of others?[41] In their letters, the protagonists of *Redgauntlet* relay the voices of others almost as often as they speak for themselves, and it is clear to the reader that they are selective regarding whose voices they take pains to represent faithfully. The novel does not cultivate an illusion of authentic and unfiltered representation of others' speech; instead, Scott's protagonists demonstrate the extent to which the advocates exert control over the narratives of those for whom they speak. Both are professionally trained in the law, and they face a balancing act between, on the one hand, representing the lowly and, on the other, distancing themselves to assert their own authority. Their manner of representing the speech of others is emblematic of the containment of underclass expression that had been perpetuated for centuries by those in society's higher tiers. The epistolary novel enabled Scott to enforce within *Redgauntlet* the prolongation of restrictions long imposed on the underclass, even as the continued viability of such restrictions was being tested in British legal and political institutions during the 1820s.

From its first pages, *Redgauntlet* engages with the relationship between the expert advocate and the socially marginal subject. The events of the novel are focalized in its first section through its protagonists, two Edinburgh law students: Darsie Latimer, an orphan who receives regular stipends from a mysterious trust, and the relatively straitlaced Alan Fairford, a trainee to become a Writer to the Signet.[42] In the banter-laced letters that begin the novel, the longtime friends discuss the vocation of advocacy. Darsie informs Alan that he has decided to abandon pursuit of a legal career; raised by a social nonentity—a reclusive, abstemious mother who refused to tell him anything about his father—he plans to travel to England to find the truth for himself. Darsie jokingly requests his companion's legal services: "Turn, then, thy sharp, wire-drawing, lawyer-like ingenuity to the same task—make up my history as though thou wert shaping the blundering allegations of some blue-bonnetted, hard-headed client, into a condescendence of facts and circumstances."[43] Alan's recitation of his story, Darsie suggests, will be more effective than Darsie's telling it on his own; it will ease his entry into a new place—England— after he gives up residence in Scotland, where he is believed to be a "natural child" or illegitimate descendant: "In a country where all the world have a circle of consanguinity, extending to sixth cousins at least, I am a solitary individual. . . . I am in the world as a stranger" (4). When represented by an advocate, Darsie suggests, those neglected by society become worthy of notice in the eyes of the law and are equipped to exercise legal agency. An advocate, in other words, can bestow some measure of legitimacy.

Complicating this straightforward endorsement of the benefits of advocacy is the intertextuality of these early letters. Early on, *Redgauntlet* is situated explicitly in the tradition of epistolary history: Darsie describes Alan and himself as "Lovelace and Belford like" (14). In aligning himself and his confidante with the morally compromised male correspondents of Samuel Richardson's epistolary masterpiece *Clarissa* (1747–48), Darsie calls to mind a predatory brand of advocacy. Richard Lovelace is, of course, infamous for controlling the expressive powers of the young woman to whom he promised protection: he intercepts and forges her letters. In his biographical account of Richardson, published a year before *Redgauntlet*, Scott excoriated Lovelace's predations. "He had committed a crime for which he deserved death by the law of the country," Scott wrote; "there is no reader but feels vindictive pleasure when Morden passes the sword through his body."[44] As the novel continues, it is revealed that Darsie, similar to Lovelace, bears an elite pedigree: he is, in fact, Arthur Redgauntlet, scion of the Scottish aristocracy and eventual heir to a grand estate. Darsie's ominous early allusion thus portends that as the novel continues, the prerogative of the elite to speak for the lowly may lapse into distortion and manipulation.

Accordingly, while the initial epistolary section of *Redgauntlet* justifies the appointment of educated professionals as advocates for those who are ill-equipped to present their own cases, later segments of the novel illustrate the dangers of entrusting justice to the powerful in contexts where there are no institutional structures or processes in place to safeguard the vulnerable. At the same time, the novel demonstrates that the voices of the marginalized must be controlled, lest they overcome the privileged mediators and arbiters by whom they are currently contained in the legal system. Yet *Redgauntlet* warns that a proper legal system must make available some means of adequate representation, if not direct expression. If the powerful are allowed to co-opt the legal system completely and distort the law to suit themselves, recourse to representation will be eliminated, and the poor will not be the only ones who suffer.

Incapacity and Hostility of the Lowly: Justifying Professional Control of Representation

Redgauntlet reflects a social reality in which, unsurprisingly, the privileged command preferential treatment in the legal arena. When he first ventures into the business of professional advocacy, Alan is visited by a prospective client: "My visitor was undeniably a lady, and probably considerably above the ordinary rank; she was concealed by a walking-cloak. . . . Her person was enveloped, and moreover, was furnished with a hood" (66–67). Eluding Alan's attempts to question her verbally, the lady—who does not give her name—insists on conveying her case through a letter and abruptly departs from Alan's office. Alan is intrigued and puzzled: "I began to stand convicted in my own mind . . . for having failed to extract the lady's real purpose—and . . . now that it was over, for thinking so much about it" (69), he writes to Darsie. The lady is one of a number of socially elevated characters in the novel— including the fur-cloaked Hugh Redgauntlet—who render themselves opaque. They minimize face-to-face communication and thwart scrutiny of their facial expressions with hoods and masks. The visitor's high status out-balances her marginalized female identity. By communicating via letter, the woman seals her narrative in uninterpolated form so that Alan cannot inter-rupt or condescend to her. Notably, Alan makes a strenuous but futile effort to extract the intentions of this privileged visitor; he takes her case seriously.

His regard for the client is further enhanced by the sizable sum she encloses in the letter as a retainer. The lady demonstrates that she is qualified to have a say in her own case, and Alan complies readily with the written instructions she peremptorily sets forth in her letter.

In contrast, Alan describes an impoverished new client, Peter Peebles, with disdain, emphasizing the man's lack of capacity to handle his own affairs. Peter is an extreme example of the marginality of the lowly in the eyes of the law: Alan describes him as "an insane beggar—as poor as Job, and as mad as a March hare!" (116). The man's "emaciated figure," "withered and blighted skin," and "features begrimed with snuff" repulse Alan, who feels "shame and embarrassment" (130) while working with him. For fifteen years, Peter has been embroiled in a dispute with a former business partner. Alan's father, also an advocate, asks Alan to represent Peter pro bono. Having run through a sequence of lawyers, each of whom refused to continue representing him, Peter is nearing the limit of the law's accommodation of him. Alan, who has misgivings about the case, may be Peter's last chance.

Alan's narration of the progress of Peter's case is the first of a series of episodes in *Redgauntlet* that give close attention to the power of the educated to mediate the speech of the marginalized. A large part of Peter's dialogue is relayed by Alan; when he is introduced, and for the duration of the epistolary sequence that forms the first section of the novel, Peter does not speak for himself, even when his words are cited verbatim. In a letter to Darsie, Alan textually reenacts a conversation with Peter: "Oh, Mr. Alan Fairford, ye are a lucky man to buckle to such a cause as mine at the very outset! it [*sic*] is like a specimen of all causes, man. By the Regiam, there is not a *remedium juris* in the practiques but ye'll find a spice o't. Here's to your getting weel through with it" (121–22), Peter exclaims in Alan's retelling. Alan's meticulous documentation of Peter's speech is a performance of "eye dialect," George Philip Krapp's term for orthography that calls attention to pronunciation.[45] Celeste Langan has shown that, earlier in his career, Scott used textual poetry as an "audiovisual medium," challenging some later theorists' notions that "presuppose that print is a more or less silent medium [that works] by silencing actual speech differences—class, provincial, and gendered vocal inflections."[46] Alan undercuts Peter's credibility by transcribing his speech meticulously. He takes care to differentiate his own refined parlance from Peter's mangled and uncouth turns of phrase; he represents Peter scrupulously, but in doing so he also ridicules him. Although Peter is sufficiently knowledgeable to cite the *Regiam Majestatem*—a time-honored compendium of the laws of Scotland—

and spouts legal terminology to assert himself as an informed participant in his case, his display of knowledge is offset by his flood of mispronounced words, which only occasionally resolve into coherent legal reasoning. Alan has the power to guide others' impressions of his client's intellectual capacity and worthiness, both on the page and in court; although he ridicules him in private, he champions his case in the legal arena. Without him, the novel makes clear, Peter is not capable of presenting a viable case.

Even as the novel paternalistically suggests that unmediated expression is not in the best interest of underserved clients such as Peter, it also questions whether the justice system should accommodate such clients in the first place. Alan describes his client as a case study of a larger societal problem: "You must have seen this original, Darsie, who, like others in the same predicament, continues to haunt the courts of justice, where he has made shipwreck of time, means, and understanding. Such insane paupers have sometimes seemed to me to resemble wrecks lying upon the shoals on the Goodwin Sands, or in Yarmouth Roads, warning other vessels to keep aloof on the banks from which they have been lost; or rather, such ruined clients are like scarecrows and potato-bogies, distributed through the court to scare away fools from the scene of litigation" (118). Whereas in Scott's earlier novel *Guy Mannering* the paupers on the receiving end of Ellangowan's harsh and unaccommodating approach to justice were depicted as helpless victims, in *Redgauntlet* Alan blames Peter and his ilk for daring to assert themselves in the legal arena; he characterizes them as "fools" but also as responsible parties who at least initially were free to make better choices. No blame is attached to the elite figures who established such a hazardous system in the first place.

The novel does not cast Alan's evaluation of Peter as a singular, biased opinion. On the contrary, little seems to distinguish Alan's point of view from that of the omniscient narrator, who gives an account of Peter's case in a subsequent nonepistolary section of the novel:

Poor Peter Peebles, whose shallow brain was altogether unable to bear the importance of the moment, kept as close to his young counsel as shadow to substance, affected now to speak loud, now to whisper in his ear, now to deck his ghastly countenance with wreathed smiles, now to cloud it with a shade of deep and solemn importance, and anon to contort it with the sneer of scorn and derision. These moods of the client's mind were accompanied with singular "moppings and mowings," fantastic gestures, which the man of rags and litigation deemed appropriate to his changes of countenance. Now he brandished his arm aloft, now thrust his fist straight out, as if to knock his opponent down. Now he laid his open palm on his bosom, and now flinging it abroad, he gallantly snapped his fingers in the air. (129–30)

The novel does not put forward Peter as a candidate for sympathy but as an exhibit of a drain on the limited time and resources of legal professionals. He needs help that the legal system cannot provide. As is the case with other characters—such as Madge Wildfire in *The Heart of Mid-lothian*[47]—Peter's poverty is implicitly linked with his mental illness.

Previous scholarship has taken a different view of *Peebles v. Plainstanes*. Noting that it is mentioned that Peter was once an affluent burgess, David Brown describes him as an unsympathetic character who "represents the 'unacceptable face of capitalism' in late eighteenth-century Edinburgh society." Brown points out that the novel indicates that Peter's business troubles stemmed from greed and fraud. "In these circumstances," Brown argues, "the application of 'justice' to Peter's case (which is implied by Alan's advocacy of his cause) seems wildly inappropriate: the law (and so, by implication, the Fairfords) is shown to be a parasite of the property system."[48] Bruce Beiderwell comments, "The law seems a petty, clumsy matter in respect to the Peter Peebles episode."[49] In light of the episodes of *The Visionary*, however, Brown's articulation of the relationship between law and property does not represent Scott's point of view. Whereas the rioters in the dream vision would have agreed with Brown, Scott saw law as property's rightful support. Far from indicting the legal system, the Peebles episode thus invites an altogether different interpretation: the fairness of Edinburgh's modern legal system is demonstrated through the pains taken to accommodate even this self-sabotaging, repulsive litigant. Peter embodies the grasping, undeserving, and unruly poor whom Scott vilifies as threatening men of property. His plight is implied to be a result of his choices rather than a condition imposed on him; his poverty is not the consequence of structural inequities that need to be rectified. Scott thus neatly preempts the placement of blame for Peter's indigence on anyone except the client himself. Peter is thus set apart from the uncomplaining, community-minded members of the underclass—the likes of Ellangowan's victims—who, in Scott's eyes, deserve more sympathy.

Under these circumstances, the novel endorses containment of recalcitrant underclass clients. Observing Peter's odd behavior, and Alan's exasperation, Alan's father resorts to paying another ne'er-do-well to bring the client to a pub to ensure that he is too inebriated to return to court. Tellingly, Alan is more persuasive in defending his client after Peter has been ejected from the room in which his lawsuit is being adjudicated. Alan has a duty to represent Peter, but the impoverished man must first submit to containment. Although Peter announces that he intends to represent his own case—"I will state it myself," he says (119)—Alan's father definitively prohibits him from acting on his wishes. The novel strongly implies that an educated and expert advocate is the only effective voice the poor can have in court.

While Alan declares, "I will plead as well for Peter Peebles, as I could for a duke" (123)—a statement that acknowledges typical disparities in legal treatment for high-born and lowly people—he feels no real loyalty to his client. Indeed, he abandons him in the midst of a pivotal court hearing: just as he is successfully stating Peter's case in court—thus giving the client his first real opportunity for justice in years—Alan is handed a letter advising that Darsie has gone missing after a riot on the border between Scotland and England. Scott has concocted a moment of high drama: on one side lies Alan's responsibility to his impoverished client, on the other his wish to help his endangered friend. The novel could hardly be more overt in staging legal representation as a contest between the demands of the poor and the well-being of the privileged. Alan departs in the midst of the trial, leaving a gallery of shocked spectators in his wake. To no avail, Peter obtains a warrant and subsequently devotes all of his time to pursuing Alan and attempting to force him to return to Edinburgh and represent him.

The protagonists are intent on insulating themselves from society's most vulnerable members, whom they invariably find repugnant or threatening. Throughout the novel, the lowly are cast as presenting an ongoing threat by dint of their proximity. At the close of a letter to Darsie, Alan marvels at how "Peter and his lawsuit have insinuated themselves so far" into his letter and at Peter's ability to "occupy my thoughts" (123). By replaying the case in letters, Alan can channel Peter's voice while keeping his distance. After he is abducted and can no longer communicate with Alan, Darsie, writing in his journal, expresses apprehension regarding the influence the marginalized could exercise upon him: "I have heard—dreadful thought!—of men . . . trepanned into the custody of the keepers of private mad-houses . . . whose brain[s], after years of misery, became at last unsettled with the wretched beings amongst whom they were classed." Vowing that "this shall not be my case," Darsie promises, "by strong internal resolution . . . to avoid exterior and contagious sympathies" (167). At another point, Darsie admits, "I ought, perhaps, to blush at recollecting what has been often objected to me by the dear friend to whom this letter is addressed, viz. the facility with which I have, in moments of in-dolence, suffered my motions to be directed by any person who chanced to be near me, instead of taking the labour of thinking or deciding for myself" (146). At such times, Scott's fascination with what the narrator calls "the relative situation of adviser and advised, protector and protected" (367), shifts to dwell on the protagonists' fear and their own need for protection.

Advocacy for Silent Sufferers

Even before Peter directly threatens Alan at the close of the novel, he imposes great strain on his advocate and the resources of the legal system. If members of the "lower orders" can challenge social hierarchy through exercising legal agency, why does Scott nonetheless appear to uphold the provision of some measure of legal representation for all comers, including the poor? The an-swer seems to be that Scott expresses particular concern for the unassertive and weak—no matter their position in society—who are easy prey for the strong. The plight of the weak is exacerbated in contexts when the rule of law is absent or vitiated by corruption.

While fractious litigants like Peter are figured as repellent, Scott has great sympathy for those who are not in a position to vocalize their grievances in a formal legal venue. Soon after Alan's abrupt exit from Peter's trial, the novel features another letter from Darsie, who—en route to England—takes refuge at a farm owned by a family of Quakers. Darsie listens as the brother, Joshua Geddes, describes withstanding assaults from fishermen in the course of a dis-pute over water rights. Joshua proclaims: "Thou knowest there may be as much courage in enduring as in acting" and wonders aloud "whether there is not more cowardice . . . in the armed oppressor, who doth injury, than in the defenceless and patient sufferer, who endureth it with constancy" (44). Joshua's remarks resonate beyond his own predicament. Certainly, the novel's valorization of quiet "endurance" over violent revolt aligns with Scott's antip-athy toward mob agitation. Yet the novel also casts endurance as something more than survival; it is imbued with dignity. Joshua is a prosperous land-owner, but in his dispute, the fishermen have the upper hand; they outnum-ber his small family and could easily overpower them. This episode shows that the lowly are not the only ones who suffer when legal representation is abridged or unavailable; those with power and property are likewise harmed by the absence of a judicial forum that can serve as a level playing field.

As the scene continues, Scott reaffirms support for restrictions on the abil-ity of the lowly to communicate grievances. In the same letter, Darsie considers animals as a category of beings whose legal agency has been wholly denied. He jokingly recounts for Alan a conversation with Joshua's sister, Rachel:

> She pointed out [each animal's] peculiarities and qualities, with the discrimination of one who had made natural history her study; and I own I never looked on barn-door fowls with so much interest before—at least until they were boiled or roasted. I could not help asking the trying question, how she could order the execution of any of the creatures of which she seemed so careful.
>
> "It was painful," she said, "but it was according to the law of their being—they must die—but they knew not when death was approaching; and in making them comfortable while they lived, we contributed to their happiness as much as the conditions of their existence permitted to us."
>
> I am not quite of her mind, Alan. I do not believe either pigs or poultry would admit that the chief end of their being was to be killed and eaten. However, I did not press the argument. (58)

In the early nineteenth-century context of the novel's composition, the suggestion that animals had personal sovereignty akin to that of human beings—and that the views of animals ought to be considered in decisions involving their lives—would have been ridiculed as a notion insupportable beyond the realm of fairy tales. Darsie and Rachel use legal terminology to introduce two distinct notions of the value of animal life: the euphemistic "law of their being" is opposed to *execution*—a term that defamiliarizes the routine processes of the abattoir. Whereas Rachel contends that the animals are ignorant—they do not know when they will die—Darsie imagines their sentience. Although Darsie's aside is a seemingly humorous, quickly passing moment, it reiterates the serious questions raised earlier in the novel. The positioning of animals resembles that of the poor: the impoverished are ill-equipped to speak for themselves in formal legal contexts, but they can be represented effectively by educated advocates. Similarly, animals have no voice to protest the "law" that determines their fate, but their opinions can be channeled and communicated in intelligible terms by human interlocuters. Darsie empathizes but is reluctant to risk losing the Geddes's hospitality by contesting Rachel's opinion.

Scott was likely aware of emerging debates over animal rights.[50] In an 1829 letter to the novelist Maria Edgeworth, Scott offers a prescient formulation of cruelty to animals: "In the practice of the bar, it is astonishing how we become callous to right and wrong. . . . I have myself often wondered how I became so indifferent to the horrors of a criminal trial if it involved a point of law. In like manner, the pursuit of physiology inflicts tortures on the lower animals of creation," he stated, drawing an explicit analogy between human litigants and animals used for scientific experimentation. An animal rights activist read from Scott's letter as evidence against the continued legality of vivisection during the Royal Commission hearings in 1875.[51]

In *Redgauntlet*, however, playful suggestions that livestock or pets are capable of thinking and feeling serve less to express concern for animal rights than to offer a limit case for societal reassessment of who counts as worthy of having a say in matters of law. When Alan imagines a cow as a party to a lawsuit (9), or Darsie describes his host's dogs as human-like dinner guests (26), the novel is not particularly interested in exploring Montaigne's famous question: "How does [man] know, by the force of his intelligence, the secret internal stirrings of animals?"[52] Instead, the novel's imaginings of animals enact slippery-slope reasoning, as if to ask: If the government were to heed the voices of the lowly and expand legal and political representation, where would such expansions of rights stop? Exactly how much power would the privileged be forced to relinquish? Scott aims to set a boundary on the scope of the debate.

Speech under Strongmen: The Privileged Lose Their Voice

In the first section of *Redgauntlet*, the educated protagonists serve as formal or informal advocates for the lowly; their letters are material emblems of their simultaneous transmission and containment of the real and imagined speech of the marginalized. The latter part of the novel, by contrast, depicts Alan and Darsie in situations in which their own expression is mediated—and usually distorted—by strongmen. The replacement in this section of the epistolary mode by an omniscient observer's "Narrative" and the abductee's "Journal"— addressed to whoever may find it—indicate that the protagonists have lost the powers of advocacy they possessed within the urban legal establishment; their own voices are now alarmingly subject to external direction and appropriation. Here, the novel indicates the dangers that arise when those in control completely abridge the expressive capabilities of those under their power. Scott presents two elaborate illustrations of this situation. One episode— Alan's captivity by smugglers—is a vision of what may come to pass if the legal system were suspended and those on the margins of society were allowed to speak and act for themselves without constraint: they would overcome the figures of traditional privilege who currently contain them within the legal system. Another episode—Darsie's abduction by his uncle Hugh Redgauntlet—demonstrates the travesties of justice that ensue when the elite co-opt the legal system and claim the prerogative to silence all below them without mediating their grievances. There is a point, Scott suggests, at which a person's ability to speak for himself is too unmediated and another at which it is too constrained. In either case, abuse of power is likely.

The groundwork is laid for these episodes by the aforementioned letter that arrived midway through Peter's trial, informing Alan that Darsie has been abducted; Alan immediately departs from the courtroom to seek Darsie. While traveling on horseback through the remote regions where his friend was last seen, Alan is forced to keep company with a group of smugglers. The unregulated borderlands between Scotland and England through which he travels offer no idyllic pastoral alternative to the orderly and humane urban legal system of Edinburgh.

In a lawless realm in which the speech of the lowly is fully authorized and unmediated, that of the privileged is silenced. The outlaws ridicule their visitor's self-identification as a man of law and presume to speak for him, a humiliating role reversal for Alan, the professional advocate. After Alan is led for the first time to the smugglers' den, a bandit questions him with suspicion; Trumbull, the lead smuggler, declares, "I will answer for this gentleman" (239). When, during the ensuing discussion, the men notice Alan's silence and seem to expect him to speak, he feels unable to do so: "Fairford now found himself called upon to say something; yet his feelings, upon finding himself thus completely in the power of a canting hypocrite, and of his retainer, who had so much the air of a determined ruffian, joined to the strong and abominable fume which they snuffed up with indifference, while it almost deprived him of respiration, combined to render utterance difficult" (239). After a futile attempt to argue against Trumbull, who insists on giving him a new name, Alan falls into "silent abhorrence" (243). He must ask permission for taking trivial liberties such as a nap—requests that are granted only grudgingly (245). Alan's time in the realm of the smugglers resembles a more fleshed-out version of the sketches in *The Visionary* of a world in which the underclass has seized power.

Whereas Alan's quest in the latter half of the novel shows the dangers imposed by the absence of any legal system, Darsie's journey in this same section illustrates the perils of a corrupt legal system. In both cases, individual liberty is imperiled for everyone except the few strongmen in control, and even the privileged and educated are unable to protest against coercion.

Darsie, too, finds himself silenced, but in a very different social context, when, in the course of his journey to England, he is swept up by a mysterious rider.

Held captive in the estate of the rider, who does not reveal his identity, Darsie becomes a petitioner in a mock trial, staged not in a courtroom but in the domestic space of the parlor of the rider's estate. After trying in vain to persuade the rider to release him, Darsie appeals directly to a visitor: a local justice of the peace. Darsie's words are stirring: "Every British subject has a right to know why he suffers restraint . . . nor can he be deprived of liberty without a legal warrant," he argues, demanding, "Shew me that by which you confine me thus" (169). The rider claims that he is providing "temporary guardianship" (174) to a disoriented stranger who wandered onto his estate. The epitome of a corrupt legal authority, Foxley scorns Darsie's attempt at self-advocacy: "Justice Foxley . . . pshawed, hemmed, and elevated his eyebrows, as if in scorn of my supplication. . . . He leaned back in his chair, and smoked his pipe with great energy, with a look of defiance, designed to make me aware that all my reasoning was lost on him" (173). Foxley accepts Redgauntlet's claim of magnanimity and commends him: "I know him to be a most responsible person—a—hay—aye—most responsible and honourable person" (174).[53]

This scene further establishes the similarity between Darsie's new position and that of lowly men, such as Peter, who navigate Edinburgh's legal system. Despite his knowledge of the law, Darsie is subjected to the coercion that those of very little means face throughout their lives. Although Darsie will eventually be recognized as nobility, up to this point he has occupied a middling social position, above the very poor and considerably below those of the highest status. Rather than igniting in him a newfound sympathy for the poor, his experience of being unable to speak for himself seems primarily to indicate how easily those currently in a position of security could be brought down to the level of the disenfranchised—were it not for the stability and fairness of the modern, urban-centered, and professionally managed Scottish legal system.

At length, the rider reveals himself to be a close relative whom Darsie has never met: Hugh Redgauntlet, the brother of Sir Henry Redgauntlet, Darsie's deceased father. Hugh Redgauntlet has spent years in the borderlands laying the groundwork for his cause: a renewed attempt to place Charles Edward Stuart, the famed Pretender, on the throne. Redgauntlet aims to groom Darsie to serve as a spokesman for his agenda; Darsie, he hopes, will convince others to mount a new Jacobite rebellion against the king. Darsie refuses to do his uncle's bidding. To pressure him to comply, Redgauntlet refuses to let his nephew speak in public or write letters. On the severing of his line of communication with Alan, Darsie shifts from composing letters addressed to a specific recipient to writing in a "Journal" in which the field of addressees is open to anyone "in whose hands soever these leaves may fall" (144). Although Darsie's journal serves as an expressive outlet for him, it is not found or read by any other character, so it provides no means of transmitting his grievances to a venue where they can be addressed. Darsie thus finds himself in a predicament analogous to that of lowly individuals who lack advocates and access to court; however vocal they may be in stating their complaints, their voices will go unheeded, so it hardly matters what they say.

In keeping with Scott's intimation that domestic interactions can prepare the way for large-scale historical change, Darsie's private rejection of Redgauntlet's demand to use his voice is later reprised in a public venue. At the denouement of the novel, Redgauntlet, accompanied by his Jacobite followers, asks Darsie to speak on behalf of the rebel forces to government officials who—seeking to preempt the uprising—have traveled to meet them. Darsie once again rejects his uncle's attempt to co-opt him as an obedient mouthpiece but remains "silent" for fear that "a direct refusal would cost him his liberty or life" (317). This moment reveals a Darsie changed by his experience of confinement; he is now cautious and self-restrained, in comparison to his carefree, outspoken persona at the novel's opening. Unable to muster support from the Jacobites, who are reluctant to risk their property rights for rebellion, Redgauntlet gives up his cause and retreats to a cloister. Darsie rests secure in the knowledge that he never let his uncle speak through him, although he fell silent when it became clear that Redgauntlet would not hear his appeals. He is now free to take his real name, which is revealed to be Sir Arthur Redgauntlet, and assume control of his family's estate. Scott presents a vision of liberty in which an individual's assertion of the right to speak for him- or herself must work in tandem with, not against, the rule of law and the upholding of property rights. When unable to avail themselves of an advocate, victims who silently endure injustice—rather than berating their superiors, violently retaliating, or destroying others' property—will eventually have their reward.

～

Early in *Redgauntlet*, barriers to communicating grievances and seeking redress afflict only the indigent, the mentally ill, or animals—that is, those whose silence and lack of power is disregarded as the natural order of things, "the law of their being." Over the course of the novel, however, the privileged and educated, too, are reduced to this subordinate position. The events experienced by Alan and Darsie are depicted as humiliating emergencies, and Scott ensures that they finally attain their rightful positions in society. As do the invincible princes of fairy tales, they sail through abduction and false imprisonment without sustaining lasting physical injury or psychological trauma. Scott's hasty resolution of the novel's counterfactual events of the peaceful Hanoverian 1760s—with years-long grievances resolved in a single chapter—seems too neat. Yet it is designed to reassure the reader of national and institutional resilience and inevitable return to a baseline of stability—a baseline that persists, Scott implies, despite the tumultuous legal and political developments under way in the 1820s, the decade of the novel's publication. Professional men and men of property will receive their due.

By contrast, the suffering of members of the "lower orders" is reported but only occasionally repaired, and their legal self-assertion is unsuccessfully attempted—or floated but never fulfilled. Darsie's conversation with Rachel Geddes regarding animals and "the law of their being" ends on a dissonant, inconclusive note. For several years, Peter awaits in vain the hearing of his case; eventually, on being offered a proposal for a settlement, he drops dead in the halls of the judiciary. No rulings, formal or informal, are delivered for these plaintiffs. That nothing is resolved by the professional or informal advocacy undertaken by the protagonists is, in Scott's view, the rightful order of things, not a failure of justice. Scott manages to have it both ways: the letters register the dignity of the animals and the humanity of Peter's broken speech, without conveying any particular support for the legal recognition and societal reordering that would undertake the difficult work of addressing their suffering. In contrast, the beggar Wandering Willie, who warns others to refrain from openly criticizing the Redgauntlet family, is rewarded for his subordination with a comfortable perch on the estate of Darsie, who is now Sir Arthur.

Belatedly, with only a few chapters remaining in the lengthy novel, Scott introduces the twist that Peter—during his earlier, prosperous years—evicted an indigent family, precipitating the death of his elderly tenant. Within the space of a few paragraphs, the novel alternates between denoting the character as "Poor Peter" and "Peter the Cruel." When confronted on this subject, Peter replies: "She might live or die, for what I care . . . what business have folk to do to live that canna live as law will, and satisfy their just and lawful creditors?" (333). His response reflects callous disregard for the tenant, who could not afford to pay rent as per his contract; it is designed by Scott to exempt readers from sympathizing with Peter. Here, speaking unmediated, Peter comes across as odious—far from the "simple-hearted, honest, well-meaning man" (133) Alan made him out to be during legal proceedings.

Building on this strained, last-minute plot twist, in the novel's final pages Scott continues to redirect any sympathy that may remain for the impoverished and outspoken litigant. Over drinks in a pub, Joshua Geddes—who has traveled to come to Darsie's aid—distracts Peter from confronting Alan; he requests the specifics of "this great law-suit of thine, which has been a matter of such celebrity" (364). Peter responds: "Celebrity? . . . It's very true that it is grandeur upon earth . . . to see the reporters mending their pens to take down the debate—the Lords themselves powing in their chairs . . . To see a' this . . . and to ken that naething will be said or dune amang a' thae grand folk, for maybe the feck of three hours, saving what concerns you and your business—O, man, nae wonder that ye judge this to be earthly glory!" (364–65). Peter's account of the reception of his case does not reflect reality, and the novel cues readers to view him with derision for his delusions of grandeur. In Peter's imagining, a marginalized person's legal complaint is sufficiently fascinating to captivate the powerful. This scenario must be cast as grandiose and rejected because it threatens the balance endorsed by Scott, in which powerful advocates control the transmission of the complaints of the lowly. If Peter's vision were to come to pass, Scott implies, the courts would be overrun by "lower class" litigants, as he worried in his personal journal: the privileged would be vulnerable to lawsuits launched by inferiors motivated by spite or greed, and their own worthier cases would be crowded out by the nuisance claims brought by their inferiors.

Here, as in other episodes throughout the novel, the concerns of the lowly receive a hearing in order to stave off harm to the privileged: Geddes initiates conversation with Peter to distract him from confronting Alan or harassing Darsie's sister Lillias. Yet Peter's story is something more than the barely tolerated ramblings of a ne'er-do-well: although Scott could not have known it, it was an accurate picture of the future: televised court sessions and sensationalistic news articles in which short-lived public attention to a marginalized person's quotidian legal struggle is construed as something of a substitute for justice. The still more audacious prospect to which Peter's musings give rise—a prospect that Scott attempted to dismiss, even as he raised the possibility and wrote it into the literary record—was an entirely different type of novel: a chronicle of a lowly person's mundane legal struggle, rendered in exhaustive, humdrum detail. For such a novel, the world was not yet ready.

CHAPTER FOUR

Masters of Passion and Tongue

White Eyewitnesses and Fear of Black Testimony
in the Proslavery Novel

When scholars discuss the literature of transatlantic slavery, they often choose to focus on writings that supported the emancipation of the enslaved: slave narratives and antislavery poems, plays, and novels. This preference is understandable, for it is fueled by two interconnected and long-standing objectives that have directed the recent course of literary studies: the wish to unearth and amplify the voices of the marginalized and the desire to find evidence that literature can change how people believe and even how they act.[1] Certainly, authors of antislavery literature demonstrated faith in the power of literature to effect social change as they targeted the hearts and minds of white readers in Britain and, later, the United States, the majority of whom had no direct contact with plantation life.[2] A key strategy used by antislavery authors to inspire sympathy in those readers was the portrayal of slaves as emotionally transparent. Enslaved characters in antislavery fiction are frequently given to open expression of the sadness and misery experienced as a result of harsh treatment at the hands of white owners and overseers. Yet as Lynn Festa, George Boulukos, Colin Dayan, and others have noted, such depictions often left the impression that blacks were creatures of emotion rather than people of reason. Consequently, such characterizations tended to reinforce the belief that blacks lacked the intellectual capacity to be recognized as legal persons.[3]

In this chapter, I consider an underexamined context for debates regarding the humanity of the enslaved and the legal agency of slaves and slaveholders by turning to sources from the opposite end of the ideological spectrum: early nineteenth-century proslavery British literature. These works have been relatively neglected, likely owing in part to what many of today's readers would deem their noxious politics.[4] In the first three decades of the nineteenth century, British publishers released a smattering of novels and fictional travelogues that argued—some subtly, some bluntly—that slavery was not inhumane, contrary to what detractors averred. Set in Jamaica or elsewhere in the West Indies and published in London and Glasgow, these literary works were crafted to forestall the end of slavery. I focus on two novels in particular: *Hamel, the Obeah Man* (1827), by Cynric R. Williams (said to be a pseudonym);[5] and *Marly; or, A Planter's Life in Jamaica* (published anonymously in 1828; one "plausible candidate" for authorship is said to be John Stewart, a resident of the island).[6] Proslavery works represented the grievances of plantation owners (known as "planters") and administrators. As such, the descriptors "pro-planter" or "anti-abolitionist" have also been applied to the genre.[7] This group feared black unrest and resented government officials in the metropole for threatening planters' liberty through means such as British Colonial Office oversight of West Indian legislation governing slavery.[8] In a last-gasp effort, proslavery authors became particularly adamant about defending slaveholder rights in the years leading up to the 1833 Slavery Abolition Act, which took effect in 1834.

At times, the proslavery novel mirrored antislavery literature in strategically devoting attention to the feelings of the enslaved and in portraying slaves as simple-minded and emotionally transparent. Yet antislavery writers depicted the enslaved as openly sad, fearful, melancholic, or suffering.[9] By contrast, proslavery novels presented as the majority slaves whose happiness was visibly evident. Furthermore, proslavery authors departed from the trope of slaves' emotional transparency in cases when it did not align with their political agenda. *Hamel* and *Marly* offer conflicting images of slaves as emotionally transparent and entirely inscrutable; the novels oscillate between attempting to promote a vision of harmonious plantation life through cheery tableaux of singing and smiling, and warning of the anger harbored by the enslaved.

In examining this literature, I highlight depictions of enslaved men and women strategically engaging in prevarication or evasive silence and demonstrate that these portrayals were developed as a public relations campaign of sorts to challenge contemporaneous pressure to admit slaves as witnesses against white defendants in West Indian courts. Beginning in 1800 and continuing into the 1820s, various British West Indian assemblies struggled to resolve questions of the legal agency of the enslaved and, particularly, their capacity to testify against whites. These debates are explicitly addressed in *Hamel* and *Marly*.

More than three decades before the American author Harriet Beecher Stowe proclaimed in *A Key to Uncle Tom's Cabin* (1853)—a guide to her best-selling 1852 novel—that "the very key of Southern jurisprudence is the rejection of colored testimony,"[10] British authors attempting to defend slavery in the West Indies recognized that undermining slave testimony was crucial to furthering their agenda. Proslavery literature thus features a significant number of black characters who are conniving, duplicitous, and capable of exercising formidable self-control. Over such subjects, whites would need to keep a firm upper hand.

This strategy of depiction, therefore, was problematic for the proslavery agenda because it humanized the enslaved and emphasized their ingenuity and reasoning ability to the extent that, at times, the white characters are easily duped or outsmarted. To exacerbate matters, proslavery authors' attempts to cast slave protagonists as simplistic and unidimensional were constrained by the literary form of the novel, with its Romantic-era emphasis on vivid representations of interiority.[11] In other words, the form of the novel itself intensified the ideological contradictions that undermined the capacity of the proslavery novel to support its political agenda. I argue that proslavery literature—and the proslavery novel in particular—thus inadvertently advanced an alternative vision of the enslaved as rational, self-controlled, and emotionally sophisticated persons, although at other times proslavery authors reaffirmed the simplistic depictions offered by antislavery sentimentalists. These authors depicted a black subject who was too dangerous to emancipate.

A Blind Spot in Literary History

From the final decades of the eighteenth century through the first decades of the nineteenth, some defenders of slavery justified the institution by claiming that black people could not act independently and appropriately in a civilized society, owing to their inferior intellectual capacity and inability to control their emotions. Slaves were often figured as children who required constant oversight.[12] Within the larger proslavery coalition, an "ameliorationist" contingent averred that they supported eventual emancipation but not before slaves were made fit to become part of civilized society.[13]

The antislavery literature that contested these arguments has been credited with helping to generate fellow-feeling for the enslaved in both Britain[14] and America.[15] A particularly important facet of this category of humanitarian writing, scholars have long contended, was its political instrumentalization of emotion.[16] However wide the gulf between the lived experience of white middle-class readers and the humiliating conditions of slavery, readers could still imaginatively relate to the feelings of enslaved people as set forth on the page.[17] Emotional similarities, according to this logic, trumped the vast chasm of racial difference manifest in physical attributes such as skin color,[18] and the literary portrayal of these similarities led white readers to recognize the personhood of the enslaved and turn against slavery. Even scholars who push back against this claim have largely maintained the focus on antislavery literature.[19] A number of critics, including Brycchan Carey and Marcus Wood, have argued that sentimental portrayals of slaves were self-indulgent and refocused attention on the feelings of white spectators.[20] Others have contended that well-meaning attempts to humanize slaves—through conveying their fear or grief—were patronizing and reinforced the very same racist notions promoted by supporters of slavery—that is, that slaves were simple, emotionally reactive, incapable of self-regulation, and prone to immediate gratification.[21]

To this day, the literary output of British proslavery writers remains curiously underexamined: while historians and sociologists including Eugene D. Genovese, Diana Paton, Orlando Patterson, and Larry E. Tise have offered accounts of proslavery political writings, speeches, and diaries,[22] they largely neglect proslavery fiction. A few literary scholars have discussed individual British proslavery works (Janina Nordius, Candace Ward, and Tim Watson);[23] applied a literary interpretive lens to proslavery texts on natural history and geography (Elizabeth A. Bohls);[24] or evaluated select fictions in light of a specifically racial theme such as miscegenation (Sara Salih).[25] In her analysis of the works of white Creole authors residing in the British West Indies, Candace Ward has noted their attempts to shape their public image through fiction as they contended with widespread views that they were "single-minded in their pursuit of money and irredeemably corrupted by their investment in slavery."[26] No previous studies have assessed British proslavery novelists' explicit commentary on the decades-long battle over the admission of black testimony in a variety of contexts, which ranged from military court-martials, to slave courts, to trials of slaveholders.[27] Proslavery novelists attempted not only to preserve slavery as an institution but, more specifically, to limit the role of the enslaved in the legal system—and thus to ensure that the ability to testify in a variety of contexts remained reserved for whites.

Slavery, Emotion, and Strategic Deception in Earlier Literature

Eighteenth-century British proslavery writing from the West Indies, ranging from natural histories and travelogues to journals, established an array of conventions that were foundational to early nineteenth-century British pro-slavery novels, which both adapted and dispensed with these existing racial tropes. Later antebellum American antislavery novels such as *Uncle Tom's Cabin* depict slaves as simple-minded, emotionally transparent subordinates. In contrast, eighteenth-century British proslavery travelogues and natural history provide a spectrum of depictions, showing the extent to which conceptualizations of black men and women as emotionally and intellectually similar to, or different from, whites were in flux. Writers of proslavery literature presented their work as eyewitness testimony—the only authentic window into the truth about how black people felt about being enslaved; yet the same texts at times portrayed slaves as emotionally inscrutable.

Some proslavery writers rejected the notion that slaves harbored any feelings at all that were not immediately apparent to white spectators.[28] Describing his time at a slave auction, Bryan Edwards acknowledged in *The History, Civil and Commercial, of the British Colonies in the West Indies* (1793) that the spectacle might appall British readers, but he assured them that sensibility was scarcely experienced by those "creatures" on sale: "Although there is something extremely shocking to a humane and cultivated mind ... I could never perceive ... that the Negroes themselves were oppressed with many of those painful sensations which a person unaccustomed to the scene would naturally attribute to such wretchedness."[29] He presents slave emotion as ephemeral, a response to the moment: "They display, therefore, on being brought to market, very few signs of lamentation for their past, or of apprehension for their future condition, but, wearied out with confinement at sea, commonly express great eagerness to be sold; presenting themselves, when the buyers are few, with chearfulness and alacrity for selection, and appearing mortified and disappointed when refused" (125–26). Edwards claimed that the slaves pay former harms no mind and experience no distressing emotions that they would benefit from hiding. When a buyer rejects one of the slaves, "the majority [of the rest of the slaves offered for sale] seem highly diverted by the circumstance; manifesting, by loud and repeated bursts of laughter, that reflection constitutes very little part of their character" (127). These slaves are cast as inwardly unfeeling and outwardly emotive. They are expressive husks with no emotional core.

Yet because Edwards uses words that savor of cultivated appearance rather than internal truth—such as *display, express, present,* and *manifest*—in his descriptions of slave emotion, he inadvertently leaves open the possibility that slaves' levity does not necessarily mean that they are as unfeeling as they appear. Today's critics, primed by performance theory, may be inclined to find significance in Edwards's wording: Is the "loud" mirth a display of bravado, a defensive reaction that effaces the shame and aggression of the enslaved men, redirecting hostility towards whites into ridicule of their fellow chattel? After all, for the enslaved, emotional expression was one of the few outlets not subject to the total control of white authorities. Given Edwards's limited focalization, he judges solely by external appearances, so we cannot know for certain. Although Edwards aims to forestall any possible concerns the reader may have regarding the feelings of the enslaved by presenting these "beings" as cargo without emotional depth, the very fact that he felt the need to address such concerns shows that his underlying premise—the marked difference between blacks and whites—was far from a settled matter.

By contrast, other eighteenth-century proslavery discourse paid close attention to indications that the enslaved harbored a complex inner world. Some authors warned that blacks hid their true feelings and that this native cunning rendered them a social menace. Yet acknowledgments of the duplicity of the enslaved, intended to warn that they represented a social threat, also undercut the goal of rendering them incapable of complex thought—a characterization that was fundamental to some proslavery arguments. Commenting on "our Creole negroes" in his landmark *History of Jamaica* (1774), Edward Long claimed, "In their tempers they are in general . . . very artful. They are excellent dissemblers, and skilfull flatterers."[30] Long's remarks that blacks retained selective memories of harm provided a template for impugning slaves' testimony of abuse by their masters: "Their memory soon loses the traces of favours conferred on them, but faithfully retains a sense of injuries; this sense is so poignant, that they have been known to dissemble their hatred for many years, until an opportunity has presented of retaliating."[31] Hector Macneill similarly claimed in *Observations on the Treatment of the Negroes, in the Island of Jamaica* (1788) that blacks were essentially duplicitous: "The negro is possessed of passions not only strong, but ungovernable; a mind dauntless, warlike, and unmerciful; a temper extremely irascible; a disposition indolent, selfish, and deceitful."[32] Echoing Long's claim that blacks had a propensity to resolve conflicts through "blind anger, and brutal rage," Macneill suggests that blacks were not naturally fit for abiding by the rule of law: "A negro in power, is so completely directed by his passions, that mercy or justice has little to do in his decisions."[33] In these earlier texts, then, we find two contradictory claims: blacks are ruled by passions, yet they can disguise

these passions whenever they seek an advantage. Motivated by "ungovernable" emotions, blacks cannot be governed as equals but, instead, must be
restrained as slaves under the strict control of whites.

Such depictions were challenged by contemporary antislavery accounts of
blacks as naturally lawful, emotionally transparent, and tranquil in the absence of whites. The anonymous author of the dramatic dialogue *No Rum!
No Sugar!* (1792) contends that blacks are characterized by "innocence, pastoral content, and simplicity when unconnected to the slave trade. . . . The natives are friendly, and may be trusted, when not deceived by Europeans."[34]
The principal participant in the dialogue, a black man, Cushoo, who was taken
as a slave in Africa, kept as chattel in Jamaica, and then freed in England,
indignantly denies reports of rampant African crime and deviance when
questioned by a white London gentleman, "Ours no rascally country—ours
very fine country! . . . We live in peace [if] white man let us alone. . . . What
make you think black men quarrel?"[35]

Texts concerned with slaves' capacity for deception reveal the stakes of
these portrayals: according to the proslavery view, slavery was vindicated as
the only currently viable means of controlling a category of human beings who
were naturally unfit for law. Other writers, in contrast, asserted that slavery
had a chilling effect on the natural affinity of black people for justice. In his
best-selling account of his voyage with Captain Cook (made available in a
popular English translation in 1786), Anders Sparrman admired the "Gunjemans Hottentots," an indigenous Khoisan people of Southern Africa: "This
little society had long been . . . without any penal laws and statutes, as well as
without crimes and misdemeanors; having been united and governed only by
their own natural love of justice and mildness of disposition."[36] He argues that
the legal structure of plantation society left no avenue for slaves to complain
of abuse and exclusively protected the "rights" of planters: "How is a slave to
go to law with his master, who is, as it were, his sovereign, and who, by the
same laws, has a right . . . to have him flogged at the whipping-post, not absolutely to death, indeed, yet not far from it; and this merely on the strength of
the master's own testimony, and without any further inquisition into the merits of the case?"[37] Sparrman contends that it is such inequity under the law,
rather than any natural propensity to criminal behavior, that distorts the natural temperament of blacks and drives them to violence: "In consequence of
this, the unhappy slaves, who are frequently endued with finer feelings and
noble sentiments of humanity, though for the most part actuated by stronger
passions than their masters, often give themselves up totally to despondency,

and commit various acts of desperation and violence."[38] Sparrman posited a direct connection between racialized restrictions on testimony and black violence.

A Decades-Long Battle: Legislative Debates over Slaves as Witnesses
Before proceeding to the novels' legal critique, it is important to understand the fervent arguments—spanning decades, court systems, and an ocean—in which they intervened. Years after eighteenth-century travelogues and natural histories offered conflicting accounts of the links among legal capacity, emotional comportment, and racial identity, proslavery advocates at the beginning of the nineteenth century found themselves enmeshed in a new debate over the legal agency of the enslaved. This debate became increasingly divisive with the passage of time. In a controversial 1800 military court case in British-held Suriname, a white military officer was sentenced to death on presumptive evidence; although the judge deemed credible the two men who stated that the officer did not commit the murder of which he was accused, the witnesses were barred from testifying because they were slaves.[39] Prohibitions on slave testimony (other than confessions) initially stemmed from theological arguments that non-Christians were not able to take the oath required of witnesses.[40] Frustrated at the impossibility of meting out justice under such conditions, and mindful that West Indian planters' political power was dwindling as their wealth decreased, military administrators pushed to change the law. In 1809, the British imperial government made a watershed decision to allow testimony from slaves in court-martial proceedings, prompted by a request from the commander in chief stationed in Jamaica for clarification regarding the admissibility of slave testimony.[41]

While this decision was driven by military necessity, antislavery advocates seized the opportunity to push for admission of enslaved witnesses in other legal cases involving white defendants, in part as a mechanism to hold accountable particularly cruel plantation owners who were shielded from justice because of the ineligibility of slave testimony against white people.[42] West Indian planters responded by presenting themselves as victims of the tyranny of the home government and expressed indignation at the prospect that final say over their legal proceedings was given to distant politicians who had never set foot on the islands.[43]

Governing powers in the British West Indian colonies were divided among a governor, a council appointed by the king, and an elected assembly whose members tended to be propertied slaveholders. As Ronald V. Sires notes, the objective of this leadership structure was to balance the interests of the central home government in England against those of the propertied residents of the West Indies.[44] Yet home government had a crucial advantage: the British Colonial Office had oversight of colonial laws and could evaluate the validity of laws passed by colonial assemblies in Antigua, Barbados, Demerara, Dominica, Grenada, Jamaica, Nevis, St. Kitts, Tobago, and other British West Indian colonies.[45] Indeed, as Russell Smandych has shown, for years such laws were weakened by the interventions of one man: James Stephen (ancestor of Virginia Woolf), a steadfast antislavery partisan. In his decades of service in the British Colonial Office, Stephen wielded the power both to argue that laws were invalid and to recommend revision.[46] Resentment of imperial control flourished in the colonies as transatlantic debates raged between West Indian assemblies and the Crown over proposals to expand the category of slave "evidence."[47]

The proslavery contingent slowly accepted that popular opinion was turning against them and that some degree of accommodation would be necessary. They consequently embarked on a multipronged public relations campaign to improve transatlantic perceptions of West Indian slavery. To prevent uprisings, and to preserve the semblance of harmony on their plantations, planters tasked themselves in the mid-1810s and 1820s with two related endeavors: first, cultivating the appearance of more rigorous monitoring of the enslaved and their living conditions (as seen in Alexander Barclay's meticulous records of his slaves' behavior in "red books")[48] and, second, the provision of means (or, at least, the semblance thereof, to placate antislavery activists) for slaves to challenge abusive masters instead of concealing fear and anger that would erupt in rebellion. An 1816 overhaul of the slave code, however, allowed slaves to make only informal complaints to magistrates and was widely viewed by antislavery activists as insufficient.[49]

Some proslavery advocates adopted an appeasement strategy, in which they openly promoted the admission of slave witnesses against whites as a concession to improve or "ameliorate" slavery in exchange for its prolongation. At the same time, however, they loaded reform proposals with onerous requirements that must be met for slaves to testify. In 1826, members of the Jamaican assembly considered legislation to admit slave testimony under very rigid preconditions that effectively reduced the pool of qualified candidates to zero; although touted as a significant demonstration of humane concern—and thus meant to appease antislavery partisans—such legislation was designed to ensure maintenance of the status quo.[50] This proposal, *An Act to*

Regulate the Admission of the Evidence of Slaves, followed the successful passage of similar legislation in Barbados and was altered from a template sent to the governor of Jamaica—William Montagu (the Duke of Manchester)—by Henry Bathurst (Earl Bathurst), a member of Parliament in charge of communications with the Jamaican government. Earlier in 1826, Bathurst had conveyed to Montagu the king's order for the dissolution of the previous Jamaican Assembly because its members rejected measures proposed by the Crown for the "improvement and manumission of slavery."[51] This was a significant blow for planters who complained of home government tyranny and advocated for self-rule. The newly constituted assembly felt pressure to persuade those watching at home in Britain that they were taking sufficient measures to make slavery more humane.[52]

A few years earlier, some proslavery writings had endorsed this type of change to the laws of slave evidence. John Stewart—possibly the author of *Marly*—touted his bona fides as a "late resident of Jamaica" on the title page of *A View of the Past and Present State of the Island of Jamaica* (1823). He reported that another proprietor of a Jamaican plantation had written a letter in favor of admitting the evidence of slaves against whites to be "a wise, safe, and salutary step." Stewart asserted: "The passions and affections of the Negroes, not being under control of reason or religion, sometimes break out with frightful violence; rage, revenge, grief, jealousy, have often been productive of terrible catastrophes; but it is only in their intercourse with each other that this impetuosity prevails; they are so far subdued by a habitual awe of the whites as to have a mastery over their passions, and, if ill treated, they brood in silence over their wrongs, watching for a favourable opportunity of revenge."[53]

Similar perspectives were expressed by other well-connected public figures. "It is necessary to confer certain privileges on the slave to give room to his mind to expand, and to propose a bounty to good conduct by stimulating his endeavours to add personal credibility to his legal competency," Henry Nelson Coleridge, the nephew of Samuel Taylor Coleridge and his uncle's sometime editor, argued in support of the slave evidence measure in his 1826 travelogue *Six Months in the West Indies, in 1825*.[54] By the mid-1820s, it benefited the propagandistic aims of proslavery writers to congratulate white West Indians for implementing new, more humane plantation practices in which the complaints of the enslaved would no longer be viciously suppressed. They omitted to mention that the 1826 act's onerous stipulations regarding the qualifications of enslaved witnesses would sustain de facto prohibition of slave testimony.[55]

Even as legislators undermined reform measures, proslavery authors attempted to shield the plantation system against an increasingly influential antislavery lobby that sponsored the publication of accounts of slaves telling of the abuse they had suffered at the hands of white masters and overseers. Although the accounts were in fact transcribed and often heavily supplemented through the contributions of sympathetic whites, they were presented as direct evidence of the iniquity of the plantation system. Those mediated narratives, which Nicole Aljoe calls "Creole testimonies," were offered up as "documentary evidence" that systemic inhumane treatment continued unabated.[56] In refuting the veracity of these popular writings, the proslavery contingent noted with indignation the sizable audience that these narratives of abuse garnered. They insisted on what Tim Watson calls "eyewitness insiderism"[57]—the primacy of their own firsthand accounts of island life—in a concerted effect to vindicate themselves.

Proslavery advocates understood that they needed to cast doubt on the credibility of the slaves who had been given a public platform by the antislavery campaign. Moreover, as they faced pressure to allow slave witnesses in judicial contexts, the proslavery contingent needed to make a compelling argument for substantial restrictions; but existing conceptions of slaves as creatures of emotion were a difficult set of priors to surmount. Prevailing notions that slaves were emotionally transparent, intellectually deficient, and lacking self-control would not bolster proplanter arguments for continuing to prohibit slave testimony. After all, if slaves were in fact simple and emotionally transparent, they would not be strategic enough to fabricate evidence persuasively and would only be able to relay exactly what they saw and heard; they would be ideal witnesses.

If the trope of the emotionally transparent slave and the claim of happy plantation life both held true, slaveholders should have been eager to promote, rather than prohibit, the admission of slave witnesses: under such circumstances, slave witnesses would offer glowing accounts of their treatment, thereby discrediting antislavery advocates' claims of pervasive and flagrant abuse. The reality, of course, was not so harmonious. Contrasting notions of slaves' emotional and intellectual capacity were presented by pro- and antislavery partisans, and it was widely understood that these notions would be pivotal to deciding the debate over whether slaves could testify.

Slaveholders therefore needed to develop a rhetoric of slave duplicity to counter pressure to accommodate slave testimony. Whereas some on the proslavery side introduced measures that claimed to accommodate slave witnesses but in fact preserved restrictions, a number of proslavery legislators openly disputed the measures. They argued that slaves would use their powers of persuasion to secure wrongful convictions of whites. The logic of their arguments resembles that of warnings during the so-called Jew Bill debates of Smollett's 1750s heyday that if foreign-born Jews were naturalized, they would band together to give false testimony that would result in the baseless conviction and execution of Christians. An 1826 session of British West Indian representatives featured a discussion regarding whether slaves could qualify as witnesses; the representative from the island of Nevis stated on the record:

> Of all the testimony I have ever read, heard, or met with, that of slaves in general has ever appeared to me to be the least correct, the least to be depended on, and at the same time, the most plausible and the most imposing. . . . They frequently possess or acquire such an extraordinary and wonderful power of invention, and even of *representing*, so as that, without an absolute breach of truth, the relation should still convey an intentional falsehood; and they will adhere to it with such rigid consistency and pertinacity, as to elude the penetration and the skill of the most expert or experienced examiner.[58]

These remarks exemplify how the special "power . . . of *representing*" attributed to slaves was invoked not to make a case for their shared humanity but to cast doubt on proposals that would have brought them within the ambit of law alongside whites. Although Nevis was part of one of the groups of smaller islands that were governed separately from Jamaica, all were part of the British West Indies, and all faced similar challenges in determining whether to change laws pertaining to slavery. Significantly, the representative from Nevis here casts tensions between slaves and whites as a contest of authorship; slaves are here credited with talents of "invention" and "representing" that rival the abilities of novelists. In a time when slaves in general were being charged with concocting "intentional falsehoods" during legislative debates, proslavery authors sought to preempt suspicions regarding the veracity of their own novelistic representations. They presented their testimony—in the form of novels and narratives—about plantation life as fundamentally more trustworthy than the claims of the enslaved.

The Counterclaim of the White "Eyewitness"

While slaves in the British West Indies of the 1820s were poised to be admitted as witnesses against white people, the islands' white inhabitants feared demotion in legal status. They were increasingly cast as criminals by antislavery activists and government officials in the metropole. Slaveholders were increasingly reviled as "unfeeling . . . [and] brutal" law-breakers.[59] In an 1827 court decision, Lord Stowell referred to slavery as "the crime of this country," although he ultimately upheld its legality.[60] An 1829 *Antislavery Monthly Reporter* review of "Pro-Slavery Writings" accused "A Jamaica Proprietor" (who had written an open letter to the Duke of Wellington seeking political support for West Indian slaveholders) of attempting "to perpetuate the crime of slavery."[61] Proponents of slavery complained that such assertions dehumanized them and reframed their lawful business as a sordid criminal enterprise. An "elderly gentleman" in *Marly* decries what he sees as attempts to "criminate the character" of West Indian slaveholders: "Those dear friends at home . . . will have us to be monsters of cruelty and tyranny rather than men pretty much like themselves."[62] Decades before Stowe and other American antislavery authors popularized the "antebellum . . . literary device that figured slavery as a crime, slaveholders as perpetrators and defendants, and slaves as victims and eyewitnesses,"[63] British proslavery authors contended with an earlier formulation of this typology.

Proslavery authors responded by recasting whites in the "eyewitness" role. As compared to the late eighteenth-century proslavery travelogue writers, the proslavery authors of the 1810s and 1820s present themselves as embedded in plantation life rather than as transitory observers. Accounts of interactions with the enslaved are less protoethnographic than close-up and intimate.[64] Throughout his *Journal of a West India Proprietor* (a record of his 1814 sojourn in his two Jamaican plantations, belatedly published in 1833), Matthew Lewis doubts that the ingratiating expressions of emotion he is offered by his slaves are genuine. His efforts to gauge the sincerity of such displays become a persistent theme throughout his journal entries. One slave "came to me with tears in his eyes, implored me most earnestly to forgive what had past, and promised to behave better for the future, 'to so good a massa.'"[65] Of another man, Lewis recalls: "He was brought to me all rags, tears, and penitence, wondering 'how he could have such *bad manners* as to make massa fret.'"[66] Still another slave "spoke to me with tears running down his cheeks" and promises to stop running away if granted easier labor.[67] In the latter case, the promise is kept. In two other incidents, however, slaves who make a show of tears had previously deceived Lewis: one runs away and makes false reports that Lewis abused him; another absconds with a large sum of money. Consequently, Lewis frequently worries that he cannot trust the black men and women who surround him.

Because of the prevalence of feigned tears, white narrators exult when they encounter what they deem to be genuine displays of emotion from slaves. In Cynric R. Williams's 1826 *A Tour through the Island of Jamaica* (the fictional travelogue that directly preceded the publication of his novel *Hamel*), the white narrator is aroused by the weeping of his slave mistress: on bidding her farewell, he relishes "the grief which Diana in vain would have concealed" and is gratified when "she soon gave up all restraint, and wept without attempting to controul her tears."[68] A standard set piece in proslavery literature is a detailed account of a slave "ball" or "jubilee"; white narrators present the spectacles—where a celebratory, unguarded mood was thought to prevail—as opportunities to witness slaves exhibiting sincere emotions. Implicitly contesting antislavery reports of ongoing plantation violence, these proslavery scenes feature happy wards delighting in festivities sponsored by kindly masters, where the only spectacle to "witness" is one of joy and entertainment. Williams's narrator makes himself the center of attention: "I slipped on my dressing-gown and mingled into their orgies, much to the diversion of the black damsels, as well as to the inmates of the house, who came into the plaza to witness the ceremonies."[69]

Recalling his wanderings through New Year's Day festivities held by his slaves in 1816, Lewis muses: "I never saw so many people who appeared to be so unaffectedly happy."[70] Yet Lewis's celebration of the "unaffected" expressivity of his slaves is counterbalanced by the unease he feels in other situations where he finds black emotion unreadable. Only in a holiday crowd, where the vigilance of the enslaved presumably is relaxed, does Lewis believe he can observe sincere emotions. His more direct encounters with slaves are fraught with deception. As the author of a best-selling Gothic novel whose celebrity stemmed from his own ability to manipulate readers' feelings, Lewis was well aware of the power of duplicity. Appearances of gratitude and good humor could be deceiving: the central plot twist of his novel *The Monk* (1796), for instance, involves the unveiling of a fawning subordinate, Matilda, as a diabolical schemer who feigns humility to gain control over and inflict violence on the man she initially hails as "Master."[71] White authors documented their various strategies—including interrogation, emotional manipulation, and surveillance—for uncovering slaves' hidden thoughts and feelings, indicating that they were aware that slaves made efforts to thwart discovery by cultivating complacent facades.

One planter, in his proslavery treatise, insisted that he conveyed "the actual state of feeling" of the enslaved, a reality wrongly ignored or dismissed in the court of public opinion.[72] In her research on historical accounts of slavery, Srividhya Swaminathan has observed, "Most proslavery writers wrote from an eyewitness position of authority."[73] In fiction, by contrast, it was not so much authority (power over slaves) as physical and temporal proximity (being nearby when slaves spoke and interacted) that proslavery authors invoked to lend credibility to their depictions of the enslaved.

The Novel: A Form Incompatible with the Proslavery Agenda?

According to many accounts of the eighteenth- and early nineteenth-century development of the novel, narrative fascination relies on an illusion of access to another person's private thoughts and genuine feelings, as opposed to those displayed.[74] As Lisa Freeman observes, "Novels . . . appear to render the inner depths, the conscious and even unconscious motives and thoughts of characters, transparent to the reader, even as, under the cloak of 'realism,' they conceal the very mechanics of character conveyance."[75] If novels in general (with obvious and abundant exceptions ranging from eighteenth-century innovations such as Sterne's *Tristram Shandy* to later experimentalism and postmodern works) "conceal" their unreality, proslavery novels are extreme case studies of this precarious balancing act. When slave characters are featured prominently, the strain is especially conspicuous.

Proslavery novelists confronted a challenge: they were working within a literary form in which producing compelling protagonists entailed suggesting that such characters had a rich inner life not visible at the surface level. As Ian Watt proclaimed, "Implicit in the novel form in general . . . [is] the premise, or primary convention, that the novel is a full and authentic account of human experience, and is therefore under an obligation to satisfy its reader with such details of the story as the individuality of the actors concerned."[76] Earlier eighteenth-century proslavery travelogues, journals, and other writings had not managed to reconcile the opposing tropes of simple-minded, guileless slaves and their strategic, deceptive counterparts. In the proslavery novel, where subjectivity was carefully rendered, tensions between political aims and the imperatives of form fostered particularly incongruous characterizations of enslaved protagonists. Proslavery authors attempted to fulfill vying objectives: adhering to the novelistic convention of endowing protagonists with a layered, complex subjectivity; helping readers to forget that they were immersed in the nonreal domain of the imagination; and rebutting activists' claims of the brutality of slavery—all while appearing to honor promises of superior verisimilitude afforded by an eyewitness vantage point. Proslavery novels thus veer between adherence to formal conventions, which mandate rendering individuated protagonists with inner depths of thought, and compliance with the white supremacist tenet that for black people such depths did not exist. When pressed into service for the proslavery cause, the novel's devotion to the development of complex characters and exploration of their motivations—a devotion that set it apart from other discursive forms such as the travelogue—generated an unintended outcome. It is in the proslavery novel, of all places, that a new type of black protagonist emerges: an enslaved black man who fascinates those around him precisely by defying racialized stereotypes of hyperemotional expressivity. His formidable powers of reason and strategic intellect enable him to threaten to seize control from the white ruling class and call into question the most fundamental premises of the British colonial race-based legal hierarchy.

White Fear and Black Secrecy in *Hamel, the Obeah Man*

An account of a doomed slave rebellion, *Hamel, the Obeah Man* is set in Jamaica during an era when planters felt compelled to defend themselves against accusations made by former slaves and antislavery activists, even as they faced continued threats of insurgence. Throughout the period, as Candace Ward and Tim Watson note, "the fear of slave uprisings was part of the common vocabulary of creole whites, an anxiety based on repeated insurrections"; uprisings large and small roiled the Caribbean from 1816 onward, from Barbados and Haiti to St. George.[77] The novel follows the parallel trajectories of three major characters: Hamel, Fairfax, and Roland. Hamel, a slave regarded as a leader of the revolt, practices magic in a remote mountain cavern, where he is free to go given his relative autonomy as a trusted plantation monitor. Oliver Fairfax, a white heir of a once eminent planter family, has returned to the island under the assumed identity of "Sebastian" to try to reclaim his ancestral estate from Filbeer, a disreputable plantation "attorney" (manager) who improperly took control of the estate after Fairfax's father died. He then infiltrates black groups on the island and ultimately leads the effort to quell the revolt. Roland, a morally bankrupt Methodist missionary, supports the uprising. Notably, both Oliver and Roland disguise themselves as black in key scenes, demonstrating the novel's anxious attention to distinctions between white and black capabilities.

One of the key reform measures proposed to mollify antislavery forces and assuage black unrest was the expansion of slave testimony. The pseudonymous author, Cynric R. Williams, adopts the novel—the dominant literary prose form of the era—to elucidate the subtle trade-offs that plantation owners faced on this issue. On the one hand, the novel suggests that planters might benefit from allowing certain kinds of slaves—the simple, emotionally expressive, and transparent type—to testify in particular situations. As mentioned, the historical record indicates that the Colonial Assembly of Jamaica modified legislation proposed by the home government so that it seemed to expand the pool of witnesses but in actuality would have disqualified most of the enslaved from testifying. The 1826 revised act was intended to appease the home government with a show of change while, for the most part, maintaining the status quo. Slave testimony was still heavily restricted; for example, slaves were barred from testifying against their owners "in any proceeding of a civil nature."[78] By slightly loosening restrictions on slave testimony, though, the new act could have made more evidence available to convict and punish slave conspirators, as well as their white Methodist missionary allies who—according to some proslavery advocates—posed the greatest threat to the continuation of the institution of slavery. Roland and Hamel explicitly state that they are using their knowledge of the rules of evidence to evade detection of their crimes.

Yet the novel touches on the substantial risks of allowing unrestricted slave testimony: devious conspirators who possess considerable emotional control and strategic skill could calibrate their testimony to manipulate the legal process and advance their objectives. But in demonstrating the need for subtlety and care in developing testimony laws, the novel defeats its own purpose: it portrays some blacks as more rational and emotionally mature than whites, calling into question the fundamental justification for slavery.

The opening scene of *Hamel* seems to portend that the novel will simply reiterate the older (and persisting) notion of blacks as guileless subordinates whose feelings and intentions are immediately apparent. The very first character to appear is a slave, Cuffy, "whose happy physiognomy bespoke the innocence and kindness in his heart, and relieved that of the spectator from the sympathy of sadness inspired by the looks of the white-faced traveler."[79] Inspection of Cuffy's countenance obviates any need either for his own verbal testimony or for rendition of his thoughts by the narrator. The cheery black youth's "features scarcely harmonized with those of his very demure and melancholy-looking master" (57)—Roland, the white Methodist missionary. The narrator warns that Roland's emotions cannot be discerned from a surface reading: "Yet the gloom on the cheek of this last was not attributable perhaps to any dignified grief or sentimentality of disposition—at least his features did not augur any such feeling. . . . Anxiety of mind, as well as natural irritability [may have caused this gloom]. . . . Whether this were the case in the present instance, will be seen in the course of our narrative" (57). From the outset, readers are led to expect that they can immediately gauge the feelings of slaves, whereas those of a white man require four hundred pages of exposition.

Many black characters in *Hamel* fall into the category—so prevalent in antislavery literature—of the emotionally transparent peon epitomized by Cuffy in the novel's opening. The mob of slaves who support Hamel's planned rebellion demonstrate the threat posed by this type: when riled up by missionaries or insurrectionists, they are easily provoked into a frenzy. They indicate the risk of rebellion that looms if the situation is not defused by providing them an outlet for their frustrations. During a meeting to plot the overthrow of Jamaica's white elites, they crown as their king Combah, the brash young male slave whose escapades are as prominent as those of Hamel in the second half of the novel. The gatherings of the enslaved devolve into chaos, as they do little more than publicly act on their anger and libidinous urges: easily distracted from the speeches of the leaders, they descend into fistfights and carousing and eventually drift away in amorous clinches.[80] This representation of slaves as emotionally reactive, mindless, rudderless on their own, and easily controlled by others is also found in antislavery texts. As Sianne Ngai has observed, when white writers such as Harriet Beecher Stowe and William Lloyd Garrison made a case for freeing slaves, they brought black characters to life "through acts resembling puppeteering"—not physically but virtually: in their writings, black characters are portrayed in hyperemotive actions such as fervent recitations of memorized Bible verses—scripted speech, rather than their own words. White antislavery authors, Ngai contends, thus ventriloquized black subjects, reducing them to conduits lacking agency.[81]

Against the backdrop of these caricatures of black manipulability, Hamel emerges as a sharply contrasting figure. He first appears before Roland—who happens on his cave while seeking shelter from a storm—not as another reassuring manifestation of the familiar stereotype of the "happy darky" but rather as a menacing enigma: "This figure stood before the lamp, whose rays served to define the outline of his person with the greatest accuracy. Of his features little otherwise could be seen, except the light gleaming from his eyeballs" (70–71). Hamel's initial entrance is also a disappearance; he is a barely discernible "figure" and "outline." When Roland asks Hamel who he is, the obeah man responds, "What you will" (71), an answer that in the guise of servility eschews disclosure. Significantly, Hamel's answer, one in a lengthy sequence of Shakespearean allusions in the novel, invokes *Twelfth Night, or What You Will*, a title that refers to a holiday when customary social hierarchies dividing servants and masters were temporarily suspended.[82] To the extent that Hamel's emotional state is apparent, it is described in terms of negation and absence: the descriptors attached to Hamel—"unmoved" (72), "unsuspicious" (74), "untouched" (72), "uncommon" (74), "no feeling" (73), "no annoyance" (72)—provide little information about his actual emotional state and, instead, render him more cryptic. Roland is "suspicious" (73) and frustrated: "It was but too evident to Roland, that the Negro had evaded his questions . . . but as the use of Obeah is denounced by law, however despised by white men, he could not attach any particular consequence to such evasion, nor justify himself in expecting any confession" (74). Hamel does not exhibit the vivacious garrulousness that was associated with obsequious slavehood in contemporaneous antislavery and later abolitionist writings. He thwarts the efforts of the white visitor to elicit speech.

Indeed, it is notable that the novel portrays some blacks (Hamel and Combah) as capable of surpassing certain whites in this capacity for selective disclosure and self-discipline. Hamel tells the villainous white attorney Filbeer, "You teach the Negroes to sing psalms and preach; now learn something from a Negro in return. Learn to be master of your passion and your tongue" (322). This "master" is not the divine presence invoked so often in the Psalms, nor is he the lord of the plantation. Instead, Hamel redefines *master* as a person who exerts control over himself and proclaims authority not through harsh commands but through his elective silence. By advocating for disciplined silence, Hamel not only places himself outside the realm of black caricatures; he also positions himself as a model for whites to emulate. As Kevin Quashie notes in his work on post-1960s African American literature, "Silence . . . is often based on refusal or protest. . . . The expressiveness of silence is often aware of an audience, a watcher or listener whose presence is the reason for the withholding—it is an expressiveness which is intent and even defiant."[83] Time and again in the novel, scenes center on Hamel's control over the narrative, as he makes the deliberate choice to selectively disclose what he knows or refrain from speech altogether in the presence of white people.

The novel's foremost villain, the white missionary Roland, is subjected to a similar lesson in black capability when, later in the novel, he is imprisoned by the island's authorities in the same jail cell inhabited by the rebel slave Combah. Initially prone to drunken fisticuffs, Combah has realized his leadership potential by learning self-discipline. Roland, overwhelmed by his own plight, bawls, his sobs resounding through the cell. Combah meditates in silence, then scolds: "If you have nothing more to say, at least wipe your eyes; stop your tears; do not disturb me with your womanish grief. We are here on a sort of equality, I own; for though I am a king, I am a prisoner like yourself; but that does not authorize you to torment me with sobbing and crying" (326). Roland admires the rebel leader: "The preacher was struck with the assurance of the Brutchie [Combah's regal title]. . . . He took a hint from his majesty's behavior" (326). Although this scene does not involve testimony in a legal context, it does highlight the alarming possibility that some slaves could tailor their self-expression to the occasion and in doing so could even gain an advantage over whites. As Roland becomes the subordinate of a black "master," the customary subject position of the slave is mapped onto him. This humiliating position, the novel implies, will be the fate of whites who let blacks get the upper hand.

The command of self-expression demonstrated by Hamel and Combah throughout the novel can be seen as indicative of the dangers of loosening restrictions on slave evidence. The rebel leaders prevaricate and resist disclosing information—maneuvers that in a court of law could challenge planters' chokehold on power. Slaves motivated to oppose the West Indian plantocracy, the novel suggests, could sabotage the operations of legal institutions. Yet the novel also implies that for the majority of slaves who are contented, the need for testimony would be rare but in some cases quite useful for the planters. Specifically, in keeping with its adherence to the ameliorationist playbook, according to which humane reforms benefited both the planters and the enslaved, the novel provides two scenarios in which the prohibition of slave testimony lets fester conditions that render the plantation more vulnerable to insurrection.

When Roland is imprisoned by the island authorities for murder and conspiracy to incite rebellion, he tells a fellow missionary who visits him in jail that he is relieved that slaves familiar with his involvement in planning the uprising cannot testify against him: "I know the *ferocity* of my enemies; I know they will strain every point to bring me to the scaffold. The Negro evidence, thank God, is nought; that is, the evidence of slaves; but Fairfax saw me—heard me; and who knows but they will take the evidence of slaves, and admit it to confound one whom they call evangelical, and hate on that account?" (330). The implication: if slaves were allowed to testify against antislavery whites who fomented discontent, such revelations would help preserve concord between masters and slaves. Cast as a deceptive, shambling race traitor, Roland exemplifies a rhetorical strategy used by proslavery advocates in the waning years of West Indian slavery: the vilification of white itinerant Methodist missionaries, who were said to incite rebellion among slaves who without such interference would remain loyal to their masters.[84] The planters' concern had some basis in truth. In 1824, the Methodist barrister Richard Matthews, a member of the Wesleyan Methodist Missionary Society, went so far as to claim that "if the slave is denied by law the protection it ought to give him, he has a right to rebel and no moral guilt can be attached to a resort to violence."[85] Significantly, the novel's more dire instances of moral turpitude—murder of a child and sexual assault of a white planter's wife—are enacted by Roland. By implicating white missionaries as the true enemy, proslavery advocates could soften their racist rhetoric so that it took on a more humane tone, while still portraying white planters as the victims with the most to lose. Yet *Hamel* continually conveys a troubled awareness that some blacks were not simply easy prey for the missionaries but, instead, were capable of exercising independent thought and even of drawing on knowledge of the law to gain advantage over whites.

In the second scenario, Hamel uses his knowledge of the slave code to elude detection by island authorities as he orchestrates the uprising. Mindful that slaves could testify against other slaves, Hamel (who can write in Arabic but not in English) asks one of his followers whether her young child can transcribe his correspondence: "The daughter was commissioned to obey Hamel's direction, but not in the presence of her mother. The wizard would have no witnesses" (327). Hamel seeks out slaves whose youth, disability (as in the supposedly mute "duppy," a black man who is shunned by other slaves, who believe him to be a ghost), or other attributes incapacitate them from serving as witnesses against him.[86] By this arrangement, Hamel produces a letter that he arranges to be delivered secretly to Combah, facilitating the continuation of their planning despite his own illiteracy and Combah's incarceration. The implication: certain restrictions on slave testimony were vulnerable to exploitation by hostile slaves.

The novel sustains to the end a thoroughgoing fascination with slaves' ability to avoid disclosure and control the narrative, despite total legal disempowerment. It concludes with a bizarre scene in which the island's white authorities are entranced by Hamel's silent embarkment from the island, as he sails toward freedom: "They rode to the top of the rocks which overhung the sea, whence they could, by the help of a spy-glass, for a long time distinguish the obeah man sitting in his canoe, in a pensive posture, gazing on the deep blue waves that heaved about him. . . . They watched him without regarding the time they so misapplied, until his little boat was diminished to a speck . . . indeed none of them could assign any reason for gazing at all" (427). In preserving Hamel's inscrutability to the novel's very last page, the author leaves readers to speculate endlessly about Hamel's thoughts and motivations—contradicting the trope, so prevalent elsewhere in the novel, of the hyperexpressive black simpleton.

The reader is bound to ask: why glorify a black insurrectionist in a proslavery novel? The aim seems to have been to reiterate that the terrifying figure of the inscrutable, duplicitous, and violent slave was a reality and to warn that, without care to keep him contained through institutional subjugation and legal mechanisms, this type of slave was ascendant. Hamel emerges as the foremost protagonist, but readers are not encouraged to adopt his point of view; instead, they are conditioned to assume the perspective of a fearful white spectator. Yet the deprivation of access to Hamel's perspective becomes increasingly noticeable as his paucity of speech is inversely correlated with his omnipresence. It is meaningful, in that light, that the novel's two most prominent white characters both cede the ground of protagonist to Hamel and thus are relegated to the "subordinated narrative position" that is usually the lot of black characters during the period.[87] Both come to resemble the enslaved in some measure—both Fairfax and Roland through their adoption of blackface, and Roland through excessive emotion. The novel seems to caution whites to further distinguish themselves from the majority of slaves, who were cast as typically intellectually deficient, emotionally transparent, and fractious.

The incongruity between the novel's proslavery politics and its characterization of the enslaved did not escape contemporary reviewers. A reviewer for *The Scotsman*, a leading Edinburgh-based newspaper founded by a lawyer who advocated reform of prisons and policing, wrote: "Our author . . . seems to disprove his own case; since a race who can present such specimens of talent as we find here in the Obeah man . . . or . . . 'the Brutchie' [Combah]—must have capacities for civilization and self-government."[88] A critic for the *Westminster Review*—who states that antislavery reports of the "misery of the slaves" are "exaggerated"—observes that the author confers "some degree of dignity to two of his black heroes" and claims that because the novelist did not take a "more moderate tone" toward the missionary, he is "liable to suspicion."[89] The reviewers agree that when representing fraught political subjects, the novelist—similar to the historian—must document social reality, not exercise creative license.

Yet there is a fundamental incompatibility between the objectives of the proslavery author of *Hamel* and what the reviewers saw as the function of the novel as a literary form. In depicting—in vivid detail—the experiences of the inhabitants of a particular time and place, *Hamel* was offered as a kind of testimony: a reality-based corrective to what it implied were the overwrought portraits of cruelty in antislavery literature. At the same time, however, it revived stock tropes and scavenged the most hackneyed conventions of romance. The novel strains to corroborate the propagandistic narrative of white planter victimhood while acknowledging the reality of the "dignity" and sophistication of black freedom fighters, and its explicit remarks on the problems caused by restrictions on slave testimony are at odds with its portrayals of some blacks as duplicitous and manipulative. The author of *Hamel* made a mistake in the choice of the novel as a literary vehicle for the proslavery agenda. Although the intention seems to have been to develop a cautionary portrayal of Methodist agitation and black autonomy that would frighten white readers in the metropole into supporting the cause of the planters, *Hamel* inadvertently made the case for black capability and humanity.

"Slave Driver" Tells All: *Marly*'s Explicit Legal Commentary

While *Hamel* only alludes to contemporary West Indian legislative controversies over slave witnesses, *Marly; or, A Planter's Life in Jamaica* addresses them explicitly. In the year between the respective debuts of the novels, the arguments had grown still more vociferous. To understand the overtness of the critique in *Marly*, it helps to begin at the end. A "Note" that forms the epilogue of the novel opens by commending Jamaica's 1826 Consolidated Slave Act, a compromise measure that was touted as combining humane reforms with protections of planter's rights.[90] The novelist states with approbation that "the Colonial Legislature of Jamaica has shewn an eagerness to improve the condition of slaves" and was considering a measure that "admitted the testimony of slaves in criminal cases against the whites" (325). Although the note mentions the two other central provisions of the 1826 reform measures—a ban on the flogging of women, and the prohibition of slave markets on Sunday, which was supposed to be a day of rest—only the slave evidence provision is considered in depth by the novel.

Marly takes an adamant position on the proposal. By the time the novel was published, the 1826 Act had failed. It had been approved by the Colonial

Assembly of Jamaica but did not survive the scrutiny of the British home government, which disallowed it. The colonial secretary, William Huskisson, relayed to the assembly the home government's concern that rules for witnesses were too restrictive: "On the important subject of the evidence of slaves, his Majesty is graciously pleased to signify his approbation of the advances which have been made towards a better system of law; but in reference to this subject, I am to observe, that this law appears to contemplate the admission of the evidence of slaves in those cases of crimes only in which they are usually either the actors or the sufferers, excluding their evidence in other cases, a distinction which does not seem to rest on any solid foundation."[91]

The epilogue to *Marly* concludes with a repudiation of Huskisson's decision as unequivocal as the preface: "The Colonial Legislature of Jamaica had acted in the revision of the Slave laws, but it seems Mr. Huskisson has thought they have not gone far enough, and therefore has returned the Act to the Island, without approval, thereby annulling what had been done in favour of the Slave" (324). Yet while *Marly* claims to support the reform of standards for slave witnesses, a number of episodes of the novel suggest, to the contrary, that the unrestricted admission of slave testimony poses a threat to the white plantocracy: most of the enslaved characters have emotional and intellectual traits that render them unable to provide unmediated verbal testimony that is both credible and informative. Although the novel acknowledges that the peace and order of society is threatened when slaves have no recourse other than violence for airing grievances regarding abuse by whites, egregiously cruel masters are depicted as rare outliers from the norm of benevolent ones. Unlike the claims of antislavery activists, the novel does not show abuse to be a pervasive problem that requires an overhaul of the justice system.

Hamel and *Marly* differ in how explicitly they address the proposed changes to the laws surrounding slave testimony, but the two novels have much in common. As we have seen, the events of the plot of *Hamel* are catalyzed by a quest: a young white hero ventures into Jamaica to pry his stolen ancestral estate from the clutches of a treacherous attorney; he courts an eligible maiden and unites with her to reestablish his family's presence on the island. This description could also serve as the synopsis for *Marly*, which details the strivings of an ambitious yet impecunious Scotsman, George Marly, who arrives in Jamaica in 1816 to reclaim his estate, Happy Fortune. When Marly was a child, his parents died at sea en route from their estate in Jamaica to England, whereupon their plantation attorney, McFathom, ceased communication and claimed the estate for himself. Years later, Marly, not yet of age,

ventures in disguise to the estate, seeking the documents certifying his ownership; he has been informed that the papers are hidden somewhere on the
property. Whereas only *Hamel* derives from the rebellion plot developed in
Walter Scott's *Waverley* (1814), both of the proslavery novels draw heavily
from the inheritance template established earlier in the novels of Maria Edgeworth and others. It is especially significant, given both authors' attempts to
redirect attention from the suffering of black slaves to the travails of propertied white slaveholders, that the novels feature white heroes—Fairfax (of
Hamel) and Marly—who are dispossessed yet trust that the legal system will
eventually recognize their rights.

Although the 1826 Slave Act is discussed at length at the end of *Marly*, the
novel is framed from the beginning as a response both to the political conflict
over slave testimony and to the broader social contest over whose word should
be believed. The preface freely acknowledges that the outcome of the conflict
hinges on establishing the credibility of white West Indians. Should readers
heed the claims of abuse from the enslaved or the indignant refutations from
the white slave driver? If black voices are allowed into the record, should they
be permitted universally or only selectively? Such concerns form the background to the novel's prefatory statement "To the Public," in which the authorial speaker directly addresses the reader: "When a Slave Driver lays down
the whip to take up the pen . . . some reason . . . may be deemed necessary. To
say he is actuated [to write] by humane motives, he is afraid will not be
credited. . . . It might afford cause for doubting his veracity; for few, indeed,
would believe him, if he fell into the common simper of whining about the
comfort of convicted felons, of brute beasts, and of the very slaves whom he
has flogged" (2). While this opening address appears to be an earnest expression of authorial anxiety—registering the extent to which British public opinion
had by 1828 been swayed by the antislavery movement—it is also a performa-
tive declaration designed to openly acknowledge and allay its audience's
doubts.[92] The white "Slave Driver" worries that as the general public and legal
institutions become receptive to the testimony of slaves, his own credibility—
and, by extension, his authority and legal standing—will be imperiled.

A new preface, added to the 1828 second edition of *Marly*, doubled down
on preemptively bolstering the author's "veracity." The authorial speaker
styles himself as "an impartial eyewitness" (326) who can "point out as clearly
and correctly as possible, the life, conditions, habits, and feelings of that race
of human beings who [were] born in slavery" (326). He vows that his novel
will refute not only the allegations made by "philanthropic enthusiasts . . .

who would make the world believe that our West India Slaves are the most miserable and discontented portion of mankind," but also more hardline pro-slavery rebuttals by those who "boldly assert that they [slaves] are the happiest and most comfortable of human labourers" (326). Given the premium the authorial speaker claims to place on factual reportage, it is remarkable that he insists that a novel is the best venue for such a project:

> It may be asked why the author has adopted such a mode [the novel] of elucidating his views. . . . He only imitates the principal writers of the day, who perhaps not unwisely imagine, that to awaken the interest and engage the attention of the mass of readers, there is nothing so effectual as the machinery of a novel. He thinks too, that essays and letters on slavery are already, probably, too numerous, and although he feels himself not altogether alive to the mysteries of *fiction* he was determined to avail himself like the generality of his publishing brotherhood, of the fashionable medium of a tale, to convey what *facts* he was enabled to pick up concerning West India matters, during a residence in Jamaica. (326–27)

A novel is a curious choice for transmitting "facts": the literary form's capacity to represent real life had been disputed and mocked since its inception. As Catherine Gallagher observes, "The novel has been . . . widely regarded as a form that tried, for at least two centuries, to hide its fictionality behind verisimilitude or realism, insisting on certain kinds of referentiality and even making extensive truth claims."[93] From the beginning, then, *Marly* unwittingly undermines its own credibility by virtue of its literary form. It purports to present "facts" in the vehicle of fiction and is labeled an "eyewitness" account by an author who shrouds his identity rather than signing his name to his work and openly attesting to its truth.[94]

The anxieties surrounding white representations of blacks are apparent in the novel's epigraph, a quotation from Shakespeare's *Othello*, in which the black tragic hero requests that the white man taking him into custody deliver an undistorted account of his life to others: "Speak of me as I am; nothing extenuate, / Nor set down aught in malice."[95] Othello, who has just murdered his white wife, Desdemona, is addressing Ludovico, the officer who has arrested him and is taking him to prison. Immediately before committing suicide, Othello requests that his full spectrum of emotions—not just the cruel, extreme ones that precipitated his monstrous crime—be represented: he declares that his emotional state ranges from placid to jealous (as "one not easily jealous, but being wrought, / Perplexed in the extreme") (5.2.343–44), from even-keeled to lachrymose (as "one whose subdued eyes, / Albeit unused to the melting mood, / Drop tears as fast as the Arabian trees") (5.2.346–48). The choice of these lines for a central place on *Marly*'s title page foreshadows the novel's close attention to the extent to which white witnesses can be relied on to accurately observe and report the emotions of blacks. By indicating his awareness of the risk of misreporting, the novelist suggests to his reader that he can be trusted to make representations that are faithful to reality, but in one of the novel's abundant self-contradictions, he simultaneously brings into view the opposite perspective: mistrust of the white narrator.

Whereas in *Hamel*, the white hero who seeks to authenticate himself as a legitimate heir is displaced from the narrative spotlight by the enigmatic Hamel and by Combah, the author of *Marly* eliminates any black protagonist-contenders who could siphon narrative attention from his white lead. This choice is prudent, because little of the charisma that other characters are said to see in George Marly is apparent to the reader. In both novels, the white hero's attempt to prove that he is a legitimate heir—despite his lack of documentation or witnesses other than himself—is shadowed by the parallel struggles of some black characters in the novel to gain some measure of legal standing. This parallel suggests an inverse relationship between the fortunes of whites and those of blacks and reflects anxiety over the threat of black ascendancy. The property claims of the white characters are as tenuous as those of their black counterparts; the claims of both are hampered because the cases hinge on the verbal testimony of a sole claimant whose credibility is impugned, as he lacks the documents to prove that the property rightfully belongs to him. Doubtful that his word alone will convince anyone to believe that he is the true owner of Happy Fortune, Marly infiltrates a soirée at the estate to attempt to find the concealed papers. Around the same point in the novel, the plantation bookkeeper adjudicates what is characterized as a "judicial proceeding" (62) between two slaves, Jupiter and Quashie; Jupiter complains that a small garden plot "that belonged to, or was occupied by, his mother Peggy" (62) had been unfairly taken over by another slave, Quashie; after each side presents its argument, the plot is "adjudged" (62) to belong to Jupiter. In a firebrand speech in the middle of the novel, a free mixed-race man laments that he and other "brown" heirs face legal obstacles in proving that they inherited property willed to them by their white fathers (162–68). These episodes illustrate differing resolutions to the same type of problem, based on one's place in the racial hierarchy: the competing verbal accounts by slaves are adjudicated favorably, albeit in an informal context; the mixed-race character cannot rely on the whiteness of his father to enforce his claim's validity in the eyes of the law; and the white protagonist is on his own for document discovery before entering the legal arena.

One of the novel's several explicit endorsements of the new legislation to admit slave testimony can be found in a lengthy speech by "Mr. Broadcote," a former resident of Jamaica who, on returning from his travels among the free laborers of India, holds forth to his white West Indian neighbors: "I consider it only an act of justice, and . . . a step which would tend to raise the negro in his own estimation . . . that his evidence should be allowed in cases where white persons are concerned" (247). Broadcote condemns as predicated on "imaginary" fantasies (247) antislavery writers' accusations "that there are numbers among us who maltreat the people under them through motives of ill-will or anger, without fear of any bad consequences resulting to them, from their studiously using the precaution of allowing no legal evidence to be present" (247). He declares, "If the testimony of negroes was once admitted, and no complaints were made by them, it would effectively prove that all such surmises ascribed to us were groundless, and it would convince the world that our characters and principles are actually as mild and humane as those of our brethren at home" (247). Implementation of reform, Broadcote declares, will reveal that such changes to the law were unnecessary.

Oscillating between avowals of support for legislation admitting slave testimony, propagandistic sketches of beaming slaves, and accounts of predatory slaves who deceive their kindly masters, the novel is an amalgam of contrasting depictions that undermine its purported realism and even its stated objectives. At certain points, *Marly* pays lip service to antislavery critics: the novel endorses, in theory, the notion that slaves are to be given some means of communicating complaints. Yet its depiction of slavery appears cultivated to promote the status quo: the novel makes a case that significant restrictions must be placed on such testimony so that it is mediated or limited by white authorities.

Distrust of the attestations of the enslaved prevails to the extent that one slave dies after his claims of illness go unheeded. Marly hears of this outcome from the white bookkeeper of a neighboring plantation: Sancho, a "pretty-strong middle-aged negro" (140) with no visible symptoms, says that he feels pain and leaves work for the plantation infirmary, but the overseer tells the bookkeeper "he does not look as if he were sick" (140), and the examining doctor concludes that the patient is healthy and dismisses him. In the plantations of the West Indies, "bookkeepers" were not accountants but rather men who were charged with direct supervision of slaves; bookkeepers had more contact with the enslaved than overseers did.[96] Twice more Sancho returns, and twice the same response is given. The bookkeeper becomes concerned and eventually defends him, averring that Sancho has earned his trust by refraining from "the habit of complaining without a reason" (141), to which, he suggests, other slaves are prone. The doctor assures him that Sancho may appear distressed but is "only sulky" (141). As the historian Joanna Bourke remarks, scientists of the era believed that blacks did not feel pain in the same way that whites did: "It's really a Catch-22. They're [Black people are] either not really feeling, and it's just reflexes, or they're feeling too much and it's exaggerated or it's hysterical."[97] Sancho is flogged multiple times for his supposed deceit. Only when speaking of Sancho at the moment of his death—when the enslaved man is silenced and can no longer advocate for himself—does the bookkeeper shift from corporeal terms to holistic description, belatedly acknowledging him not simply as an inspected body but as an "unhappy negro." In an unusually elaborate autopsy, "the coroner . . . with a jury and several surgeons" (142) slices open the body of the enslaved man. As with modern-day refugees whose stories of torture are questioned—"Their narratives were systematically questioned; their body was therefore summoned to testify"[98]—the flesh is regarded as the sole valid witness. The group concludes that Sancho's feelings of pain were genuine and stemmed from a hitherto undetected "disease."

While this finding vindicates Sancho, the novel is hardly issuing a directive to believe the claims of the enslaved; instead, it implicitly commends the judgment of the bookkeeper, who is portrayed as knowledgeable of the character of the slaves whom he manages, responsive to their complaints, and willing to speak up for them when authorities make decisions not in their best interests. The implication is that slaves do not need a formal venue for registering grievances because compassionate supervisors will communicate on their behalf. The problem is the relatively distant authorities who are not as familiar with the slaves and their needs: in this particular instance, the doctor, who makes only occasional visits, and the overseer, both of whom had less direct contact with slaves than did the bookkeeper. In other cases, the distant and disparaged authority is the meddlesome home government issuing directives from England via the Colonial Office. The routine discrediting of slaves' complaints—inferior versions of testimony that had to suffice for those denied access to the legal sphere—is reflected in the bookkeeper's narrative choices as he tells Marly of Sancho's case: he directly quotes the white plantation authorities, who give only condensed and paraphrased (and thus distorted) versions of what Sancho said. Sancho's speech is never quoted verbatim.

If one strategy used by the novel to foreground white perspectives and undermine black testimony (while claiming to support it) is to relay the words of white supervisors rather than those of black subordinates, in other episodes a similar effect is achieved by observing and reporting the behavior of slaves from a distance instead of questioning them directly. When a regiment of British troops arrives in Jamaica to be stationed in barracks in Marly's neighborhood, they are mindful of reports by antislavery activists of inhumane treatment: "They attentively observed the negroes at work on numerous plantations . . . and studiously looked for the misery which they had been taught would meet their eye at every step, confirmed by the groans and lamentations of the people" (274). The visitors are relieved: "When the reverse of the expected picture was only to be seen, when the smiling countenances of the blacks, and the merry chorus of the song which they heard chaunted, proclaimed happiness, they could hardly believe they were in a slave country. Their former belief was naturally somewhat staggered by the evidence of their eyes and ears" (274–75). Can the soldiers trust what they see? They are only inquisitive so far as to probe gently into their initial misgivings; they fail to consider that the coercive reach of West Indian planters was similar to that of their American southern counterparts, who "employed an extensive notion of discipline that included everything from the task system to the modes of singing allowed in the field."[99] The trope of the spontaneously expressive, emotionally transparent slave is reaffirmed only because the soldiers keep their distance.

In other episodes of the novel, however, even force will not elicit the desired transparency from the enslaved. Concern surfaces repeatedly among the plantation staff—who, unlike the visiting soldiers, have regular proximity to the enslaved—regarding the refusal of the enslaved to voice their true thoughts and feelings. More than once, whites administering corporal punishment are foiled in their attempts to elicit cries of pain; instead, the enslaved persist in declaring that they are impervious to whippings. It may seem surprising that episodes of punishment are included at all in a proslavery novel that frequently insists that planters treat their slaves gently, but in *Marly*, unlike *Hamel*, slaves are whipped. Perhaps the later novel's acknowledgment of the reality of corporal punishment reflects the extent to which, in a year's time, pressures to acknowledge the realities of slavery had grown even more forceful. After one such flogging, "the whole gang immediately . . . [were] joining in the usual chorus on such occasions, of,—'I don't care a damn, oh!—I don't care a damn, oh!'" (138). The white overseer loses his emotional composure as his attempts to retain control via whip are met with saucy expletives from the slaves: he "bore it for a short time apparently without concern; [but] his choler at last getting up, he hurried to his mule" (138–39) to flee. The next day, he returns, only to become "evidently enraged" (139) at a young slave boy who tries to prevent him from flogging the boy's mother; but he quickly repents his initial angry reaction: "Even *he* felt indignant at the idea of ordering a boy of twelve . . . to be punished, merely for showing strong and natural affection" (139; original emphasis). Once again, he "instantly rode off . . . cheered with the customary song of 'I don't give a damn, oh!'" (139). The overseer loses his moral authority as he descends to the emotional reaction that is supposedly characteristic of blacks, while the slaves retain their composure. An almost identical dynamic is observed by Marly in an early scene featuring the overseer's predecessor: "All [of the slaves] received the same punishment, without distinction of sex or age. The negroes said very little, but the moment the Busha's [overseer's] back was turned to go away, the whole line commenced singing in a general chorus, as if they regarded him not, 'I don't care a damn, oh! I don't care a damn, oh!' and this must have sounded in his ears for at least five minutes, before he could get beyond the reach of hearing" (92).

The novel appears to imply through such episodes that punishments inflicted on the slaves were gentle and effected no real harm, but some twenty-first-century readers may perceive these scenes not as comical vignettes of plantation life, after which harmony is quickly restored, but rather as evidence that slaves felt underlying, unabated hostility toward the whites who controlled their lives but felt compelled to express their resentment indirectly. A critic reviewing the new edition of the novel in 2006 noted that this aspect of the scene appears to escape the author: "The writer is insistent in portraying the slaves as a happy, carefree lot. He constantly refers to their singing, using it to remark on their happiness and seems even oblivious to the rebelliousness of their singing 'I don't care a damn oh' after being whipped."[100] Notably, the reviewer here takes the novel as a documentation of historical reality rather than as a work of fiction—just as the preface suggests it should be construed. Although the novelist may have intended to render the slaves' reaction as "childlike" (as the critic notes), the black children in these scenes exhibit more control over their verbal responses than their white overseer does. Such episodes inadvertently challenge the demarcation of white and black self-command invoked to justify racialized legal hierarchy.

No complaints to authorities arise from these floggings, and the novel's sole instance of slaves registering a formal allegation of abuse in a legal context is a false claim. When an impecunious planter gives his slaves an extra day off each week to cultivate their own provisions, they complain to the authorities that he has deprived them of food: "Although they availed themselves of their owner's goodness, and as they well knew, at very considerable cost to him, . . . they made a formal complaint to a Magistrate against him for failing to provide them with fish and clothing, in terms of the Statute" (209). Here, provision of a race-specific alternative to formal testimony—a measure intended to help the enslaved obtain justice after abusive treatment—instead opens the judiciary to fabricated accusations against whites. Blacks' capacity for deception, the novel suggests, is another reason for withholding liberty from slaves and for regarding their attestations with skepticism.

Yet the novel concedes that there must be some means of giving vent to complaint, for still other episodes in *Marly* demonstrate concerns that slaves harbored undisclosed resentments that would erupt into violence if not otherwise elicited. Reflecting on news that a crew of slaves has been executed for murder, the narrator recalls that they were overworked by their harsh master, known to islanders as "Cruel Grandison"; the slaves eventually ambushed Grandison in his bedroom and strangled him. The narrator launches into a lurid flashback of their planning of the crime. Of the mastermind, he states, "Cambridge was of a resentful, revengeful disposition, and in consequence, his whole thoughts kept brooding over the degradation he had suffered, and in planning schemes for an effectual retaliation" (201). Even as the narrator weaves a fantasy of transracial omniscience, in which he can peer into the minds of slaves, his perspective is self-consciously limited and externally situated. He refers in general terms to "disposition" and "thoughts," instead of scripting the slaves' private dialogue or ventriloquizing their thoughts. In a novel that addresses the controversy over slave testimony, it is significant that throughout the episode, the conspirators' words are not relayed as direct quotations: the single exception occurs when Cambridge insults his master to his face as he adjusts the rope around Grandison's neck.

Whereas *Marly*'s happy slaves are an undifferentiated throng (as are those of *Hamel*), each conspirator is individuated with a name, national origin, and distinct emotional temperament or formative experience. Cambridge, "an old African Negro, a Coromantee, who had long been head driver" (227), is joined by "Nelson, a thoughtless, fearless boy"; "Jack, a Mundingo, a middle aged negro who had been flogged along with him"; "Ned, a Mungola, who had no hesitation in [joining the conspiracy]"; and "a Moco, of the name of Sam" (228). The conspirators are characterized as rational and strategic (the narrator focuses on their "ideas," "thoughts," and "secrets" rather than their skin color or physical brawn), and their plot is facilitated by their ability to refrain from disclosing secrets: "Such ideas in some of their bosoms had long lain latent, and only required a spark to inflame, and a proper leader to direct it" (202). After Cambridge recruits his partners, "These five concealed their secret so effectually in their own breasts, that no suspicions transpired throughout the day, while each was ruminating on the best mode of accomplishing their end" (202). The men's pact not to disclose the plot to the master features just as much of a betrayal as does his strangulation.

Once the conspirators are captured, convicted, and bound for execution, the narrator dwells on their insouciance on the scaffold:

> When the day of terminating their existence came round, no signs of compunction in [any] of these three were visible. While on the road towards the fatal tree, they appeared equally unconcerned, as if they had been going to their daily work. Though they had never heard of the principles of Stoicism, they were truly Stoics. They smoked their cigars, chatted, and laughed to each other, as if nothing whatever was to happen to them. Even upon the fatal spot, these victims betrayed neither fear nor repentance. Nay, so far from it, they insulted those who had charge of them, and gloried in the crime for which they were to suffer an ignominious death. Jack was the first who mounted the fatal ladder. He did so, not with fear and trembling, but with the most cool indifference, jesting and laughing with those around him, and exulting in the part he had performed in depriving his master of his life. (205)

The narrator is disturbed by the conspirators' lack of remorse: are they hiding grief and fear? Or do they feel no shame as they glory in their deeds? The "cool indifference" displayed by the conspirators is the opposite of the effusive subservience of happy slaves. Yet the narrator suggests that this is a facade for the true feelings that the conspirators stubbornly refuse to "betray" to an audience of white onlookers.

That this entire episode is the narrator's fearful fantasy of black powers of self-command and disciplined nondisclosure becomes more evident when the scene from the novel is compared to two real-life parallel Jamaican legal cases of 1823 and 1824, both of which were discussed in the British Parliament in 1826, only two years before the publication of *Marly*. Historical records show that crews of slaves were unjustly executed for plotting to kill their masters based on the false testimony of other slaves, who were either reporting hearsay or trying to distract from their own infractions. Denied due process and repeatedly interrogated, the accused nonetheless refused to admit their guilt or accept plea bargains. Eventually, they were hanged on a public scaffold. British Members of Parliament subsequently convened a session to inquire into the miscarriages of justice occurring on the island. *Marly*'s account of the fictional execution of Cambridge and his crew strongly resembles the description in a December 1823 letter of one of the real-life hangings of wrongly accused slaves. The letter was sent by Colonel Henry Cox, who had been charged with leading a militia to put down slave insurrections, to William Bullock, secretary of the Duke of Manchester; its contents were reprinted in the official transcript of the 1824 Parliamentary debates on slave trials, from which the following excerpt is taken:

> Industry, December 25, 1823.—
>
> ... They all declared they would die like men, and met their fate with perfect indifference, and one laughed at the clergyman, Mr. Cook, when he attempted to exhort him under the gallows.... —Your's, &c. H. Cox.[101]

Although the original transcript also features other, longer parts of the letter, only this excerpt is reproduced in the official Hansard record, set off as a block quotation from the rest of the narrative to impart its significance.

Review of the above transcript shows that while the execution scene in *Marly* is an accurate representation of the 1826 execution, the novel alters the most important facts of the original case, in which a misbegotten trial, based on perjured testimony provided by slave witnesses who accused others to protect themselves from punishment, resulted in the state-sanctioned murder of innocent slaves.[102] The novel reshapes this travesty of justice into a triumphant proslavery legend: a righteous tale in which the safety of the white community is restored when a slave, actuated by feelings of contrition, reveals the plot to the inquisitors of the white plantocracy: "Sam, tormented by the thoughts of crime in which he had been an actor," breaks down, confesses, and implicates his guilty cohorts (204). A real-life judicial ignominy is thus reshaped to fit the template of "happy slave" tales described by George Boulukos, such as Maria Edgeworth's "The Grateful Negro" (1804), in which one slave reveals another's plot to murder their master.[103] Betrayals of fellow slaves are recast as acts of fidelity honoring benevolent masters who, by dint of their generosity, are undeserving of disloyalty, let alone violent retribution.

A central episode of a novel that purports to make the proslavery case for slave testimony is thus a distortion of a historical episode that centered on the lies of slave witnesses.

Taken together, these instances of the novel's engagement with questions regarding the racialized standards of testimony reveal *Marly* to be a case of projection, in which anxieties regarding the credibility of the white proslavery "impartial eyewitness" narratives are filtered through discussions of the trustworthiness of black witnesses. Yet the novel's contemporary reviewers were taken in by the authorial speaker's touting of his own credibility: in terms that echo the author's prefatory claims, the reviewers consistently praised *Marly*'s "authenticity" and "impartiality" as its singular distinction. A reviewer for the *Athenaeum*, a London literary magazine, wrote: "Whether we ought or not to place any confidence in the authenticity of the more important parts of this singular publication we know not, but it is very evidently the production of a man[,] whatever might be his situation, well acquainted with West Indian matters, and the routine of Negro management." The reviewer notes with approval "the coarseness in the style and the manner of the work, which goes far, indeed, to make us believe that he really belonged to the fraternity [slave drivers] with whom he claims connection." Moreover, the reviewer finds, "in the close view it enables us to take of the people who are employed in the management of slaves, it appears deserving of perfect credit for authenticity."[104] Somewhat mystifyingly, the reviewer abruptly shifts from praising *Marly* to conclude that although the novel features proslavery arguments, it could furnish evidence in favor of antislavery efforts, because it showed that slavery degraded the character and capacity of black people. Living as free persons, the reviewer claimed, black people would rise to their natural competency.[105]

An evaluation in the *London Weekly Review; and Journal of Literature and the Fine Arts* similarly lauded the novel as a truthful account of slavery: "The book provides a rare and minute picture, in the Dutch style . . . of a state of society so extraordinary, that we believe the very fact of its existence will become a matter of dispute to a future and more civilized age. The picture is the more rare and valuable [in] that it seems to be completely impartial."[106] A reviewer for the *Atlas* was still more profusely complimentary:

This [novel] really is what the title indicates—a minute and faithful picture of the life of a planter in Jamaica. We are not deluded by general descriptions and high-colored sketches; we are not entrapped into an Abolitionist pamphlet by a collection of controversial lectures under the disguise of a tour—we are truly and justly set down in a planter's settlement. . . . The Slave question, when discussed, is treated temperately and impartially; but better than all, the true state of this class of people is delineated through familiar pictures, on a minute scale, which bear every mark of veracity on the face of them. . . . Though the scene is in its details perhaps fictitious, the nature of the work is of that kind that we are certain it would not have been introduced had it not been an exact resemblance in its general features to real scenes.[107]

This reviewer enthusiastically endorses the author's choice of the literary form of the novel. In highlighting "authenticity" as the key criterion of value in proslavery writings, reviews of *Marly* echoed phrasing from earlier reviews of antislavery works, such as the ex-plantation heir and abolitionist John Riland's 1827 *Memoirs of a West-India Planter*. In his preface, Riland had presented his text as a series of testimonies, "modeled on the rules of a British court of justice," by antislavery "witnesses who give their names" to dispute the "ocular testimony" of "anonymous" proslavery clergymen.[108] A reviewer of Riland's work commented, "Of course, the narrative is understood as fictitious; but the incidents which it comprises, and the general colouring, are substantiated by the testimony of the most unexceptionable witnesses." The reviewer was pleased by the memoir's inclusion of "a mass of important and authentic information respecting the actual state of slavery in our West India colonies."[109] Challenging some reviewers' designation of antislavery partisans as unimpeachable "witnesses," the "Slave Driver" author of *Marly* successfully persuaded at least some readers that his account of slavery was credible.

Credible toward what end, though? The novel is so inconsistent in its various stagings of slaves' intellectual and emotional capacities—both as witnesses and, by extension, as subjects fit to be emancipated and subsequently entrusted with other types of legal agency—that while the reviewers believed it gave an authentic picture, it was unclear how that picture should be interpreted. Perhaps these inconsistencies fostered rather than diminished the reader's trust in the perspective of a self-described "Slave Driver." After all, *Marly* acknowledges—albeit in occasional, sanitized episodes—slave discontent, the plotting of violent uprisings, and abusive masters. Yet the novel fails to make an airtight case for the implications of these contradictions for changes to laws concerning testimony and, more broadly, for the future of slavery as an institution—such that at least one reviewer came away from it deploring slavery.

⌒

This chapter has examined the contradictions between the proslavery novel's avowed support for measures that expanded slave testimony and its attempts to undermine the credibility of the enslaved. These contradictions become more apparent over the course of each novel, owing to the authors' refusal to consistently abide by any single account of slaves' intellectual and emotional capacity; instead, conflicting tropes—the emotionally transparent peon and the duplicitous, scheming ingrate—proliferate in both novels. Proslavery authors meant to alarm the public with depictions of the threat that emancipated slaves would pose to whites, but the unintended and paradoxical outcome was a rendition of complex subjecthood—a richness of representation of black people that was largely absent from sentimental antislavery literature composed for the express purpose of advocating for the humanity of the enslaved.

Whereas some critics claim that antislavery portrayals of slaves expressing conspicuous emotion transmitted the message that slaves were relatable as human beings, proslavery literature was more likely to feature slaves capable of the emotional reserve and strategic behavior that, contradicting its own agenda, upheld them as dignified, self-controlled, and potentially formidable storytellers in the courtroom. Proslavery literature thus offers us unintentional proof that sometimes it is disconnection from, not intimacy with, marginalized protagonists that engenders novel conceptions of personhood and, by extension, makes the case for expanded legal agency.

Proslavery novels are more than mere historical curiosities; they epitomize—and test the limits of—the capacity of the novel form to represent, or at least adumbrate, not only hidden motives and feelings but also grievances that would never be recognized by the legal institutions of political regimes that assign human beings to social segments to which rights are unequally distributed. The narrative structure of *Hamel* and *Marly*, in which black characters displace or threaten to displace the white heroes, reflects proslavery writers' concerns that if slavery were to end, and proper restrictions were not imposed, whites would be eclipsed by the black people whom they meant to subordinate.

The proslavery novel highlights the link between two key elements that would come to be identified with the nineteenth-century ascendance of the novel form: first, preoccupation with interiority, and, second, attention to the paradigmatic conflict between self and society. Slaveholders in the West Indies attempted to restrict slave testimony so that they could remain in control and continue a way of life that they sensed was in imminent danger of being outlawed by legal authorities back home. At the close of his magisterial work on the origins of the English novel, Michael McKeon declared, "The autonomy of the self consists in its capacity to enter into largely negative relation with the society it vainly conceives itself to have created, to resist its encroachments and to be constructed by them. The work of the novel after 1820 is increasingly to record this struggle."[110] McKeon does not refer to slavery here, but his statement applies to the conflicts that engulfed the West Indies at this historical moment. Whether the resisters of encroachment were white slaveholders decrying a distant government's outlawing of their livelihood on islands they had settled, or enslaved people refusing to disclose their true thoughts and emotions to the persecutors whose crops, mansions, and children they raised, of no novelistic subgenre is McKeon's statement more true than for the British proslavery novel on the eve of its obsolescence, as emancipation loomed.

Abiding the Law

In 2012, Britain's then-prime minister David Cameron began a speech to the European Court of Human Rights by articulating a triumphant chronology, beginning with the Magna Carta, of Britain's expansions of the rights of the marginalized. In this rendition of history, the eighteenth century took pride of place: "By the eighteenth century," he stated, "it was said that: 'this spirit of liberty is so deeply implanted in our constitution, and rooted in our very soil, that a slave the moment he lands in England, falls under the protection of the laws, and with regard to all natural rights becomes instantly a freeman.'"[1] Having quoted that famous passage from the first chapter of William Blackstone's *Commentaries on the Laws of England* (1760–65),[2] Cameron declared, "The same spirit led to the abolition of slavery." He then reiterated the continuity between past and present: "these beliefs have animated the British people for centuries, and they animate us today." This glowing narrative of the eighteenth century as an era defined by a driving desire for equality for all can be found in a number of widely influential scholarly treatments, from Lynn Hunt's *Inventing Human Rights* to Steven Pinker's *Enlightenment Now*. Hunt claims that novels played a vital role in this history: "Novels taught their readers nothing less than a new psychology and in the process laid the foundations for a new social and political order."[3] Pinker similarly identifies the novel as one of several keys to "understanding the legacy of modernity": "Many novels from the mid-18th to the early 20th century played out the struggle of individuals to overcome the suffocating norms of aristocratic, bourgeois, or rural regimes."[4] Both Hunt and Pinker laud the works of Samuel Richardson as the first in a series of novels that were key vectors of the ideals that shaped this historical moment.

Yet the account of history offered by Cameron, Hunt, and Pinker is, of course, only one version of the story of the eighteenth-century legal and cultural legacy. I have demonstrated that complications to this narrative of a magnanimous "spirit of liberty" can be found in a different set of late eighteenth-century and early nineteenth-century novels—contemporaneously prominent (although now, in a number of cases, disparaged or neglected) works imbued with conservative ideology. These novels instead identified the privileged as society's most vulnerable members. Unlike those who were satisfied with social order based exclusively on lineage, however, conservative authors advocated a distribution of rights that also took merit into account. They supported a vision of law in which legal agency was reserved for privileged people whose character and actions showed them to be deserving of it. The conservative authors thus seem to offer an early prototype of the twenty-first-century "cognitive elite" who "operate like the gods of myth in the same physical environment as the ordinary, subject citizen, but in a separate realm politically"—a type whose ascendance David Rees-Mogg and James Dale Davidson prognosticated in the libertarian manifesto *The Sovereign Individual*.[5] This aspect of the conservative conceptualization of the proper distribution of rights starkly contrasts with the vision offered by the humanitarian novelists.

Yet inordinate focus on the differences among humanitarian and conservative authors of the era can obscure the ground on which they converged: both groups believed that law should empower private citizens to seek justice and that it was important to uphold standards of due process. Certainly, conservative novelists did not support the extension of rights to all. Even so, humanitarian and conservative authors faced a shared enemy: authoritarians—such as corrupt judges or domineering political leaders—who rationalized arbitrary application of the law or force by declaring the importance of maintaining "order." Authoritarians believe that the central role of law is to preserve social order and that obedience to the law is what qualifies a citizen for government protection of person and property. Conservative and humanitarian authors alike perceived the threat that self-serving individuals or political cabals could assume control of the law either locally or nationally and target all manner of people at whim.

Abiding by the law is no guarantee of safety in conservative novels. Certainly, in reality poor and nonwhite persons were particularly stigmatized as unruly and dangerous. In the novels I have examined, however, privileged characters are markedly vulnerable to arbitrary enforcement and application of the law. As are their lowly counterparts in humanitarian fiction, characters of higher status in conservative novels are continually arrested, charged with invented crimes, and indefinitely detained. These characters, too, become frustrated when they realize that their legal agency is limited—or perpetually subject to revocation—based on factors beyond their control, such as gender or jurisdiction. Smollett's Sir Launcelot finds himself incarcerated by a jail-keeper with little concern for due process. Smith's heroine Althea is terrorized by a lawyer who breaks into her home, intent on searching it despite having no warrant. In the proslavery novels, scions of West Indian planter families are dismayed to learn that their estates have been seized by cunning "attorneys" who circumvent the law. Darsie's plea that Redgauntlet is holding him captive is ignored by the justice of the peace. Under authoritarian conditions, the novelists indicate, status and merit offer little protection against unjust treatment.

The antipathy toward authoritarianism shared by eighteenth-century humanitarian and conservative authors is significant to our political future, for the cultural and legal legacy of the eighteenth century has been invoked to rouse support for government policies that are authoritarian in nature. The quotation in the opening paragraph of this epilogue is from the first part of Cameron's speech, which aligns with the Hunt-Pinker view of history. Cameron, however, was softening up his audience of European human rights advocates en route to announcing a departure from supporting the Court's mission. Shortly after the above-cited passage, Cameron abruptly altered his tone. Britain, he warned, needed to turn away from protecting the rights of others—in this case, "foreign nationals who threaten our security"—and reprioritize the protection of "law-abiding citizens."[6] In his deft transition from lauding historical expansions of rights to recommending a departure from that legacy, Cameron suggested that the eighteenth-century humanitarian devotion to expanding legal agency had for too long held sway, and he sought to revise the balance of power. He implied that nativist emotion, rather than the considered deliberation of the courts, would now determine who deserved rights.

Such a call for preferential treatment for "law-abiding citizens" formed the core of the vision of justice promoted decades earlier by the US president Ronald Reagan. In a 1973 address to a convention of prominent businessmen and government officials, Reagan (then governor of California) stated, "One legislator accused us of having a 19th-century attitude on law and order. Well, now, that is a totally false charge. I have an 18th-century attitude. That is when the Founding Fathers made it clear that the safety of law abiding citizens should be one of government's primary concerns."[7]

Decades apart, the two leaders offered completely different interpretations of eighteenth-century history: whereas Cameron insinuated that the protection of law-abiding citizens had been eroded during the period, Reagan saw such protection as a core value of the era—a value that he intended to reinstate. Both politicians' versions of the eighteenth-century legacy were lacking: while Cameron's account of history was selective, Reagan's was ill-founded. Although Reagan identified himself as a proponent of "eighteenth-century ideas" regarding justice, reports indicate that he had little direct knowledge of the period writings that addressed these ideas. When the journalist James Conaway asked one of Reagan's policy advisors, Richard V. Allen, to describe what guided the leader's decisions, Allen stated, "I mean, I don't know if he's actually *read* Burke. But he has a great accumulation of knowledge . . . he appoints people to read books for him, and if they don't, they're in trouble."[8] Nevertheless, Reagan justified his legal worldview by citing its supposed historical origins.[9]

Reagan's "eighteenth-century" authoritarian-lite vision of government is more accurately described as rooted in Thomas Hobbes's seventeenth-century conceptualization of the social contract, which remained influential throughout the eighteenth century. Yet without vigilance this protective framework could itself become the threat. Benjamin R. Barber argues that Hobbes's "fear of anarchy leads him to embrace an authoritarian conception of the state."[10] In a similar vein, David van Mill observes: "Perhaps the most enduring criticism of Hobbes's political philosophy is that it provides for an absolute sovereign that poses a great threat to individual freedom."[11]

Conservative novelists exhibit a comparable preoccupation with the question of how best to maintain social order. They seem to share with Reagan the opinion that only a select group should be granted legal agency. The authors' notion of who qualifies for membership in this group is self-serving: in their view, the category of those most deserving of rights and protection under the law overlapped substantially with the category of the affluent or high-born—that is, people similar to themselves. Yet the novelists' perspective of who counted as deserving was somewhat flexible. In a society in which legal agency was jealously rationed, conservative authors supported this stringency, but they also endorsed carve-outs for niche demographics that had demonstrated their value to society, including wealthy Jewish émigrés (as apparent in Smollett's commentary on the Jewish Naturalization

Act and his pathbreaking Jewish character, the generous merchant Joshua Manasseh) and female members of the gentry who had fallen on hard times through no fault of their own (as evidenced by Smith's repudiation of the barriers to women's participation in legal concerns). Such rewards for good behavior extend to the enslaved: in *Marly*, a well-behaved and industrious slave named Jupiter successfully argues for his right to "possession of a spot of ground which had belonged to, or had been occupied by his mother, Peggy."[12] As part of the estate, this section of the provision grounds officially remains, of course, the property of the planter, and the scene is designed to advance the novel's propagandistic depiction of humane treatment; but it is nonetheless significant that the plantation bookkeeper sees fit to resolve this pseudo-inheritance case through "judicial proceedings," as the narrator describes it, tongue in cheek.

Conversely, the conservative novelists offer withering portraits of those among the affluent or high-born who abuse their privilege and make no contribution to larger society: the "fine lady" whose insatiable consumerism and manipulation of everyone with whom she comes into contact is denounced in *Sir Launcelot Greaves*; Smith's weak-willed, easily influenced Lord Montreville, who sacrifices to greed the best interests of his niece Emmeline; and his belligerent son Lord Delamere, who resorts to abduction and violence when he cannot obtain what he desires. Scott characterizes Sir Hugh Redgauntlet as likewise inclined to bend others to his will. The proslavery novelists, for their part, take a dim view of the "home manufacturers"—leaders of industry resident in England—who derive "wealth and prosperity" from the colonies, while failing to support them.[13]

In contrast to the emphasis placed by the conservative novelists on initiative, honesty, and emotional control as criteria for the acquisition of legal agency by the marginalized, history has shown that authoritarians are in practice generally interested in granting legal agency only to those from specific demographics. That is, rights are linked primarily to identity, rather than to virtuous action or behavior. To the extent that behavior matters, what counts most are professions of loyalty to the leader or ruling group—and actions that confirm it. Yet to cast their vision of government in terms more palatable to a general audience, politicians with authoritarian leanings often prefer to give lip service to the importance of proper action and behavior, and avoid terms that explicitly link legal agency with identity. Political scientists claim that throughout his career, Reagan used "dog whistle" terminology that seemed facially neutral, but actually freighted with racial and classist undertones,[14] to reframe governmental decisions over whose rights to protect as a battle between wholesome, hardworking patriots and violence-prone, free-riding denizens of the inner city. Because such phrasing seems to denote behavior rather than race or class—traits over which bearers have no control—it does not give rise to objections, as would more explicitly identitarian language. In particular, the catchphrase "law-abiding citizens"—revived in 2016 by Donald Trump[15]—is construed by some scholars as a euphemism for native-born whites, usually of middle-class or higher station.[16] Both Cameron and Reagan seem to have used "law-abiding" as a rallying cry to push back against the rhetoric of "civil rights" for all. Reagan's 1973 address reaffirmed the "silent majority" retrenchment after the 1960s civil rights era in the US; Cameron's 2012 speech foreshadowed his 2014 call to repeal the Human Rights Act passed by Britain in 1998.[17]

Countering such rhetoric, other politicians made well-intentioned efforts to assure the public that most members of minority communities follow the law. In 2017, Prime Minister Theresa May's spokesman said: "The overwhelming majority of Muslims in this country are law abiding people who abhor extremism in all its forms."[18] A year later, in 2018, there was a spike in the occurrence of *law-abiding* in Parliamentary speeches.[19] The descriptor was typically applied to minority groups, such as Muslims or black men, who are criminalized in the public imaginary. Although the members of Parliament were attempting to defend the stigmatized communities, the strained yoking of "law-abiding" with a minority identity label inevitably conveyed a reminder that minority groups are typically regarded as lawless or undeserving of protections of rights. Yet the MPs did not challenge the premise that legal agency must be earned, rather than guaranteed by default for human beings in general.

Eighteenth-century usage of *law-abiding*, however, casts further doubt on twentieth- and twenty-first-century right-wing constructions of eighteenth-century values. The *Oxford English Dictionary* definition has not been updated since 1902; it lists 1839 as the year of the first recorded instance of *law-abiding*. Yet the term can be traced back at least to the 1750s, when the first texts discussed in this book were published.[20] In a 1756 sermon, the Aberdeen minister John Bisset counseled: "In your dealings with your duty, and with the law, which commandeth it, you are not to flee the command, as the broken debtor doth the face of the creditor, like them who are not law abiding. But you are now through Christ on your side, to welcome every command and charge of the law, as being in some capacity to speak to it, and give it some satisfying answer."²¹ In this mid-eighteenth-century sermon, to be "law-abiding" is to welcome the law as a guiding force and to seek to comply with it—and to correct course when one has erred. Instead of an Old Testament scenario of inevitable punishment of wrongdoers by a harsh, unforgiving divine law, the passage envisions a New Testament process of realignment with a benevolent, life-giving law through reparative conduct. Although those who have erred cannot reinterpret or alter the command, they can respond to it through confession or justification. This notion of law-abidingness as an attainable property of action earned through humility and spiritual resolve to fulfill one's "duty"—rather than a fixed property of identity, a racial birthright—could hardly be more distant from the term that reentered the vernacular in the 1960s.

Elsewhere, the term was used pejoratively. In "A Letter on Colonization" (1834), a man tells a "Christian slaveholder" that by choosing to obey the legal prohibition against educating his human chattel, he is failing to honor the moral imperative to prepare them for emancipation: "You are a law-abiding man, too—you will not violate the law clandestinely," he remarks. "How, then, tell me, are *you* preparing your slaves for this important change?"²² Here, *law-abiding* is used as an epithet; the speaker implies that humane concern for those under one's care should take precedence over adherence to the letter of the law. These examples indicate that the eighteenth-century connotations of the term were more complex and morally substantive compared to those that were attached to it on its mid-twentieth-century revival.

The above passage derives from a text that would have been considered radically humanitarian in its day, but the conservative novelists similarly condoned challenges to laws or judicial practices that they deemed unjust. In each of the novels under discussion in this study, protagonists defy authoritarian figures. Emmeline refuses to comply with Delamere's demands and does not cooperate with Lord Montreville's lawyers. Sir Launcelot frees all of the prisoners of Sir Anthony's private asylum and forces the corrupt Judge Gobble to retire. The author of *Marly* rebukes British Secretary of State for War and the Colonies William Huskisson by name for "annulling" revisions of the law passed by the Jamaican Assembly.²³ Darsie refuses to serve as a spokesman for Redgauntlet's campaign to restore the Pretender, Charles Edward Stuart, to the throne; and the Pretender himself loses his loyal followers of several decades when he haughtily avows that their "allegiance . . . is due to me as my birth-right," and refuses to heed any of their suggestions: Redgauntlet laments that "your Majesty is so unwilling to concede" on small points.²⁴

Resistance to authoritarians, as portrayed in literary works that span the political spectrum, is a key part of the eighteenth-century literary heritage.

By considering not only canonical humanitarian novels but also their conservative counterparts, as well as forgotten political and religious texts, it becomes clear that knowledge of both of these novelistic genealogies is key to reckoning with politicians' schematic and apparently incompatible accounts of the nature of the eighteenth-century legacy. In this study, I have detailed how conservative authors foregrounded the plights of characters whose status or class privilege does not prevent them from seeing themselves as beleaguered minorities. These high-born wanderers, wealthy aliens, disinherited heirs, and aggrieved expatriates experience regular obstacles to exercising legal agency as they navigate a changing world where familiar conceptions of who deserves allegiance and obeisance no longer prevail. Yet the dangers typically faced by these privileged characters—arbitrary application of the law and suspension of rights—resemble some of the humiliations and injustices endured by women, the enslaved, the poor, and other members of marginalized groups in humanitarian fiction. As the eighteenth-century past becomes ever more distant, it is imperative that scholars correct the record and remind the general public—most of whom do not have the privilege of reading books for a living—of the more nuanced legacy to which we all are heirs. Recognition of the common ground between conservative and humanitarian values could help facilitate the drawing together of disparate interests into a coalition to oppose the specter of authoritarianism. For such a feat of literary reconciliation, the hour is late, but the venture is possible still.

Introduction • *A Neglected Inheritance*

1. Ian Watt famously noted "the novel's serious concern with the daily lives of ordinary people." Ian Watt, *The Rise of the Novel: Studies in Defoe, Richardson, and Fielding*, 2nd American ed. (1957; Berkeley: University of California Press, 2001), 60. Ruth Perry observes that although "the eighteenth-century novel has been criticized for being concerned only with the lives of the wealthy or at least the middle class, . . . poverty is represented in eighteenth-century fiction" in a variety of contexts: "whether in the country or in the city, whether cottagers or impoverished persons of the 'better sort,' whether living alone or caring for children or old parents." Ruth Perry, "Home Economics: Representations of Poverty in Eighteenth-Century Fiction," in *A Companion to the Eighteenth-Century English Novel and Culture*, ed. Paula R. Backscheider and Catherine Ingrassia (Oxford: Blackwell, 2005), 441–58, 441, 442. Nancy Armstrong traces in the eighteenth-century novel a preoccupation with women as "the emergent social group." Nancy Armstrong, *Desire and Domestic Fiction: A Political History of the Novel* (Oxford: Oxford University Press, 1987), 97. See also Catherine Gallagher's claim regarding the importance of nonreferentiality in the work of a number of prominent female eighteenth-century novelists: "A story about nobody was nobody's story and could be entered, occupied, identified with by anybody." Catherine Gallagher, *Nobody's Story: The Vanishing Acts of Women Writers in the Marketplace, 1670–1820* (1994; Berkeley: University of California Press, 1995), 168.

2. For the selection of *Pamela; or, Virtue Rewarded* and *Clarissa; or, The History of a Young Lady*, as well as *The Interesting Narrative of the Life of Olaudah Equiano, or Gustavus Vassa, the African* as landmark works in the literary tradition of what would come to be known as human rights discourse, see Lynn Hunt, *Inventing Human Rights: A History* (New York: Norton, 2005), 41, 66. In some cases, such texts—identified by Hunt and others with the human rights tradition—include elements that challenge such categorization. In the case of *The Interesting Narrative*, scholars' attempts to interpret Equiano's work as an early instance of human rights discourse are complicated by his self-reported complicity in the slave economy. Similar complications are found in *Things as They Are; or, The Adventures of Caleb Williams* (1794), a novel identified with social justice concerns. For an early association of *Caleb Williams* with the discourse of "the new world of human rights," see Frederick R. Karl, *The Adversary*

Literature: The English Novel in the Eighteenth Century: A Study of Genre (New York: Farrar, Straus and Giroux, 1974), 259. In recent years, other scholars have remarked that the novel undermines "Godwin's ostensible intention of promoting a liberal model of human rights." Charlie Bondhus, "'An Outlandish, Foreign-Made Englishman': Aristocratic Oppression and Ethnic Anomaly in *Caleb Williams*," *Eighteenth-Century Fiction* 23, no. 1 (2010): 163–94, 167. Gerold Sedlmayr, instead, attributes this intention to Caleb, the protagonist, and sees Godwin as indicating problems inherent to human rights ideology. See Gerald Sedlmayr, "Ownership of the Body, the Sacralization of the Person, and the Right to Bodily Integrity in William Godwin's *Caleb Williams*," *European Romantic Review* 27, no. 3 (2016): 375–84, esp. 376–77.

3. See, e.g., Suzanne Keen, *Empathy and the Novel* (Oxford: Oxford University Press, 2007).

4. By "conservative," I have in mind J. G. A. Pocock's definition: "'Conservatism' . . . is based on the claim that human beings acting in politics always start within a historically determined context, and that it is morally as well as practically important to remember that they are not absolutely free to wipe away this context and reconstruct human society as they wish." J. G. A. Pocock, introduction to Edmund Burke, *Reflections on the Revolution in France* (Indianapolis: Hackett, 1987), vii–lvi, vii. Because "conservative" may be conflated with contemporary political party labels, I considered alternatives. One possibility, "traditionalist," was eliminated because it denotes more extreme right-wing political positions in the Spanish literary tradition. In the end, "conservative" seemed to be the best option, despite its limitations.

5. Sandra Macpherson, *Harm's Way: Tragic Responsibility and the Novel Form* (Baltimore: Johns Hopkins University Press, 2012), 24.

6. Adam Smith, *The Theory of Moral Sentiments*, rev. ed. (1790), ed. D. D. Raphael and A. L. Macfie (Oxford: Clarendon, 1976), 52. Scholarship on the importance of eighteenth-century conceptualizations of sympathy to humanitarian movements neglects the extent to which Adam Smith and later eighteenth-century politicians, including John Adams, insisted that sympathy for the affluent and powerful was a compelling motivating force for political action. For correctives to such neglect, see recent work in political theory: Luke Mayville, *John Adams and the Fear of American Oligarchy* (Princeton, NJ: Princeton University Press, 2016); Dennis Rasmussen, "Adam Smith on What Is Wrong with Political Inequality," *American Political Science Review* 101, no. 2 (May 2016): 342–52; and Corey Robin, *The Reactionary Mind: Conservatism from Edmund Burke to Donald Trump* (2011; Oxford: Oxford University Press, 2017). For an argument that the prevalence of sympathy for the rich relative is overestimated in the present day relative to sympathy for the poor, see Spencer Piston, *Class Attitudes in American Politics: Sympathy for the Poor, Resentment of the Rich, and Political Implications* (Cambridge: Cambridge University Press, 2018).

7. Ta-Nehisi Coates describes "the fear that passed through the generations . . . [and] the sense of dispossession" besetting African American communities deprived of "the [American] Dream" and disregarded by "the [white] heirs of slaveholders." Ta-Nehisi Coates, *Between the World and Me* (New York: Random House, 2015), 43. Charles E. Loeser writes that "sovereign citizens believe that the United States government has perpetrated a massive fraud to deprive its citizens of their liberty." Charles E. Loeser, "From Paper Terrorists to Cop Killers: The Sovereign Citizen Threat," *North Carolina Law Review* 93, no. 4 (2015): 1106–39, 1124.

8. Robert Nichols, "Theft Is Property! The Recursive Logic of Dispossession," *Political Theory* 46, no. 1 (2018): 3–28:3.

9. Although Charlotte Smith has been characterized as a "radical" author owing to her poetry and prose work for children, I classify the specific novels discussed in this study as conservative. Certainly, her prose writing for children displays humanitarian interests, such as concern for the enslaved and indignation at those who fail to heed the distress of the poor. Likewise, her poem *The Emigrants* (1793) argued, in the face of hostile nativist complaint, for welcoming refugees from persecution in France. Yet her novels uphold social hierarchy and depict as villains those who threaten it: lower-status male professionals whose machinations enable their marriage into privileged families, or irresponsible scions who place at risk their family's wealth and reputation. Furthermore, there is little concern in the novels for the plight of those born into desperate poverty; on the contrary, the once-proud families seeking to regain their extensive estates are presented as the focal point of sympathy. Events of Smith's personal life give rise to the impression that self-interest at times guided or qualified her views in ways that undermine characterization of her as radical. She negotiated the sale of 171 slaves to benefit her family's finances and even argued with the prospective buyer over the price of individual slaves; see Adriana Craciun, *British Women Writers and the French Revolution: Citizens of the World* (Houndmills, Basingstoke, Hampshire: Palgrave Macmillan, 2005), 173. The wave of French emigrants, whose cause she advocated, was largely aristocratic, including the chevalier Alexandre de Foville, who married her daughter Augusta and provided illustrations and other support for Smith's writing. For a nuanced articulation of a critical view of Smith's political sensibilities as "radical," see Angela Keane, *Women Writers and the English Nation in the 1790s: Romantic Belongings* (Cambridge: Cambridge University Press, 2004). Keane notes that although Smith "allied herself tentatively with the radical ideals of cosmopolitan patriots," she also took a skeptical view of "the internationalism of Godwinian radical philosophy" (8).

10. Frank O'Gorman, *The Long Eighteenth Century: British Political and Social History, 1688–1832*, 2nd ed. (1997; London: Bloomsbury Academic, 2016), 3.

11. I thank an anonymous reader for the press for helping to elucidate this concept of legal agency.

12. H. L. A. Hart, *The Concept of Law*, 3rd ed. (1961; Oxford: Oxford University Press, 2012), 167 (emphasis in original).

13. As indicated by his original French subtitle ("Naissance de la prison," which translates to "The Birth of the Prison," Foucault was more concerned with the prison as an institution than with the individual human actors within it. He does not see power as a capacity attributable to individual human agents; instead, he gives an account of "un système d'assujettissement." This system of subjugation operates via "la technologie politique du corps" (that is, the political technology of the body), which he describes as delocalized: "diffuse, rarement formulée en discours continus et systéma-tiques. . . . De plus on ne saurait la localiser ni dans un type défini d'institution, ni dans un appareil étatique." Michel Foucault, *Surveiller et punir: Naissance de la prison* (Paris: Gallimard, 1975), 30, 31, 31. For a rebuttal to the prevalent assumption that Foucault rejects an agential account of power, see Amy Allen, *The Politics of Our Selves: Power, Autonomy, and Gender in Contemporary Critical Theory* (New York: Columbia University Press, 2008), chap. 2.

14. See, e.g., Hal Gladfelder's work on highwaymen and other criminal figures: "the fascination with protagonists shaped by deviant strayings from the path of normality is integral to the contemporaneously emerging genre of the novel." Hal Gladfelder, *Criminality and Narrative in Eighteenth-Century England: Beyond the Law* (Baltimore: Johns Hopkins University Press, 2001), 6.

15. Jonathan Grossman has demonstrated that *Caleb Williams* and other Romantic-era novels inaugurated "a form of justice newly rebuilt . . . around the storytelling forum of trials." Jonathan Grossman, *The Art of Alibi: English Law Courts and the Novel* (Baltimore: Johns Hopkins University Press, 2002), 49. Late eighteenth- and nineteenth-century trials relied on what Alexander Welsh calls "strong representations"—cases built on a persuasive narrative woven from circumstantial evidence. See Alexander Welsh, *Strong Representations: Narrative and Circumstantial Evidence in England* (Baltimore: Johns Hopkins University Press, 1992), 8–10. Jan-Melissa Schramm has shown that whereas in early modern criminal trials, "artless" testimony directly from the defendant was the primary factor in shaping impressions as to whether he or she was innocent, defense lawyers in the eighteenth and early nineteenth centuries took a prominent role in trials (at least for defendants who could afford counsel), shaping stories that would convince others of their clients' innocence. This development was reflected in Romantic-era and Victorian novels. Jan-Melissa Schramm, *Testimony and Advocacy in Victorian Law, Literature, and Theology* (Cambridge: Cambridge University Press, 2000), 23. See also John H. Langbein, "The Prosecutorial Origins of Defence Counsel in the Eighteenth Century: The Appearance of Solicitors," *Cambridge Law Journal* 58, no. 2 (July 1999): 314–65.

16. See John Bender, *Imagining the Penitentiary: Fiction and the Architecture of Mind in Eighteenth-Century England* (Chicago: University of Chicago Press, 1987); and John Bugg, *Five Long Winters: The Trials of British Romanticism* (Stanford, CA: Stanford University Press, 2014). For an overview of the American context in the late eighteenth century and early nineteenth century, see Caleb Smith, *The Prison and the American Imagination* (New Haven, CT: Yale University Press, 2009), 7–14.

17. See David Lemmings, *Professors of the Law: Barristers and English Legal Cultures in the Eighteenth Century* (Oxford: Oxford University Press, 2000), 36, 41, 43.

18. See Joseph Slaughter, *Human Rights, Inc.: The World Novel, Narrative Form, and International Law* (New York: Fordham University Press, 2009), 25.

19. Preface to *List of Proceedings in the Court of Requests, Preserved in the Public Record Office*, vol. 1 (no. 21 of *Lists and Indexes, Public Record Office*) (London: Mackie, printed for His Majesty's Stationer's Office, 1906), iv. I adopt the section title phrase "arc of the legal universe"—which is in turn modified from the notion of the "arc of the moral universe" popularized by Martin Luther King, Jr.—from Mark S. Cady, "The Vanguard of Equality: The Iowa Supreme Court's Journey to Stay Ahead of the Curve on an Arc Bending towards Justice," *Albany Law Review* 76, no. 4 (2013): 1991–2001, 1991.

20. "In the history of civil litigation in England, the steep decline in business that occurred between the later 17th century and 1760 . . . was a feature of all jurisdictions that have been looked at, and in all of them it was apparently dramatic." Christopher W. Brooks, "The Longitudinal Study of Civil Litigation in England, 1200–1996," in *Litigation Past and Present*, ed. Sharyn Roach Anleu and Wilfrid Prest (Sydney: University of New South Wales Press, 2004), 24–43, 33.

21. Christopher Brooks, "Litigation, Participation, and Agency," in *The British and Their Laws in the Eighteenth Century*, ed. David Lemmings (Woodbridge, Suffolk, UK: Boydell and Brewer, 2005), 155–81, 162. Compare the early seventeenth-century context: "Despite widespread and traditional complaints about both the exorbitance of lawyers' fees and the legal system's overall discrimination against the poorer sort, it was not usually claimed during our period that the poor were actually priced out of the courts." Wilfrid R. Prest, *The Rise of the Barristers: A Social History of the English Bar 1590–1640* (Oxford: Clarendon, 1986), 20.

22. See David Lemmings, *Law and Government in England during the Long Eighteenth Century: From Consent to Command* (London: Palgrave Macmillan, 2011), 59.

23. See Douglas Hay, "War, Dearth, and Theft in the Eighteenth Century: The Record of the English Courts," *Past and Present* 95 (May 1982): 117–60, 147–48. By contrast, Allyson Nancy May contends that fees hamstrung the accused: "Even those accused who employed counsel suffered under a disadvantage: being poor, they were usually unable to raise the requisite fees until the last minute, so their defense was hastily assembled." Allyson Nancy May, *The Bar and the Old Bailey, 1750–1850* (Chapel Hill: University of North Carolina Press, 2003), 187. Yet Hitchcock and Shoemaker note, "The fact that several hundred were able to pay counsel in the 1780s, many of whom were in lower-class occupations . . . is testimony to both the desperation and the combativeness of Old Bailey defendants in those years." Tim Hitchcock and Robert Shoemaker, *London Lives: Poverty, Crime, and the Making of a Modern City, 1690–1800* (Cambridge: Cambridge University Press, 2015), 359. See also Lemmings, *Professors of the Law*, 215.

24. Hitchcock and Shoemaker, *London Lives*, 271. The extent to which prosecutions rose or fell year-to-year, as well as the relative importance of various causes of the increase, is debated by scholars.

25. Hitchcock and Shoemaker, *London Lives*, 8, 6. See also Robert B. Shoemaker, "The Old Bailey Proceedings and the Representation of Crime and Criminal Justice in Eighteenth-Century London," *Journal of British Studies* 47, no. 3 (2008): 559–80: "The intended readership of the Proceedings, those whose purchases funded its publication, were London's property-owning classes—the men and women who were most likely to be the victims of the thefts dominating the Old Bailey's dockets" (565). Regarding the 1690–1800 year range, higher-resolution chronological data would be preferable, of course; further research is needed to determine whether the class distribution of prosecutors changed after the statutes of the 1750s and 1778.

26. Hitchcock and Shoemaker, 6.

27. Drew D. Gray, *Crime, Prosecution, and Social Relations: The Summary Courts of the City of London in the Late Eighteenth Century* (Houndmills, Basingstoke, Hampshire: Palgrave Macmillan, 2009), 8, 26–27, 20. Hitchcock and Shoemaker comment on another resource available to the poor in Middlesex, the so-called "trading justices": "often men of lower status than the gentlemen who traditionally served" were given to "welcoming complaints from the poor and resolving them informally whenever possible." The scholars argue that these judges filled a need in a broken system: "While their detractors saw in the dramatically increasing activity of trading justices from the mid-1760s little more than venality and corruption, it should be viewed instead as a reflection of growing demand for personalized judicial services from a population

alienated from the new variety of justice being dispensed at the rotation offices and Bow Street." Hitchcock and Shoemaker, *London Lives*, 319, 320.

28. Gray, *Crime, Prosecution, and Social Relations*, 169, 29–30; and Hitchcock and Shoemaker, *London Lives*, 18–19. See also Gray Peter King, *Crime and the Law in England, 1750–1840: Remaking Justice from the Margins* (Cambridge: Cambridge University Press, 2006).

29. Douglas Hay, "Master and Servant in England: Using the Law in the Eighteenth and Nineteenth Centuries," in *Private Law and Social Inequality in the Industrial Age: Comparing the Legal Cultures of Britain, France, Germany, and the United States*, ed. Willibald Steinmetz (Oxford: Oxford University Press, 2000), 227–64, 228. Yet Hay remarks that, unsurprisingly, "the law of master and servant" tended to favor employers: "The provision of penal sanctions for the servant, and not for the master, became the most contentious part of the law. The worker in the breach was often treated as a criminal; the master rarely was" (229).

30. Malcolm M. Feeley and Deborah L. Little, "The Vanishing Female: The Decline of Women in the Criminal Process, 1687–1912," *Law and Society Review* 25, no. 4 (1991): 719–57, 720.

31. As summarized by David Lemmings, "The English propensity for litigiousness was already marked in the Middle Ages, and recourse to the law increased still more in the sixteenth century, remaining high until the seventeenth." Lemmings, *Law and Government in England*, 56–80, 57.

32. Delineation of these functions as key aspects of the novel's development can be traced in the work of Ian Watt and of Michael McKeon. Watt claims that foundational to the novel is "the concept of individualism," which "posits a whole society mainly governed by the idea of every individual's intrinsic independence both from other individuals and from that multifarious allegiance to past modes of thought and action denoted by the word 'tradition'—a force that is always social, not individual." Ian Watt, *The Rise of the Novel*, 60. McKeon contends, "The social significance of the English novel at the time of its origins lies in its ability to mediate—to represent as well as contain—the revolutionary clash between status and class orientations and the attendant crisis of status inconsistency." Michael McKeon, *The Origins of the English Novel, 1600–1740*, 15th anniv. ed. (1987; Baltimore: Johns Hopkins University Press, 2002), 173–74. Nancy Armstrong argues that "the history of the novel and the history of the modern subject are, quite literally, one and the same." Nancy Armstrong, *How Novels Think: The Limits of Individualism from 1719 to 1900* (New York: Columbia University Press, 2005), 3.

33. Hunt argues that novel reading fostered "the ability to identify across social lines." Hunt, *Inventing Human Rights*, 40.

34. Elizabeth Anker has articulated the novel's capacity to "indict the many privileges and exclusions that procure legibility for the logic of rights." Elizabeth Anker, *Fictions of Dignity: Embodying Human Rights in World Literature* (Ithaca, NY: Cornell University Press, 2012), 81. Joseph Slaughter contends, "In contrast with the weakness of legal apparatuses, cultural forms like the novel have cooperated with human rights to naturalize their common sense—to give law the Gramscian force of culture." Slaughter, *Human Rights, Inc.*, 25.

35. Eric Heinze, *Hate Speech and Democratic Citizenship* (Oxford: Oxford University Press, 2016), 93.

36. Daniel Stout, *Corporate Romanticism: Liberalism, Justice, and the Novel* (New York: Fordham University Press, 2018), 11.

37. Mark Schoenfield, "Romantic Justice: Law, Literature, and Individuality," in *A Concise Companion to the Romantic Age*, ed. Jon Klancher (New York: John Wiley and Sons, 2009), 119–40, 137.

38. From his analysis of instances of "rights" and related terminology in ECCO (Eighteenth-Century Collections Online), a sizable corpus of eighteenth-century print culture, de Bolla finds that "the Anglophone eighteenth century . . . was never really confronted with the specific problem of making 'human rights' conceptually coherent. All this is to note that the mobility of a conceptual structure may have both enabling and disabling aspects: On the one hand, a 'fuzzy' concept allows one to think outside the parameters currently available . . . while at the same time it prevents the coalescence of a new conceptual form that will generate a truly transformative worldview." Peter de Bolla, *The Architecture of Concepts: The Historical Formation of Human Rights* (New York: Fordham University Press, 2013), 65. For similar transformations over time of the meaning of liberalism, see Helena Rosenblatt, *The Lost History of Liberalism: From Ancient Rome to the Twenty-First Century* (Princeton, NJ: Princeton University Press, 2018), esp. pp. 42–72.

39. See Samuel Moyn, *The Last Utopia: Human Rights in History* (Cambridge, MA: Belknap Press of Harvard University Press, 2010), 20.

40. It is odd that British proslavery novels have until recently been neglected, given that proslavery natural history (by Edward Long, for instance) and other writings have been analyzed in depth by a number of scholars. The relatively scant research focusing on these novels may perhaps be attributed not only to today's readers' discomfort with their noxious politics but also to the relatively modest consumer demand for these novels in their own era, compared to antislavery works. Publishers' records do not indicate that there was more than one edition of *Hamel* or more than two editions of *Marly*—the novels of proslavery propaganda discussed in this study. (Thanks to John Tofanelli at Butler Library at Columbia University for his advice regarding publishers' records.)

41. While in the interim some scholars have addressed the gap indicated by Ian Duncan's criticism, it remains relevant: "Literary historians of the period have failed, by and large, to give a persuasive account of the connections between its dominant aesthetic movement and its ascendant literary genre; a failure compounded by the persistent neglect of its major novelist, Scott. For it is Scott . . . whose transformations of romance decisively transformed the novel." Ian Duncan, *Modern Romance and the Transformations of the Novel: The Gothic, Scott, Dickens* (Cambridge: Cambridge University Press, 1992), 4–5. In his foundational account of novel history, by contrast, Lukács relegates Scott to a dismissive aside: "Such [utopian] longings can indeed be satisfied, but their inner emptiness becomes apparent in the work's lack of idea, as is, for instance, the case with Walter Scott's novels, well-told though they are." György Lukács, *The Theory of the Novel: A Historico-Philosophical Essay on the Forms of Great Epic Literature* (1915; Cambridge, MA: MIT Press, 1971), 115.

42. See James A. Delle, *The Colonial Caribbean: Landscapes of Power in Jamaica's Plantation System* (Cambridge: Cambridge University Press, 2014): "some of the great planters left Jamaica for England, leaving their estates under the control of agents, later to be known in Jamaica as attorneys" (43; see also p. 69).

43. Walter Scott, "Prefatory Memoir to Smollett," in *The Novels of Tobias Smollett, M.D., viz. "Roderick Random," "Peregrine Pickle" and "Humphry Clinker,"* 10 vols., ed. Walter Scott (London: Hurst, Robinson, 1821), 1:i–xlii, i.

44. Katie Trumpener observes, "Scott's *Waverley* redacts Smith's *Desmond* both directly and indirectly, under the influence of the national tale that Smith's novel helps to shape." She compares "Smith's description of the ill-managed aristocratic estate of midrevolutionary France" with "Scott's description, at the end of *Waverley*, of the stately home despoiled during the Jacobite revolution" and remarks, "Like *Desmond*, *Waverley* uses set-piece comparisons to describe the collapse of aristocratic authority. Yet its political inferences end up reversed, Tory rather than Jacobin—a conservative rebellion, not a progressive one." Katie Trumpener, *Bardic Nationalism: The Romantic Novel and the British Empire* (Princeton, NJ: Princeton University Press, 1997), 139, 140. Note that while the political sentiments expressed in *Desmond* align with Jacobin ideology, Smith's other novels treated in this study align with a conservative desire: the reestablishment of a once-powerful family in its ancestral estate.

45. For connections between Maria Edgeworth and antislavery literature (as opposed to the proslavery literature addressed in this study), see Kate Cochran, "'The Plain Round Tale of Faithful Thady': *Castle Rackrent* as Slave Narrative," *New Hibernia Review / Iris Éireannach Nua* 5, no. 4 (Winter 2001): 57–72; and Susan B. Egenolf, "Maria Edgeworth in Blackface: *Castle Rackrent* and the Irish Rebellion of 1798," *ELH* 72, no. 4 (Winter 2005): 845–69.

46. For the variety of courts, see Edward Long, *The History of Jamaica. Or, General Survey of the Antient and Modern State of the Island: with Reflections on Its Situation Settlements, Inhabitants, Climate, Products, Commerce, Laws, and Government,* 3 vols., (London: T. Lowndes, 1774), 1:9–10); and Diana Paton, "Punishment, Crime, and the Bodies of Slaves in Eighteenth-Century Jamaica," *Journal of Social History* 34, no. 4 (Summer 2001): 923–54, 925.

47. John Finlay, *Legal Practice in Eighteenth-Century Scotland* (Leiden: Brill, 2015), 110. For resistance to modern-day impositions of "clear-cut distinctions" among institutions and types of law of centuries past, particularly regarding the Scottish legal tradition, see Lindsay Farmer, *Criminal Law, Tradition, and Legal Order: Crime and the Genius of Scots Law, 1747 to the Present* (Cambridge: Cambridge University Press, 1997), 31.

48. See Edward Gieskes, *Representing the Professions: Administration, Law, and Theater in Early Modern England* (Newark: University of Delaware Press, 2006), 210. [G. Gordon], *The Case of Bankrupts* (1734), cited in Lemmings, 240.

49. Edward Gibbon, "Remarks on Blackstone's Commentaries, Referred to in Mr. Gibbon's Memoirs," in *The Miscellaneous Works of Edward Gibbon, Esq., with Memoirs of His Life and Writings,* 5 vols. (London, 1814), 5:545–47, 545.

50. Wai Chee Dimock, *Residues of Justice: Literature, Law, Philosophy* (1996; Berkeley: University of California Press, 1997), 8.

51. See Robert Henryson, "The Sheep and the Dog," in *The Poems of Robert Henryson,* ed. Denton Fox (Oxford: Clarendon, 1981), 47–54, 51, lines 1258–59. For an appraisal of the fable as a "pointed satire on legal corruption" that relies on "detailed social figuration, with animals representing various social groups," see Edward Wheatley, "Scholastic Commentary and Robert Henryson's 'Morall Fabillis': The Aesopic Fables," *Studies in Philology* 91, no. 1 (Winter 1994): 70–99, 83–84.

52. An editorial in a prominent periodical warned that the IRS was "targeting conservative groups." "Will Predatory IRS Be Brought to Justice?" editorial, *Investor's Business Daily*, 10 August 2016, www.investors.com/politics/editorials/will-predatory -irs-finally-be-brought-to-justice.

53. Another example (of many) of rhetoric in which victimhood is invoked, in the context of immigration policy debates, as a rationale for exercise of power: during a televised debate in 2016 among Republican presidential candidates, Senator Marco Rubio declared, "The entire system of legal immigration must now be reexamined for security first and foremost" to thwart would-be terrorists who "have a sophisticated understanding of our legal immigration system and are able to use that system against us." "Transcript: Sixth Republican Top-Tier Debate 2016," *CBS News*, 15 Jan. 2016, www.cbsnews.com/news/transcript-sixth-republican-top-tier-debate-2016.

54. Jennifer Rubin, "Conservative Victimhood," *Washington Post*, 17 Sept. 2013, www.washingtonpost.com/blogs/right-turn/wp/2013/09/17/conservative-victimhood /?utm_term=.c50bb3a4b5d0.

55. See, e.g., Stephanie Russo, "'Where Virtue Struggles Midst a Maze of Snares': Mary Robinson's *Vancenza* (1792) and the Gothic Novel," *Women's Writing* 20, no. 4 (2013): 586–601; and Allen W. Grove, "Coming Out of the Castle: Gothic, Sexuality and the Limits of Language," *Historical Reflections/Réflexions Historiques* 26, no. 3 (Fall 2000): 429–46.

Chapter 1 • Bad Citizens and Insolent Foreigners

1. Tobias Smollett, *The Life and Adventures of Sir Launcelot Greaves*, ed. Robert Folkenflik (Athens: University of Georgia Press, 2002), 3. All subsequent citations from the novel refer to this edition and will be noted parenthetically in the text.

2. For society's most vulnerable, legal agency could be secured, paradoxically, through public declaration of one's utter destitution: the phrase *in forma pauperis* (in the form of a poor man) refers to procedure established by statute, implemented in 1495, which held that an impoverished would-be plaintiff could obtain legal representation if two lawyers signed an affidavit that the prospective litigant had a net worth of fewer than five pounds and thus qualified for gratis legal representation. Those who lost their cases could be publicly whipped, forced to repay costs, or, in the eighteenth century, imprisoned— punishments that were meant to discourage fraud but, of course, discouraged those who qualified from availing themselves of the option. The very need, however, for a process for identifying those who were truly deserving of legal assistance indicates the extent to which such worthiness was far from self-evident. See Joan Mahoney, "Green Forms and Legal Aid Offices: A History of Publicly Funded Legal Services in Britain and the United States," *Saint Louis University Public Law Review* 17, no. 2 (1998): 223–40, 226. Legal scholars have demonstrated that obtaining counsel *in forma pauperis* was not a viable solution for many poor litigants and thus did little to level the playing field of an inequi- table legal system. David L. Shapiro notes, "In civil matters, formidable barriers con- fronted a litigant who wished to proceed in forma pauperis, barriers compounded by substantial restrictions on gratuitous services for the poor prior to the twentieth century." Criminal defendants could not avail themselves of the remedy because they had to represent themselves in court. David L. Shapiro, "The Enigma of the Lawyer's Duty to Serve," *New York University Law Review* 55, no. 5 (Nov. 1980): 735–92, 745.

3. See Seyla Benhabib, *Transformations of Citizenship: Dilemmas of the Nation State in the Era of Globalization: Two Lectures* (Amsterdam: Koninklijke van Gorcum, 2001), 54. Marianne Noble studies the unique, now-defunct English institution of the "mixed jury" for insights into how "the preservation of customs as practices served to separate communities and to distinguish their members from one another" in a context where "communities were . . . lacking in physical and geographical definition and containing few guidelines as to who their own 'citizens' were." In pre-fourteenth-century English courts, Jews, foreigners, and others were judged by members of their particular community, as well as by local English people. Alien persons were seen as having the same right as did nonaliens to be judged by the customs of the community to which they belonged. Marianne Noble, *The Law of the Other: The Mixed Jury and Changing Conceptions of Citizenship, Law, and Knowledge* (Chicago: University of Chicago Press, 1994), 14, 2. Christopher Warren explores "the problematic of the made," that is, of the "constructedness" both of international law and of "the ways differing genres distribute international subject-hood and object-hood." Christopher N. Warren, *Literature and the Law of Nations: 1580–1680* (Oxford: Oxford University Press, 2015), 14, 23.

4. Benhabib, *Transformations of Citizenship*, 54.

5. Hannah Arendt, "The Decline of the Nation-State and the End of the Rights of Man," in *The Origins of Totalitarianism*, new ed. (1951; New York: Harcourt, Inc./ Harvest, 1994), 267–302, 296.

6. George Morrow Kahrl, *Tobias Smollett, Traveler-Novelist* (Chicago: University of Chicago Press, 1945), 51. J. Paul Hunter identifies Smollett as "a historian and journalist," noting that "because novelists as writers in an emerging species were consciously seeking ways of finding and engaging an audience for their work, the so-called subliterary 'background' was more than a cultural context and potential 'source' of subject matter and technique. . . . Most early novelists learned their craft as didacticists by writing in one or more of the approved subkinds." J. Paul Hunter, *Before Novels: The Cultural Contexts of Eighteenth-Century English Fiction* (New York: Norton, 1990), 296, 295.

7. Paul-Gabriel Boucé comments: "It is difficult to raise these novels [*Fathom* and *Greaves*] to the first rank, but they deserve to emerge from the darkness and quasi-oblivion to which a hasty and superficial reading has relegated them for two centuries." Paul-Gabriel Boucé, *The Novels of Tobias Smollett*, trans. Antonia White in collaboration with the author (London: Longman, 1976), 190.

8. A representative example: in opening his introduction to the latest edited edition of *Ferdinand Count Fathom*, Jerry C. Beasley notes, "*Ferdinand Count Fathom* in particular suffered neglect at the hands of reviewers and readers; and Smollett, after two comparative failures in a row, wrote no more fiction for seven years. Now it is true that *Ferdinand Count Fathom* has always been considered one of its author's lesser achievements." Jerry C. Beasley, introduction to Tobias Smollett, *Ferdinand Count Fathom*, ed. Jerry C. Beasley and O M Brack Jr. (Athens: University of Georgia Press, 1988), xix–xliii, xix. Summarizing critical perspectives in 1977, John Sekora wrote, "Because he did not publish an important novel between 1751 and 1771, it has generally been assumed that he had entered an arid period, writing much but accomplishing little." John Sekora, *Luxury: The Concept in Western Thought, Eden to Smollett* (Baltimore: Johns Hopkins University Press, 1977), 11.

9. See, e.g., the emphasis on Smollett's innovations in satire in Ronald Paulson, *Satire and the Novel in Eighteenth-Century England* (New Haven: Yale University Press, 1967), 165–218. For Smollett and the picaresque, see Robert Donald Spector, *Tobias George Smollett* (New York: Twayne, 1968), 107–26; and John Skinner, *Constructions of Smollett: A Study of Genre and Gender* (Newark: University of Delaware Press, 1996), 119–40; and, more recently, Richard Squibbs, "Tobias Smollett's *Ferdinand Count Fathom*: The Purpose of Picaresque," *Eighteenth-Century Fiction* 30, no. 4 (Summer 2018): 519–37. Some scholars question the categorization of Smollett's work as picaresque: see Donald Bruce, *Radical Doctor Smollett* (London: Victor Gollancz, 1964), 166–68; and Simon Dickie, "Tobias Smollett and the Ramble Novel," in *English and British Fiction, 1750–1820*, ed. Peter Garside and Karen O'Brien (Oxford: Oxford University Press, 2015), 92–108, 103. For a recent overview of Smollett studies, see Richard J. Jones, "Tobias Smollett and the Work of Writing," *Literature Compass* 15 (2018): 1–10.

10. See, e.g., K. G. Simpson, "The Scot as English Novelist," in *Smollett: Author of the First Distinction*, ed. Alan Bold (London: Vision, 1982), 64–105; and the discussion of "transculturation" in *Humphry Clinker* in Charlotte Sussman, *Consuming Anxieties: Consumer Protest, Gender and British Slavery, 1713–1833* (Stanford, CA: Stanford University Press: 2000), 81–109, 85–92.

11. E. Anthony Wrigley observes, "During the eighteenth century the urban hierarchy of England was turned upside down. The new industrial towns and port capitals of the north and the midlands thrust their way past all rivals other than London." E. Anthony Wrigley, "Urban Growth and Agricultural Change: England and the Continent in the Early Modern Period," in *The Eighteenth-Century Town: A Reader in English Urban History, 1688–1820*, ed. Peter Borsay (1990; repr. New York: Routledge, 2014), 39–82, 78. He states: "The upsetting of the old urban hierarchy in England was, at the time, an event without precedent in European history. Elsewhere the exact ranking of major cities in each country varied from time to time, but it was rare for tiny settlement[s] to develop into major centers. . . . The history of urban growth in England was distinctive. The contrast with the course of events elsewhere in Europe was especially notable between 1600 and 1750, since the paralysis which affected all but the largest towns on the continent was absent in England" (79). Peter Borsay explains that in scholarship on the population growth of towns in England and Wales, "critical attention has focused on the role of migration, since (given the high mortality rates found in towns) it was only this that could have instigated the level of urban increase achieved during the eighteenth century." Peter Borsay, introduction to *The Eighteenth-Century Town*, 1–38, 7. From analysis of diocesan court deposition data that yield what he calls "a nice cross-section of southern and midland England," Peter Clark has found that between 1660 and 1730, almost two out of every three deponents changed their parish or domicile at least once in their lives; on average, only 34.9 percent of men never changed residences, compared to 30.3 percent of women, and farthest moves were much more likely to have been intracounty or beyond, rather than intratown. Peter Clark, "Migration in England during the Late Seventeenth and Early Eighteenth Centuries," *Past and Present* 83 (1979): 57–90, 64, 65, 67.

12. Bradin Cormack, *A Power to Do Justice: Jurisdiction, English Literature, and the Rise of Common Law, 1509–1625* (Chicago: University of Chicago Press, 2007), 38.

13. Meanwhile, a widow—a member of one of the protected classes explicitly mentioned by Clarke—is unmasked, at the very end of the novel, as one of the novel's villains: she uses her sophisticated knowledge of the law to deprive Captain Crowe of his inheritance.

14. T. H. Marshall, "Citizenship and Social Class," in *Citizenship and Social Class and Other Essays* (Cambridge: Cambridge University Press, 1950), 1–85, 14, 10. As Marshall acknowledges, "To make the eighteenth century cover the formative period of civil rights it must be stretched backwards to include Habeas Corpus, the Toleration Act, and the abolition of the censorship of the press; and it must be extended forwards to include Catholic Emancipation, the repeal of the Combination Acts, and the successful end of the battle for the freedom of the press associated with the names of [William] Cobbett and Richard Carlile. It could then be more accurately, but less briefly, described as the period between the Revolution and the first Reform Act" (14–15).

15. Marshall, 10–11.

16. The influence of Smollett's history writings is evidenced by the immense popularity for his first multivolume historical work, *The Complete History of England*. Richard J. Jones notes "the spectacular sales of Smollett's *Complete History*, which may at its height have reached 10,000 numbers per week." Richard J. Jones, "Continued Continuations of Complete Histories: Tobias Smollett and the Work of History," *Journal for Eighteenth-Century Studies* 41, no. 3 (Sept. 2018): 391–406, 392. The mistaken impression persists that Smollett's historical work was merely a resumption of David Hume's *The History of England*. Although Thomas Cadell published a 1785 edition of Smollett's work (*The History of England from the Revolution to George the Second*) with a title page proclaiming it was "designed as a continuation of Mr. Hume's History," Richard Jones claims that Cadell's statement misrepresents both authors' works, which were originally published independently; see Jones, "Continued Continuations," 391–92.

17. According to John Locke, anyone "travelling freely on the Highway" within the borders of a given state is required to abide by the laws of that state. John Locke, "The Second Treatise of Government: An Essay Concerning the True Original, Extent, and End of Civil Government," in *Two Treatises of Government* [1689], ed. Peter Laslett, 2nd ed. (Cambridge: Cambridge University Press, 1988), 366. Yet mere location within a state's borders does not amount to membership within that state: "Nothing can make any man so, but his actually entering into it by positive engagement, and express promise and compact" (367).

18. Amy Buzby, "Locking the Borders: Exclusion in the Theory and Practice of Immigration in America," *International Migration Review* 52, no. 1 (Spring 2018): 273–98, 275.

19. Stanley Ayling, *John Wesley* (Cleveland, OH: William Collins, 1979), 318.

20. David Feldman, "Migrants, Immigrants, and Welfare from the Old Poor Law to the Welfare State," *Transactions of the Royal History Society* 13 (2003): 79–104, 84. Wesley deplored the obstacles confronting poor people attempting to afford legal representation or access to justice. In a 1745 essay, he wrote, "Suppose a great man, with or without form of law, does wrong to his poor neighbour. What will you do? Sue his lordship at common law? Have the cause tried at the next sessions or assizes? Alas! Your own neighbours, who know the whole case, will tell you, 'You are out of your

senses.' . . . Without *money*, you can have no more *law*; *poverty* alone utterly shuts out *justice.*" John Wesley, *A Farther Appeal to Men of Reason and Religion*, pt. 2 [1745], in *The Appeals to Men of Reason and Religion and Certain Related Open Letters*, ed. Gerald R. Cragg (Oxford: Clarendon, 1975), 233.

21. Feldman, 84.

22. John Wesley to Ezekiel Cooper, 1 Feb. 1791, in *The Letters of the Rev. John Wesley*, ed. John Telford, 8 vols. (London: Epworth, 1931), 8:259–60, 260.

23. Benedict Anderson, *Imagined Communities: Reflections on the Origin and Spread of Nationalism*, rev. ed (1983; London: Verso, 2006), 6. Anderson is describing in his own words—and objecting to (and perhaps distorting)—Gellner's comment that "nationalism . . . invents nations where they do not exist." Ernest Gellner, *Thought and Change* (Chicago: University of Chicago Press, 1964), 168. Frederick Buell defends Gellner's phrasing (opposed by Anderson to "imagining" and "creating"): "The term has to be startling to foreground the artificiality, or better, the 'artifactuality,' of national communities and cultures. Moreover, in a postmodern context, 'fabricated' no longer implies a deviation from 'true.' It quickly becomes a normative term, not a term for violation of a norm." Frederick Buell, *National Culture and the New Global System* (Baltimore: Johns Hopkins University Press, 1994), 43.

24. Anderson, 6.

25. Tobias Smollett, *The Adventures of Ferdinand Count Fathom*, ed. Jerry C. Beasley and O M Brack Jr. (Athens: University of Georgia Press, 1988), 144–45. Subsequent citations are from this edition and will be given parenthetically in the text.

26. The original edition is Ferdinand Tönnies, *Gemeinschaft und Gesellschaft* (Leipzig: Fues's Verlag, 1887). The edition cited here is Ferdinand Tönnies, *Community and Society*, trans. Charles P. Loomis (East Lansing: Michigan State University Press, 1957), 33–35.

27. Adam Smith, *The Theory of Moral Sentiments*, rev. ed. (1790), ed. D. D. Raphael and A. L. Macfie (Oxford: Clarendon, 1976), 223. Evan Gottlieb notes that in lauding such developments, Smith does not acknowledge that assimilation was coerced rather than freely chosen by the Highlanders he uses as examples. Evan Gottlieb, *Feeling British: Sympathy and National Identity in Scottish and English Writing, 1707–1832* (Lewisburg, PA: Bucknell University Press, 2007), 37–38.

28. This solution was considered and ultimately rejected by the German legal theorist Samuel Pufendorf, whom Smollett frequently cites. Pufendorf's monumental treatises reflected on the rights of refugees and foreign travelers in the wake of the 1648 Treaty of Westphalia (which stemmed the tide of refugees fleeing the carnage of the Thirty Years War, during which German territories lost 40 percent of their population to other Continental nations). Pufendorf profoundly influenced eighteenth-century discourse on sovereignty. See Eve Lester, *Making Migration Law: The Foreigner, Sovereignty, and the Case of Australia* (Cambridge: Cambridge University Press, 2017), 69.

29. For the mid-eighteenth-century British context in which an individual's social value was typically correlated with that person's status, see Michael McKeon, *The Origins of the English Novel*, 15th anniv. ed. (Baltimore: Johns Hopkins University Press, 2002), xxii–xxiii.

30. Jacques Derrida, "Autoimmunity: Real and Symbolic Suicides—A Dialogue with Jacques Derrida," in *Philosophy in a Time of Terror: Dialogues with Jürgen Habermas*

and Jacques Derrida, ed. Giovanna Borradori (Chicago: University of Chicago Press, 2003), 94. For a more medically accurate revision of Derrida's model and consideration of the application of the autoimmunity metaphor to "the laws determining the functioning of the social body," see Andrea Timár, "Derrida and the Immune System," in "Terror(ism) and Aesthetics," ed. György Fogarasi, Zoltán Cora, and Ervin Török, special issue, *Et al.: Critical Theory Online* (2015): http://etal.hu/en/archive/terrorism -and-aesthetics-2015/derrida-and-the-immune-system.

31. Sussman, *Consuming Anxieties*, 84.

32. Ian Campbell Ross, "Smollett and the Jew Bill of 1753," *American Notes and Queries* 16, no. 4 (Dec. 1977): 54–55, 55.

33. See Misty Anderson, *Imagining Methodism in Eighteenth-Century Britain: Belief, Enthusiasm, and the Borders of the Self* (Baltimore: Johns Hopkins University Press, 2012), 200–203; and Byron Gassman, "Religious Attitudes in the World of Humphry Clinker," *BYU Studies* 6, no. 2 (1965): 65–72.

34. See Richard Falk, "The Making of Global Citizenship," in *The Condition of Citizenship*, ed. Bart van Steenbergen (London: Sage, 1994), 127–40, 134, 135.

35. The reverse, of course, is also seen when refusal to uphold legal responsibilities occasions relatives' distancing. Joan I. Schwarz observes the centrality to Richardson's masterpiece of "disruptions in the traditional legal transactions" initially expected to take place between Clarissa and her relatives. Joan I. Schwarz, "Family Dynamics and Property Acquisitions in *Clarissa*," in *Reading the Family Dance: Family Systems Therapy and Literary Study*, ed. John V. Knapp and Kenneth Womack (Newark: University of Delaware Press, 2003), 111–34, 111.

36. At the close of each of these works, community relationships, rather than membership in a family, is emphasized: when Greaves weds Aurelia at the close of *Greaves*, their families (all deceased, save for Aurelia's evil uncle) go unmentioned, and the spotlight is not on the newlyweds' love for each other but on the villagers' grateful homage to their benefactors.

37. Aileen Douglas, *Uneasy Sensations: Smollett and the Body* (Chicago: University of Chicago Press, 1995), 117.

38. Although Walter Scott emphasizes Smollett's speed of composition and downplays his legal experience as factors in the novel's composition, he does note that "Smollett's recent imprisonment in the King's Bench, for the attack on Admiral Knowles, enabled him to enrich his romance." Walter Scott, *Lives of the Novelists*, vol. 1 (Philadelphia: H. C. Carey / New York: Collins and Hannay, 1825], 81–141, 115. Alice Parker observes that Smollett was familiar with the environment even before he became an inmate: "Smollett's novels are rich in characters, scenes, and situations having to do with prisons and courts. He acquired some knowledge of prisons long before he was committed to the King's Bench for libel. The descriptions of the Fleet and the Marshalsea in his first three novels are as full as that of the King's Bench Prison in *Sir Launcelot Greaves*, which is certainly based upon his own experience. On the contrary, what he has to say about the 'Bastile,' a prison which he could hardly have known at first hand, is not nearly so rich in details." Alice Parker, "Tobias Smollett and the Law," *Studies in Philology* 39, no. 3 (July 1942): 545–58, 545.

39. Susan Byrne, *Law and History in Cervantes' "Don Quixote"* (Toronto: University of Toronto Press, 2012), 5.

40. Robert Folkenflik writes, "On or about 28 November 1760, midway through the serial publication of *Sir Launcelot Greaves*, Smollett was committed to the King's Bench Prison, where he remained for nearly three months. Certainly, his time in prison influenced the setting of chapters 20 and 21 of *Sir Launcelot Greaves*; it may also have furnished him with models for his characters." Robert Folkenflik, introduction to *The Life and Adventures of Sir Launcelot Greaves*, by Tobias Smollett, ed. Barbara Laning Fitzpatrick (Athens: University of Georgia Press, 2002), xvii–liv, xix. Folkenflik notes "an earlier misleading comment in the *Westminster Magazine* (1775) suggesting that Smollett wrote *Sir Launcelot Greaves* in prison" but concludes, "Probably a few chapters, perhaps more, were completed during Smollett's months in the King's Bench Prison" (xix). Folkenflik posits that "Scott was probably being unfair" in his account of Smollett retiring to dash off copy for the novel an hour before the post came to collect it, but he acknowledges that "Smollett did work quickly" (xix).

41. Smollett to the Hon. Alexander Campbell, 23 February 1753, *Letters of Tobias Smollett*, ed. Lewis M. Knapp (Oxford: Clarendon, 1970), 21–26, 23. All subsequent citations from the letter refer to this edition and will be noted parenthetically in the text.

42. Smollett to Campbell, 25.

43. Eighteenth-century libel cases adhered to the earlier premise that "it is not material whether the libel be true." *De libellis famosis*, 3 Co. Rep. 254, 255, pt. 5, fol. 125, 77 Eng. Rep. 250, 251 (1605). See also Robert Post, "The Social Foundations of Defamation Law: Reputation and the Constitution," *California Law Review* 74, no. 3 (May 1986): 691–742, 704.

44. Tobias Smollett, *The Adventures of Peregrine Pickle*, ed. John P. Zomchick and George S. Rousseau (Athens: University of Georgia Press, 2014), 223.

45. Lewis Mansfield Knapp, *Tobias Smollett: Doctor of Men and Manners* (Princeton, NJ: Princeton University Press, 1949), 158.

46. According to Ronald Paulson, "Fathom is to some extent that traditional figure of the English picaresque, the criminal who unwittingly serves to reveal the folly of his dupes as well as his own knavery." Ronald Paulson, *Satire and the Novel in Eighteenth-Century England* (New Haven, CT: Yale University Press, 1967), 188. I argue that Fathom's criminality occasions another exposure as well: that of the injustice proliferating in the courts.

47. In devising this absurd scenario, Smollett establishes Fathom's outsider status as the defining aspect of his identity. Although statutes were implemented in Britain after 1700 to guarantee that a father who was a natural-born British subject passed this status on to his children born abroad, there were no such provisions for maternal descent. See Susan Staves, "Resentment or Resignation? Dividing the Spoils among Daughters and Younger Sons," in *Early Modern Conceptions of Property*, ed. John Brewer and Susan Staves (London: Routledge, 1995), 194–218, 208. As several eighteenth-century legal cases clarified, "The key to being 'natural born' was the child's father; having a natural born mother but an alien father left the child an alien." Mary Brigid McManamon, "The Natural Born Citizen Clause as Originally Understood," *Catholic University Law Review* 64, no. 2 (2015): 317–58, 327.

48. Mistaken for a man who, despite growing up entirely abroad, laid claim to the English throne based on ancestral right, Fathom's plight compels the reader to see that self-recognition can never be enough to establish one's belonging and rights within a community.

49. For foreign defendants in eighteenth-century England, "interpreters did not have to be neutral parties. They could be . . . most disturbingly, the principal witness against the person requiring their services." Karen A. Macfarlane, "Understanding Justice: Criminal Courtroom Interpretation in Eighteenth-Century London and Twenty-First-Century Toronto," *TTR: Traduction, terminologie, rédaction* 20, no. 2 (2007): 271–99, 282. The availability of interpreter services correlated with status: "In matters involving people of high status, there was more consideration," noting the multiple interpreters provided to a Polish count accused of murder, "but most criminal trials did not involve defendants with such social or financial resources" (Macfarlane, 281).

50. Proceedings in Courts of Justice Act 1730, St. 4 Geo. 2 c. 26. See also Ana Aliverti and Rachel Seoighe, "Lost in Translation? Examining the Role of Court Interpreters in Cases Involving Foreign National Defendants in England and Wales," *New Criminal Law Review* 20, no. 1 (Winter 2017): 130–56.

51. See José Ortega y Gasset, "La picardía original de la novel picaresca," in *Obras completas*, vol. 2 (Madrid: Catédra, 1962), 121–25; cited in Gordana Yovanovich, *Play and the Picaresque: "Lazarillo de Tormes," "Libro de Manuel," and "Match Ball"* (Toronto: University of Toronto Press, 1999), 50.

52. Todd M. Endelman, *The Jews of Georgian England, 1714–1830: Tradition and Change in a Liberal Society* (Ann Arbor: University of Michigan Press, 1979), 15–17.

53. Harm Reijnderd Sientjo van der Veen, *Jewish Characters in Eighteenth-Century English Fiction and Drama* (Groningen: J. B. Wolters' Uitgevers-Maatschappij, 1935), 45–46.

54. J. Hillis Miller, *Communities in Fiction* (New York: Fordham University Press, 2014), 22.

55. Dana Y. Rabin, *Britain and Its Internal Others, 1750–1800: Under Rule of Law* (Manchester: Manchester University Press, 2017), 50. See also Clive Parry, *British Nationality Law and the History of Naturalisation* (Milan: Università di Milano, 1954), 22. J. Mervyn Jones remarks: "From the seventeenth century up through the passing of the Aliens Act [in] 1844 . . . acts were passed naturalizing certain specified classes of aliens. Apart, however, from these special Acts of Parliament there was no method of becoming naturalized." J. Mervyn Jones, *British Nationality Law*, rev. ed. (Oxford: Clarendon, 1956), 64.

56. G. H. Maynadier, introduction to Smollett, *The Adventures of Count Fathom* [note title altered from Smollett's original], vol. 8 of *The Works of Tobias Smollett*, 12 vols. (New York: Jenson Society, 1907), xiii–xxxi, xv–xvi.

57. In the 1930s, for example, Harm Reijnderd Sientjo van der Veen devoted an entire chapter to Smollett's depiction of Jewish characters, claiming that Smollett wrote "the first pleasant words for the Jews in English literature" (van der Veen, *Jewish Characters*, 41). He claimed that the portrayal in *Ferdinand Count Fathom* showed Smollett's support for the Jewish Naturalization Bill: "Of all the eighteenth century novelists none perhaps paid so much attention to the Jews as Tobias Smollett. . . . Fortunately this attention was not all of the kind described in the preceding chapter, in which we saw in what black colours the Jew is invariably painted by the early eighteenth century prose writers" (van der Veen, 37).

Writing in the 1960s, Tuvia Bloch tempered this claim: "The episodes in which Joshua [Manasseh] appears permit us to infer little more than that Smollett was attempting to support the promoters of the so-called Jew Bill"; she further states:

"Certainly there is no evidence of Smollett's strong humanitarian spirit in the commentary he wrote [in *Continuation*] on the passage and repeal of the Bill, which in fact disclosed why he should not have hesitated to insert pejorative remarks about the Jews in his later works." Tuvia Bloch, "Smollett and the Jewish Naturalization Bill of 1753," *American Notes and Queries* 6, no. 8 (April 1968): 116–17, 117. I agree that Smollett's aims were not "humanitarian" but identify a different reason for his support.

In the late 1970s, Ian Campbell Ross in turn reproached Bloch's claim as wrongly drawing a connection between the bill and the novel: "Bloch's suggestion has not been questioned. . . . The Act, however, was not introduced into parliament [*sic*] until some six weeks *after* the publication of Smollett's novel" (Ross, "Smollett and the Jew Bill of 1753," 54). Yet Ross does not consider the larger context. As Thomas W. Perry observed earlier, "Of course the Jew Bill of 1753 did not come into existence simply because the London Sephardim suddenly perceived in that year that their problems with regard to naturalization and alien duties could be solved only by such legislation. As early as 1746 the Spanish and Portuguese Synagogue had appointed a standing 'committee of deputies' to lobby, as we say nowadays, for a change in the naturalization laws; and doubtless the subject had been discussed in the community long before that." Thomas W. Perry, *Public Opinion, Propaganda, and Politics in Eighteenth-Century England: A Study of the Jew Bill of 1753* (Cambridge, MA: Harvard University Press, 1962), 17.

In the 1990s, Frank Felsenstein argued that while Smollett's novel could not have reflected debate over the bill itself, "Smollett may have been aware that the Naturalization Bill was pending," as Smollett alludes to the bill in *The History and Adventures of an Atom* (1769). Yet Felsenstein states, "Manasseh is, however, perhaps the earliest noble Jew in English literature. . . . Elsewhere, the [Jewish naturalization] controversy barely impinges directly on the works of 'canonical' writers." Frank Felsenstein, *Anti-Semitic Stereotypes: A Paradigm of Otherness in English Popular Culture, 1660–1830* (Baltimore: Johns Hopkins University Press, 1995), 309–10n64.

58. Endelman, *Jews of Georgian England*, 14, 15–19; H. S. Q. [Henry Straus Quixano] Henriques, *The Return of the Jews to England; Being a Chapter in the History of England* (London: Macmillan, 1905), 76–78.

59. Avinoam Yuval-Naeh, "The 1753 Jewish Naturalization Bill and the Polemic over Credit," *Journal of British Studies* 57, no. 3 (July 2018): 467–92, 468–69.

60. *Wells v. Williams*, 1 *Lord Raymond*, 282, cited in H. S. Q. Henriques, *The Jews and the English Law* (Oxford: Printed by Horace Hart, at the University Press, 1908), 189.

61. Tobias Smollett, *Continuation of the Complete History of England*, 5 vols. (London: Printed for Richard Baldwin, 1760–61, 1765), 1:142.

62. Smollett, 1:143.

63. Smollett, 1:144.

64. Archaicus [pseud.], *Admonitions from Scripture and History, from Religion and Common Prudence, Relating to the Jews* (London, Printed for R. Baldwin, jun., 1753), 26.

65. Britannia [pseud.], *An Appeal to the Throne against the Naturalization of the Jewish Nation* (London: Printed for J. Bouquet, 1753), 22.

66. Smollett, *Continuation*, 2:144.

67. See Perry, *Public Opinion*, 134–61. Also see Endelman, *Jews of Georgian England*, 114; and chapter 6 of David Katz, *The Jews in the History of England, 1485–1850* (Oxford: Clarendon, 1994).

68. "Matthew Bramble to Dr. Lewis, September 20," in Tobias Smollett, *The Expedition of Humphry Clinker*, ed. Thomas R. Preston and O M Brack Jr. (Athens: University of Georgia Press, 1990), 265.

69. The two had reconciled after an earlier quarrel.

70. One contemporary assessment was an unsigned three-sentence article published by the *Critical Review*, which was edited by Smollett, and lauded the playwright as a "genius" but lamented that the play "could have been shorter . . . and more entertaining. . . . It may not set the galleries in a roar." *Critical Review*, Feb. 1757, 159–60 (repr. in *Tobias Smollett: The Critical Heritage*, ed. Lionel Kelly [London: Routledge and Kegan Paul, 1987], 115). A still terser one-sentence account in the *Monthly Review* simply marveled that the play had, "by some unnatural accident, . . . [been] exhibited eight nights." *Monthly Review*, Feb. 1757, 179 (repr. in Kelly, 116). The play's reputation did not improve in the nineteenth century: the entirety of a representative account reads: "This F. was written by Smollett—it has considerable merit, but it is better calculated for representation than perusal, and for the amusement of the gallery than the pit—is a very illiberal attack on the French." John Genest, *Some Account of the English Stage, from the Restoration to 1830*, 10 vols. (Bath: Printed by H. E. Carrington, 1832), 4:480.

71. Paul-Gabriel Boucé, *The Novels of Tobias Smollett*, trans. Antonia White (London: Longman, 1976), 24–25. The play is mentioned in Evan Gottlieb, *Feeling British: Sympathy and National Identity in Scottish and English Writing, 1707–1832* (Lewisburg, PA: Bucknell University Press, 1997), 72–73; and Frédéric Ogée, "'Channelling Emotions': Travel and Literary Creation in Smollett and Sterne," special issue, *Studies on Voltaire and the Eighteenth Century* 292 (1991): 27–42, 28–29, 30.

72. Byron Gassman comments in the only edited edition of the play: "As is evident from the play's later references to Grotius and Pufendorf . . . Smollett's wide reading had familiarized him with the basic concepts and elementary jargon of seventeenth- and eighteenth-century international law." Tobias Smollett, *Poems, Plays, and "The Briton,"* ed. O M Brack Jr. and Byron Gassman, assisted by Leslie A. Chilton (Athens: University of Georgia Press, 1993), 468n20. Smollett later referred to the work of Pufendorf (whose surname he spells as "Puffendorf") and Grotius in *The History and Adventures of an Atom*: "The judicious and learned Puffendorf, in his book *De Jure Gentium & Naturali*, declares, that a man's honour is not so fragile as to be hurt either by a box on the ear, or a kick on the breech, otherwise it would be in the power of every saucy fellow to diminish or infringe it.—It must be owned, indeed, Grotius *De Jure Belli & Pacis*, says, that charity does not of itself require our patiently suffering such an affront." Tobias Smollett, *The History and Adventures of an Atom*, ed. O M Brack Jr. and Robert Adams Day (Athens: University of Georgia Press, 1989), 100.

73. Hugo Grotius, *The Free Sea*, trans. Richard Hakluyt, ed. David Armitage (Indianapolis: Liberty Fund, 2004). Grotius claims that no nation can claim possession (*dominium*) over the sea or jurisdiction (*imperium*) to prevent others from navigating it.

74. Samuel Pufendorf, *Of the Law of Nature and Nations* (London: Printed for J. Walthoe, R. Wilkin, J. and J. Bonwicke, S. Birt, T. Ward, and T. Osborne, 1729), 241. Perhaps he is reflecting on his own experience, when a young man, of being unlawfully arrested by Swedish authorities in retaliation toward the German government.

Pufendorf devotes attention specifically to the plight of "travellers" and "strangers" throughout his writings.

75. Tobias Smollett, *The Reprisal: or, The Tars of Old England*, in *Poems, Plays, and "The Briton,"* ed. O M Brack Jr. and Byron Gassman, assisted by Leslie A. Chilton (Athens: University of Georgia Press, 1993), 173–218, 1.3.183. All citations of *The Reprisal* refer to this edition and are referenced by act, scene, and page; subsequent citations will be given parenthetically in the text.

76. See Gottlieb, *Feeling British*, 73.

77. Smollett, *Continuation*, 3:383–84.

78. Greaves's self-description has significant connotations: a coadjutor bishop is "an assistant to an old and infirm bishop" (*OED*) and is expected to assume the position after the latter's retirement or death, so that there will be no period of vacancy before a successor is appointed. The implication could be that Greaves anticipates that his own benevolent rule will replace the obsolescent, defective rule of law. For the theological definition of *coadjutor*, see Colin Buchanan, *The A to Z of Anglicanism* (Lanham, MD: Scarecrow, 2009), 102. See also Robert Martin Adams, *The Land and Literature of England: An Historical Account* (New York: Norton, 1983), 517.

79. For the dispute over the extent to which Smollett's translation was his own, see Martin C. Battestin, "The Authorship of Smollett's *Don Quixote*," *Studies in Bibliography* 50 (1997): 295–321.

80. Tobias Smollett, *The Life and Adventures of Sir Launcelot Greaves*, ed. Barbara Laning Fitzpatrick (Athens: University of Georgia Press, 2002), 15. All citations of the novel refer to this edition unless otherwise indicated; subsequent citations will be given parenthetically in the text.

81. Smollett, *Sir Launcelot Greaves*, 17.

82. Folkenflik, introduction, xxx.

83. Alice Parker, "Tobias Smollett and the Law," *Studies in Philology* 39, no. 3 (July 1942): 545–58, 558.

84. Fabel argues that "Smollett's criticism is directed not at the government, nor here at the agents of the government, but rather against the vindictiveness of individuals, particularly heartless creditors, who distort the purposes of what is evidently, for Smollett, thoroughly sound law. It should be noted that . . . there is no quarrel with institutions as they existed, unless manned by oppressors, and there is great faith in the laws of England."

85. See Ronald Paulson, *Satire and the Novel in Eighteenth-Century England* (New Haven, CT: Yale University Press, 1967), 190; Robin Fabel, "The Patriotic Briton: Tobias Smollett and English Politics, 1756–1777," *Eighteenth-Century Studies* 8, no. 1 (1974): 100–114, 106; and Thomas A. Critchley, *A History of Police in England and Wales* (Montclair, NJ: Patterson Smith, 1972), 18.

86. Philip Stevick, "Stylistic Energy in the Early Smollett," *Studies in Philology* 64, no. 5 (Oct. 1967): 712–19, 719, 717.

87. Stevick, 718.

88. Sharyn Roach Anleu and Wilfred Prest, "Litigation: Historical and Contemporary Dimensions," in *Litigation: Past and Present*, ed. Wilfred Prest and Sharyn Roach Anleu (Sydney: University of New South Wales Press, 2004), 1–23, 1.

89. Ann M. Carlos and Jennifer Lamping, "Conformity and the Certificate of Discharge: Bankruptcy in Early Eighteenth-Century England" (unpublished manuscript prepared for the 2010 annual meeting of the Economic Historians Association), 3.

90. Ian P. H. Duffy, *Bankruptcy and Insolvency in London during the Industrial Revolution* (New York: Garland, 1985), 17.

91. Earl F. Briden, "Smollett and the Bankruptcy Laws," *Notes and Queries* 223 (Feb. 1978): 45–47, 46, 45.

92. Smollett, *Continuation*, 3:34.

93. Smollett, 3:35. Lamenting in a subsequent volume of the *Continuation* that a clause in the 1761 Act of Insolvency, which facilitated amnesty for debt, "was an encouragement to idleness and profligacy, in the minds of the vulgar," Smollett nevertheless deemed the act a net positive: "it . . . prevents great numbers from abandoning their country, and reunites to the community many useful members, of whose talent and industry it would otherwise be totally deprived" (4:205).

94. David Hume, *The History of England from the Invasion of Julius Caesar to the Revolution in 1688*, "a new edition, corrected," 6 vols. (London, 1762), 6:119.

95. See Kevin Costello, "Habeas Corpus and Military and Naval Impressment, 1756–1816," *Journal of Legal History* 29, no. 2 (2008): 215–51, 216.

96. Smollett, *Continuation*, 2:221–22.

97. Charles Butler, *An Essay on the Legality of Impressing Seamen* (London, 1777), 6–7. See also Daniel J. Ennis, "Naval Impressment in Tobias Smollett's *Roderick Random*," *Albion* 32, no. 2 (Summer 2000): 232–47, 235.

98. Paul D. Halliday, *Habeas Corpus: From England to Empire* (Cambridge, MA: Belknap Press of Harvard University Press, 2010), 35.

99. Peter Murrell, "Design and Evolution in Institutional Development: The Insignificance of the English Bill of Rights," *Journal of Comparative Economics* 45 (2017): 36–55, 42.

100. Indeed, it would be suspended yet again in 1794, 1798–1801, and 1817 (Murrell, 42).

101. See Giorgio Agamben, *State of Exception* (Chicago: University of Chicago Press, 2005), 39.

102. J. Hillis Miller, "Derrida's Politics of Autoimmunity," *Discourse* 30, nos. 1 and 2 (Winter and Spring 2008): 208–25, 208.

Chapter 2 • *Covert Critique*

1. For "the eighteenth-century decline in access to the courts," see David Lemmings, *Law and Government in England during the Long Eighteenth Century: From Consent to Command* (Houndmills, Basingstoke: Palgrave Macmillan, 2011): during the late sixteenth and early seventeenth centuries, "even those groups normally excluded from taking active roles in the institutions of government, such as married women, copyhold tenants, and people with insufficient wealth to pay tax, found active voices as prosecutors" in a number of courts. "The impact of the rising costs and increasingly labyrinthine processes . . . placed the courts beyond the reach of most potential litigants during the early eighteenth century" (72).

2. Writing in the 1960s, Harrison L. Steeves echoed the views of some of Smith's contemporaries and anticipated other critics: "She was not without invention . . . but

no one who has read Mrs. Smith's novels is likely to think of her as more than a respectable bread-and-butter novelist with an appraising eye for literary vogue." Harrison L. Steeves, *Before Jane Austen: The Shaping of the English Novel in the Eighteenth Century* (1965; London: George Allen and Unwin, 1966), 317. Melissa Sodeman lauds what other readers have seen as a defect: Smith's "novels figure their derivative nature as a formal effect of exile, styling their repetitive narratives and entrenched form as an aesthetic of estrangement and alienation." Melissa Sodeman, *Sentimental Memorials: Women and the Novel in Literary History* (Stanford, CA: Stanford University Press, 2015), 81.

3. See, e.g., Judith Davis Miller's characterization of Smith's work as "providing what is essentially commentary on and exemplification of Godwin's philosophy." Judith Davis Miller, "The Politics of Truth and Deception: Charlotte Smith and the French Revolution," in *Rebellious Hearts: British Women Writers and the French Revolution*, ed. Adriana Craciun and Kari E. Lokke (Albany: State University of New York Press, 2001), 337–63, 340.

4. According to William Magee, Smith was "the most frequently and profoundly [influential] of any of [Austen's] predecessors." William Magee, "The Happy Marriage: The Influence of Charlotte Smith on Jane Austen," *Studies in the Novel* 7, no. 1 (1975): 120–32. Bishop C. Hunt Jr. was one of the first scholars to identify Charlotte Smith as "an important early influence" on Wordsworth. Bishop C. Hunt Jr., "Wordsworth and Charlotte Smith," *Wordsworth Circle* 1 (1970), 85–103, 85.

5. See Loraine Fletcher, *Charlotte Smith: A Critical Biography*, rev. ed. (Houndmills, Basingstoke, Hampshire: Palgrave, 2001), 54–58, 66, 87–88, 91, 153, 237, 287–88, 337–38.

6. The reviewer also stated: "The pathos is weakened by the author's adverting too often to perplexities in her own situation . . . and the plaintive strain, though interesting when lightly touched, is too monotonous to be long dwelt upon, though by the most skillful finger. Herself, and not the French emigrant, fills the foreground; begins and ends the piece." Unsigned review of *The Emigrants*, *Critical Review* (Nov. 1793), in the compendium *The Critical Review; or, Annals of Literature, Extended and Improved* (London: A. Hamilton, 1794), 9:299–302, 299–300.

7. Florence May Anna Hilbish, "Charlotte Smith, Poet and Novelist (1749–1806)" (PhD diss., University of Pennsylvania, 1941), 199.

8. Judith Phillips Stanton, introduction to *The Collected Letters of Charlotte Smith*, ed. Judith Phillips Stanton (Bloomington: Indiana University Press, 2003), xiii–xxxii, xv.

9. Melissa Sodeman, "Charlotte Smith's Literary Exile," *ELH* 76, no. 1 (Spring 2009): 131–52.

10. Stephen C. Behrendt rightly names Smith alongside Byron, Shelley, and other Romantic-era poets and authors who cultivated "that variety of 'indirect' or 'staged' autobiography that so effectively melds personal revelation with fictionalizing as to render the one often indistinguishable from the other. . . . The notorious pleading prefaces to Charlotte Smith's novels further illustrate how an author stages an authorial presence and persona for a reading audience that is permitted to 'see' the author almost exclusively in terms of what that author *seems* to present for inspection." Stephen C. Behrendt, "'I Am Not What I Am': Staged Presence in Romantic Autobiography," in *Romantic Autobiography in England*, ed. Eugene Stelzig (Farnham, Surrey: Ashgate, 2009), 145–60, 148. Jacqueline Labbe posits a difference between Smith's

self-positioning in her poetry and in her novels: "For editors of the novels Smith is an . . . interventionist in the formation of literary histories, and chronicler of manners, mores, and events. For editors of the poetry, Smith is a woman speaking from a specifically female position of need, loss, and sorrow, less an interventionist than a victim, less a chronicler than an *experiencer* of events." Jacqueline Labbe, preface to *Charlotte Smith in British Romanticism*, ed. Jacqueline Labbe (London: Pickering and Chatto, 2008), 1–11, 5.

11. Laruelle observes, "La victime a toujours été un *objet, mais non de connaissance*. Elle commence seulement à l'être, au mieux de pitié ou de déploration, de mémoire et de ritualité" (The victim has always been an *object, but not of knowledge*. [The victim] is regarded at best as an object of pity or lamentation, of memory and ritual). François Laruelle, *Théorie générale des victimes* (Paris: Mille et une nuits, 2012), 56–57; emphasis in original; my translation.

12. William Godwin, "Preface to the Present Edition," in William Godwin, *Fleetwood: or, The New Man of Feeling* (London: Richard Bentley, 1832), iii–xiv, vii–viii.

13. William Ray, "Reading Women: Cultural Authority, Gender, and the Novel. The Case of Rousseau," *Eighteenth-Century Studies* 27, no. 3 (Spring 1994): 421–27: "Impressionability was considered a natural quality in women, who were thus naturally more susceptible to the romantic content and affective intricacies of the novel" (423). See also Lynn Hunt, *Inventing Human Rights: A History* (New York: Norton, 2005), 67–68.

14. Charlotte Turner Smith, *What Is She?* [1799], in *What Is She? Conversations Introducing Poetry; [and] A Natural History of Birds*, ed. Judith Pascoe, vol. 13 of *The Works of Charlotte Smith*, ed. Stuart Curran (London: Pickering and Chatto, 2007), 1–58, act 3, scene 5, 35. All citations of *What Is She?* refer to this edition and are referenced by act, scene, and page.

15. Smith, *What Is She?* 3.5.35, 3.5.85.

16. Some of the foremost scholars of Romanticism touch briefly on Smith's interest in the law. Stuart Curran writes, "A sense of the legal system as an arbitrary machine of power operating without any essential relation to equity runs deep in Smith's writing. It is augmented by her recognition that the law is a social code written by men for a male preserve, and that the principal function of women within its boundaries can only be to suffer consequences over which they have no control." Stuart Curran, introduction to *The Poems of Charlotte Smith* (Oxford: Oxford University Press, 1993), xxi. Michael Gamer asserts that Smith's translation of the pitavals "thematically . . . coincides with her lifelong concerns with injustices of the legal system and the victimization of women." Michael Gamer, "Maria Edgeworth and the Romance of Real Life," in "The Romantic-Era Novel," ed. Amanda Gilroy and Wil Verhoeven, special issue, *Novel* 34, no. 2 (2001): 232–66, 238–39.

17. See Fuson Wang, "Cosmopolitanism and the Radical Politics of Exile in Charlotte Smith's *Desmond*," *Eighteenth-Century Fiction* 25, no. 1 (2012): 37–59; and Harriet Guest, *Unbounded Attachment: Sentiment and Politics in the Age of the French Revolution* (Oxford: Oxford University Press, 2013), 16–44. For earlier work see Miller, "Politics of Truth."

18. See Katharine M. Rogers, "Inhibitions on Eighteenth-Century Women Novelists: Elizabeth Inchbald and Charlotte Smith," *Eighteenth-Century Studies* 11, no. 1 (Autumn 1977): 63–78.

19. See Mary Wollstonecraft, *The Wrongs of Woman; or, Maria* in *Mary, Maria, and Matilda*, ed. Janet Todd (New York: New York University Press, 1992), 55–148, 142–45.

20. Frances Burney, *The Wanderer; or, Female Difficulties*, ed. Margaret Anne Doody, Robert L. Mack, and Peter Sabor (Oxford: Oxford University Press, 2001), 152. As Doody remarks in passing, "Elinor might have made a good wife for a lawyer; if life were different, she might have been a good lawyer herself." Margaret Anne Doody, *Frances Burney: The Life in the Works* (New Brunswick, NJ: Rutgers University Press, 1988), 335.

21. Thanks to an anonymous reader for suggesting the possibility that Elinor is a namesake. See "Pedigree of Rev. Sir Edward Repps Jodrell, Bart.," in *Visitation of England and Wales: Notes*, ed. Joseph Jackson Howard and Frederick Arthur Crisp (Privately printed, 1896), 1:113–15.

22. Charlotte Turner Smith to William Tyler [steward of her trustee, Lord Egremont], c. 1 Nov. 1802, in Stanton, *Collected Letters*, 484–86, 486.

23. Charlotte Turner Smith to William Tyler, "received 30 September 1802," in Stanton, *Collected Letters*, 465–70, 466.

24. Nathan Isaacs, "The Merchant and His Law," *Journal of Political Economy* 23, no. 6 (June 1915): 529–61, 540.

25. James Van Horn Melton, *The Rise of the Public in Enlightenment Europe* (Cambridge: Cambridge University Press, 2001), 81–86.

26. Legal dictionaries were available in earlier centuries; for an open-access online trove of such works, see the Law Dictionary Collection of the University of Texas Law School, available through the Tarlton Law Library's Jamail Center for Legal Research: https://tarlton.law.utexas.edu/law-dictionaries/common-law. Their common law legal dictionary section begins with *Exposiciones terminorum legum anglorum* (London: printed by John Rastell, c. 1523), a playwright and lawyer.

27. Giles Jacob, preface to *The Student's Companion: or, The Reason of the Laws of England* . . . (London: Printed for E. and R. Nutt and R. Gosling for T. Corbett, 1725), i–vi, ii–iv, v.

28. Giles Jacob, preface to *Every Man His Own Lawyer: or, A Summary of the Laws of England, in a New and Instructive Method, under the Following Heads* . . . (London: Printed by E. and R. Nutt, and R. Gosling, for J. Hazard, 1736), v–vi, v.

29. Preface to *A Treatise of Feme Coverts; or, The Lady's Law* (London: Printed for E. and R. Nutt, and R. Gosling, 1732), vii.

30. *A Treatise of Feme Coverts*, 81.

31. Jacob, *Every Man His Own Lawyer*, title page.

32. *A Treatise of Feme Coverts: or, The Lady's Law. Containing All the Laws and Statutes Relating to Women, under Several Heads* (1732), vi–vii.

33. Fletcher, *Charlotte Smith*, 82–83.

34. Susanne Kord, *Murderesses in German Writing, 1720–1860: Heroines of Horror* (New York: Cambridge University Press, 2009), 13.

35. Wolfgang Schild, "Relationen und Referierkunst: Zur Juristenausbildung und zum Strafverfahren um 1790," in Jörg Schönert, ed., *Erzählte Kriminalität* (Tubingen: Niemeyer, 1991), 159–76, 170, cited in Kord, 13.

36. François Gayot de Pitaval, "Lettre de l'auteur servant de défense aux *Causes célèbres* et de réponse a deux ecrivains périodiques," in François Gayot de Pitaval, ed., *Causes célèbres et intéressantes, avec les jugemens qui les ont décides*, 18 vols. (Paris, 1740), 15:1–22, 10.

37. Sarah Maza, *Private Lives and Public Affairs: The Causes Célèbres of Prerevolutionary France* (Berkeley: University of California Press, 1993), 25.

38. See François Richer, "Avertissement," in *Causes célèbres et intéressantes, avec les jugemens qui les ont décidées,* ed. François Richer, 22 vols. (Amsterdam: Michel Rhey, 1773), 3: ii-vii, v. "Le seul désir que m'anime est de me faire lire par tout le monde: mais jamais je ne trouverai mauvais que tout le monde n'embrasse pas mes opinions. Il me suffit de pouvoir les croire fondées en raison & en preuve, & de pouvoir montrer au lecteur impartial." (The only desire that motivates me is that my work be read by all the world; but I would never be distressed if everyone does not agree with my opinions. It is enough for me to be able to believe that they are founded in reason, and to be able to share them with an impartial reader.)

39. David Lemmings, *Professors of the Law: Barristers and English Legal Culture in the Eighteenth Century* (Oxford: Oxford University Press, 2000), 89.

40. Charlotte Turner Smith, preface to *The Romance of Real Life,* in *"Manon L'Escaut: or, The Fatal Attachment"* (1786); and *"The Romance of Real Life"* (1787), ed. Michael Gamer with assistance from Karla M. Taylor, vol. 1 of *The Works of Charlotte Smith* (London: Pickering and Chatto, 2005), 129–30, 120. All subsequent citations of *The Romance of Real Life* refer to this edition and are referenced parenthetically in the text.

41. Angela Wright, *Britain, France and the Gothic, 1764–1820: The Import of Terror* (Cambridge: Cambridge University Press, 2013), 53.

42. Gamer, "Maria Edgeworth," 238.

43. Article 42 in the "Monthly Catalogue for October 1787," *Monthly Review* 77 (1787): 328.

44. Wright, *Britain, France and the Gothic,* 55.

45. The Gothic does have a track record of registering legal critique, as shown most recently by Bridget Marshall. See Bridget Marshall, *The Transnational Gothic Novel and the Law, 1790–1860* (Farnham, Surrey: Ashgate, 2011), 1–16. Yet these critiques, when extant, are typically veiled.

46. For the tale of Jean Boucaux, an enslaved man in Saint-Domingue who attempts to gain his freedom when he travels to France with his master, see François Gayot de Pitaval, "Liberté réclamée par un Negre, contre son Maître qui l'a amené en France," in *Causes célèbres* (Paris: Theodore le Gras, 1739) 13:526–627. In the preface to that volume, Gayot de Pitaval approves of Boucaux's efforts: "La troisième Cause est celle du Nègre qui réclame sa liberté; dépoüillé de ce précieux présent que la nature fait à l'homme, il l'a demandé à la Justice, il l'a réussi à persuader les Juges" (The third case is that of a black man who reclaimed his liberty; deprived of that precious gift bequeathed by nature to mankind, he demanded it from the law and succeeded in persuading the judges). Gayot de Pitaval, "Avertissement," in *Causes célèbres,* 13:i-xix, xii-xiii; translation mine). Note that Pitaval refers to liberty not as a boon granted out of generosity but rather as a natural right of which the man was deprived. Smith's choice not to include the slave's story in her translated edition may have been because her family owned slaves in Barbados.

47. I calculated this number by analyzing the forty-five stories in Gayot de Pitaval, *Causes célèbres et intéressantes, avec les jugemens qui les ont décidées,* new ed., vol. 8 (Paris: [F.] Delaulne, 1789).

48. Statistics for the German sources are from Jules de Doncker, "Collecting Criminal (Stereo-)Types: Eighteenth- and Nineteenth-Century 'Causes célèbres' as Anthologies," *German Life and Letters* 70, no. 1 (Jan. 2017): 115–36, 128.

49. Martin Dinges, "The Uses of Justice as a Form of Social Control in Early Modern Europe," in *Social Control in Europe: 1500–1800*, vol. 1, ed. Herman Roodenburg and Pieter Spierenburg (Columbus: Ohio State University Press, 2004), 159–75.

50. Susanne Pohl-Zucker, *Making Manslaughter: Process, Punishment, and Restitution in Wüttemberg and Zurich, 1376–1700* (Leiden: Brill, 2017), 9.

51. Charlotte Turner Smith, *Emmeline, or, The Orphan of the Castle*, ed. Loraine Fletcher (Peterborough, Ontario: Broadview, 2003), 47. All subsequent citations of *Emmeline* refer to this edition and are referenced parenthetically in the text. While romances and prayer books were also printed in this black-letter type, it ceased to be used in most volumes in these genres at least half a century earlier than the phase-out of black letter for law materials.

52. Derek T. Leuenberger, "'Their Only Protector and Support': Protection and Dependency in Charlotte Smith's *Old Manor House*," *European Romantic Review* 28, no. 2 (2017): 139–61, 142.

53. Charlotte Turner Smith, *The Old Manor House*, ed. Jacqueline M. Labbe (1793; Peterborough, Ontario: Broadview, 2002), 512. All subsequent citations of *The Old Manor House* refer to this edition and are referenced parenthetically in the text.

54. See, e.g., W. A. Champion, "Recourse to the Law and the Meaning of the Great Litigation Decline, 1650–1750," in *Communities and Courts in Great Britain, 1150–1900*, ed. Christopher Brooks and Michael Lobban (London: Hambledon, 1997), 179–98.

55. See Edward F. J. Tucker, *Intruder into Eden: Representations of the Common Lawyer in English Literature, 1350–1750* (Columbia, SC: Camden House, 1984); and Lemmings, *Professors of the Law*, 198. The affluence of the opposition could have a chilling effect on the availability of counsel. Similar barriers to legal representation were seen elsewhere in the British Empire in the second half of the eighteenth century. In the American colonies in the 1760s, Native American and poor white tenants were thwarted in their attempts to seek relief from the exploitative practices of wealthy landlords, as the historian Murray Rothbard reports: "Not only were the judges packed against the Indians and the tenants, but the grand Indian sachem, Daniel Ninham, was unable to retain a lawyer because every attorney in the province had been bought by the landlords." Murray N. Rothbard, *Conceived in Liberty* [1975–79] (Auburn, AL: Ludwig von Mises Institute, 2011), 926.

56. The historian Christopher W. Brooks comments, "By 1730 attorneys were no longer extending credit to less well-off litigants . . . [marking] the decline of a practice which had been important in fuelling the late Elizabethan and early Stuart boom in litigation." Christopher W. Brooks, *Lawyers, Litigation and English Society Since 1450* (London: Hambledon, 1998), 48.

57. Lemmings, *Law and Government in England*, 59; see also Lemmings, *Professors of the Law*, iv.

58. See Joan Mahoney, "Green Forms and Legal Aid Offices: A History of Publicly Funded Legal Services in Britain and the United States," *Saint Louis University Public Law Review* 17, no. 2 (1998): 223–40: "In order to be eligible for legal assistance, paupers had to swear that they were not worth more than £5, excluding their clothes

and the matter at issue, and if they lost they might be given the option of paying costs or being whipped, at least until the eighteenth century" (226).

59. See Adriana Craciun, *British Women Writers and the French Revolution: Citizens of the World* (Houndmills, Basingstoke, Hampshire: Palgrave Macmillan, 2005), 173.

60. Cheryl Nixon, "Gender, Law, and the Birth of Bourgeois Civil Society," in *Law and Literature*, ed. Kieran Dolin (Cambridge: Cambridge University Press, 2018), 124–41, 135.

61. Charlotte Turner Smith, preface to *Marchmont*, ed. Kate Davies and Harriet Guest, vol. 9 of *The Works of Charlotte Smith*, ed. Stuart Curran (London: Pickering and Chatto, 2006), 3–6, 4–5. All subsequent citations of *Marchmont* refer to this edition and are referenced parenthetically in the text.

62. For the foreign origins of eighteenth-century vampires, see Samantha George and Bill Hughes, introduction to *Open Graves, Open Minds: Images of the Undead from the Enlightenment to the Present Day* (Oxford: Oxford University Press, 2013), 1–23, 8–9. For the scorpion as "embodiment of evil" in Middle Eastern literature, see Jürgen Wasim Frembgen, "The Scorpion in Muslim Folklore," *Asian Folklore Studies* 63, no. 1 (2004): 95–123, 98–103. For the provenance of the upas tree, see Iain Bamforth, "The Upas Tree," *PN Review* 41, no. 1 (2014): 57–60, 58.

63. The speaker of the poem expresses sympathy for aristocratic families escaping from France, comparing wealthy debtors to poor ones:

> The exil'd Nobles, from their country driven,
> Whose richest luxuries were their's [sic], must feel
> More poignant anguish, than the lowest poor,
> Who, born to indigence, have learn'd to brave
> Rigid Adversity's depressing Breath!

Charlotte Turner Smith, *The Emigrants*, in Curran, *The Poems of Charlotte Smith*, book 1, 135–48, 146, lines 310–14. Elsewhere in the poem, she attributes the Revolution in part to

> Men, whose ill acquired wealth
> Was wrung from plunder'd myriads, by the means
> Too often legaliz'd by power abus'd. (book 1, 145, lines 282–84)

64. Albert J. Schmidt, "The Country Attorney in Late Eighteenth-Century England: Benjamin Smith of Horbling," *Law and History Review* 8, no. 2 (Autumn 1990): 237–71, 238. One could become a law clerk without attending university. To prevent unqualified clerks from going into business, "An Act for the Better Regulation of Attorneys" was passed in 1729, but it was constantly flouted (237). From the earliest years of the eighteenth century, it became difficult for Parliament and judges to keep track of and regulate the number and activities of attorneys, especially as the profession expanded rapidly beyond London; thus, a significant number of men were able to work as attorneys despite little or no training. See Michael Miles, 'Eminent Attorneys': Some Aspects of West Riding Attorneyship c. 1750–1800" (PhD diss., University of Birmingham, British Library/EThOS, 1982), 33–34. Given the antidemocratic elements in some of the novels explored in this book, it is striking that the role of the legal profession in a society's "institutional structure" has been identified by some scholars such as Peter Grajzl and Peter Murrell as an index of "democracy and social stability":

Grajzl and Murrell state in their discussion of the rise of the legal profession in England at the beginning of the long eighteenth century, "Professional power substitutes for weak democracy, an observation consistent with events during England's Glorious Revolution." Peter Grajzl and Peter Murrell, "Lawyers and Politicians: The Impact of Organized Legal Professions on Institutional Reforms," *Constitutional Political Economy* 17, no. 4 (2006): 251–76, 252.

65. The preface's foreign animal and botanical motifs of the scorpion and upas tree transplanted to English grounds reflect contemporary preoccupation with boundary delimitation. "After the acts of enclosure in the eighteenth century," Eve Darian-Smith contends, "the garden, as a particular feature of the landed estate, continued to operate as an aesthetic metaphor for a social elite's legal capacity to civilize, cultivate . . . exclude, dominate, and ultimately make inequalities appear more plausible and acceptable." Eve Darian-Smith, *Bridging Divides: The Channel Tunnel and English Legal Identity in the New Europe* (Berkeley: University of California Press, 1999), 404–5.

66. According to Schmidt, "The key to understanding Georgian country attorneys lay in their acquisition of the conveyancing business and withdrawal from litigation. An expertise in drawing up wills, trusts, and family settlements, in facilitating land purchases and sales, and, especially, money-lending—these rather than litigation made the attorney a confidante of well-to-do families." Schmidt, "The Country Attorney," 238.

67. See Stephen Landsman, "Rise of the Contentious Spirit: Adversary Procedure in Eighteenth Century England," *Cornell Law Review* 75, no. 3 (March 1990): 497–609: "The growing presence of counsel at criminal trials led to a significant decentralization of responsibility in litigation and diminution of judicial power" (519).

68. Indeed, the only pitaval from the perspective of a poor man that Smith adapted for *The Romance of Real Life* is a servant of "general integrity" who has served his mistress for twenty-nine years: he is falsely accused of murdering her and stealing her money. He dies in jail before it is revealed that her own relatives murdered her to obtain their inheritance. The memorialization of his fidelity becomes a public spectacle: "Such was the grief universally expressed by all ranks of people, and such the concourse who attended his corpse to the grave, that it seemed to become a public cause, even before the real culprit was discovered." See "James Le Brun," in Charlotte Turner Smith, *The Romance of Real Life*, ed. Michael Gamer and Karla M. Taylor (London: Pickering and Chatto, 2005), 259–74, 259, 272.

69. Stern observes: "During the seventeenth and eighteenth centuries . . . the general warrant [was] a means of licensing wide-ranging searches into citizens' houses, papers, and effects, even when the authorities lacked any well-founded basis for investigating a particular suspect. Initially left relatively unchallenged, the general warrant would become the object of intense criticism in the eighteenth century for many reasons." Simon Stern, "Fanny Hill and the 'Laws of Decency': Investigating Obscenity in the Mid-Eighteenth Century," *Eighteenth-Century Life* 43, no. 2 (April 2019): 162–87, 178.

70. Levy comments that in the 1500s and 1600s, "Beale, Coke, and Hale . . . invented a rhetorical tradition against general searches, which Sergeant William Hawkins and Sir William Blackstone continued [in the eighteenth century]. But the rhetoric was empty; the tradition had almost no practical effect." According to Levy, pronouncements on searches were aspirational rather than reflecting the reality of law, as

illustrated by the fact that Coke's own home was searched while he was dying, and his valuables were forcibly seized. "In fact," Levy states, "English law was honeycombed with parliamentary enactments that relied on warrantless general searches" in the mid- to late 1700s. Leonard W. Levy, "Origins of the Fourth Amendment," *Political Science Quarterly* 14, no. 1 (1999): 79–101, 81. For a contrasting point of view of warrant enforcement, also citing cases such as *Wilkes v. Wood* (1763), see Mark A. Graber and Howard Gillman, *The Complete American Constitutionalism*, vol. 1, *Introduction and the Colonial Era* (Oxford: Oxford University Press, 2015): "The common law in the eighteenth century sharply limited searches of private residences. . . . Rules that governed search warrants were strict" (486).

71. Levy, "Origins of the Fourth Amendment," 79.

72. For the feminist critique of liberal nonintervention, see Susan Moller Okin, "Humanist Liberalism," in *Liberalism and the Moral Life*, ed. Nancy L. Rosenblum (Cambridge, MA: Harvard University Press, 1989), 39–53, 45.

73. Michael Taussig, *Law in a Lawless Land: Diary of a Limpieza in Colombia* (Chicago: University of Chicago Press, 2003), 30.

74. Unsigned review of *Marchmont*, in *The Critical Review; or, Annals of Literature* (London, 1797), 256–60, 256.

75. Unsigned review of *Marchmont*, in *Monthly Visitor and Entertaining Pocket Companion*, vol. 1 (London, 1797), 92–94, 94.

76. For contemporary calls for reform of Chancery, see Michael Lobban, "Preparing for Fusion: Reforming the Nineteenth-Century Court of Chancery," *Law and History Review* 22 (2004): 389–427. Smith was ahead of her time in calling attention to barriers to justice in Chancery. Dickens's critique in *Bleak House*, by contrast, included outdated information and did not prompt reform: "When *Bleak House* appeared, Chancery's most cumbersome machinery was already abolished, and the way was clear for the modern fusion of law and equity." Allen Boyer, "The Antiquarian and the Utilitarian: Charles Dickens vs. James Fitzjames Stephen," *Tennessee Law Review* 56, no. 3 (April 1989): 595–628, 623. Thanks to an anonymous reviewer for calling attention to objections to Dickens's portrayal of legal affairs.

77. For additional details of Smith's legal experiences, see Fletcher, *Charlotte Smith*, 153, 210, 215, 237, 257.

78. Ian Watt, *The Rise of the Novel: Studies in Defoe, Richardson, and Fielding* [1957] 2nd American ed. (Berkeley: University of California Press, 2001), 24.

79. Barbara C. S. Shea states in her analysis of attorney's liens, "Fee collection is a recurring problem at two stages of representing a client: prior to litigation or resolution of the problem and subsequent to litigation. In the first situation, most frequently the client discharges the attorney or the attorney chooses to withdraw and the client refuses to pay." Barbara C. S. Shea, "Attorney's Liens: A Practical Overview," *Bridgeport Law Review* 6 (1985): 77–121, 77.

80. John Leubsdorf claims that it was during the eighteenth century that this particular coercive practice became an option for attorneys: although barristers could not assess retaining liens, "solicitors, by contrast, may assert a retaining lien, but their right to do so was unclear at the outset of the eighteenth century and was established definitively only during that century." John Leubsdorf, "Against Lawyer Retaining Liens," *Fordham Law Review* 72, no. 4 (2004): 849–83, 851.

Chapter 3 • Letters of the Law

1. See David Daiches, "Scott's *Redgauntlet*," in *From Jane Austen to Joseph Conrad*, ed. Robert C. Rathburn and Martin Steinmann Jr. (Minneapolis: University of Minnesota Press, 1958), 49; and Magnus Magnusson, *Scotland: Story of a Nation* (New York: Harper Collins, 2000), 637.

2. A Scottish newspaper reported: "The celebrated ventriloquist paid a visit to Abbotsford [Scott's estate], where he entertained his distinguished host, and other visitors, with his unrivalled imitations." The account from a "Scotch newspaper, 1830" accompanies the poem in numerous collections, including Walter Scott, *The Poetical Works of Sir Walter Scott, Bart., in Twelve Volumes* (Edinburgh: Adam and Charles Black, 1855–59, 1857), 10:363–64. The poem originally appeared in the 1824 edition of the *Edinburgh Annual Register*.

3. Scott, *Poetical Works*, 10:363–64.

4. Vattemare was said to be especially skilled at portraying lowly beings: one reviewer of the extravaganza commented, "His most original and extraordinary efforts, without doubt, are his imitations of animals, dogs barking, cats mewing, a child crying." Unsigned review, *Theatrical Observer*, 17 April 1822, 522. He also portrayed scenes of resistance to authority: another notable segment of his act featured the auditory illusion of a servant attempting in the vestibule to prohibit a tardy ticket-holder—an elite diplomat—from entering the auditorium in which the show was performed.

5. Robert Poole, "French Revolution or Peasants' Revolt? Petitioners and Rebels in England from the Blanketeers to the Chartists," *Labour History Review* 74, no. 1 (April 2009): 6–26, 6. Poole begins his list of important events in the year of Peterloo with a mention of Scott's writings: "1819, the year of Peterloo, was also the year of *Ivanhoe*, Walter Scott's reworking of the Robin Hood legend with its influential tale of resurgent Saxon chivalry" (22).

6. Robert Poole, "'By the Law or the Sword': Peterloo Revisited," *History* 91, no. 302 (April 2006): 254–76, 254.

7. Walter Scott, *The Visionary*, 1819. Facsimile of the first edition, ed. with an introduction by Peter Garside (Cardiff: University College Cardiff Press/Regency Reprints I, 1984), 48. All subsequent citations of *The Visionary* refer to this edition and are referenced parenthetically in the text.

8. Judith Wilt, *Secret Leaves: The Novels of Walter Scott* (Chicago: University of Chicago Press, 1985), 146–51. Ian Duncan, *Scott's Shadow: The Novel in Romantic Edinburgh* (Princeton, NJ: Princeton University Press, 2007), 261.

9. Andrew Lincoln, *Walter Scott and Modernity* (Edinburgh: Edinburgh University Press, 2007), 202.

10. See Harry E. Shaw, "Is There a Problem with Historical Fiction (or with Scott's *Redgauntlet*)?" *Rethinking History* 9, nos. 2–3 (June/September 2005): 173–95, 182.

11. For reevaluation of "the complex relationship between history, the narrative that is inexorably true, and romance" (109) in Scott's novels, see Ian Duncan, *Modern Romance and the Transformation of the Novel* (1992; Cambridge: Cambridge University Press, 2005), esp. 51–176. The implications of Scott's treatment of history for twentieth-century historicism are discussed in James Chandler, *England in 1819: The Politics of Literary Culture and the Case of Romantic Historicism* (Chicago: University of Chicago

Press, 1999). For Scott and cultural memory, see Catherine Jones, *Literary Memory: Scott's Waverley Novels and the Psychology of Narrative* (Lewisburg, PA: Bucknell University Press, 2003). Scott's views on the union between England and Scotland are examined in Evan Gottlieb, *Feeling British: Sympathy and National Identity in Scottish and English Writing, 1707–1832* (Lewisburg, PA: Bucknell University Press, 2007). A treatment of Scott's novel as a reflection of contemporary ideas of nationhood and civic virtue can be found in Yoon Sun Lee, "Giants in the North: 'Douglas,' the Scottish Enlightenment, and Scott's *Redgauntlet*," *Studies in Romanticism* 40, no. 1 (Spring 2001): 109–21. For reflections on Scott's novels as commentary on local and global trade, see Ayşe Çelikkol, "Free Trade and Disloyal Smugglers in Scott's *Guy Mannering* and *Redgauntlet*," *ELH* 74, no. 4 (Winter 2007): 759–82.

12. H. L. A. Hart, *The Concept of Law* (Oxford: Oxford University Press, 1961), 158. Lincoln rightly notes that although "Scott officially endorses the humanitarian sentiments . . . of his moderate heroes," the novelist's engagement with matters of virtue and social convention is complicated by skepticism, irony, and doubt as to whether there exist universal moral principles that determine what counts as moral behavior. Lincoln, *Walter Scott and Modernity*, 188.

13. Walter Scott to Maria Edgeworth, 4 Feb. 1829, repr. in John Gibson Lockhart, *Memoirs of the Life of Sir Walter Scott, Bart.*, vol. 2 (Philadelphia: Carey, Lea and Blanchard, 1837), 632–34, 634.

14. Walter Scott, entry for 12 Dec. 1825, *The Journal of Sir Walter Scott*, ed. W. E. K. Anderson (Oxford: Clarendon, 1972), 34–35.

15. See Lincoln, *Walter Scott and Modernity*, 10. Lincoln mentions Scott's awareness of "the growing independence and class consciousness of the lower orders" (68).

16. Charles Dickens, *Bleak House*, ed. Stephen Gill (Oxford: Oxford University Press, 1998), 737. See also Jan-Melissa Schramm, *Testimony and Advocacy in Victorian Law, Literature, and Theology* (Cambridge: Cambridge University Press, 2000), 105–23, esp. 119.

17. Alexander Welsh, *Strong Representations: Narrative and Circumstantial Evidence in England* (Baltimore: Johns Hopkins University Press, 1992), 8.

18. Edlie Wong, "'Freedom with a Vengeance': Choosing Kin in Antislavery Literature and Law," *American Literature* 81, no. 1 (2009): 7–34, 23.

19. David Marshall, *Sir Walter Scott and Scots Law* (Edinburgh: William Hodge, 1932), 64. Marshall argues, "This description of Ellangowan's activities is, indeed, almost a dramatized version of Sir George Mackenzie's account of the duties of a local magistrate" (63).

20. Walter Scott, *Guy Mannering; or, The Astrologer* [1815], ed. P. D. Garside (Edinburgh: Edinburgh University Press, 1999), 33.

21. "Sir Walter Scott and Scots Law," *Scottish Law Review* 47 (May 1931): 46–56, 87–96, 123–28, 158–68, 158. The article was published anonymously across multiple issues of the journal, beginning in October of 1930.

22. See George Mackenzie, *The Laws and Customs of Scotland in Matters Criminal*, ed. Olivia F. Robinson (1678; Edinburgh: Stair Society, 2012), 307; see also John W. Cairns, "Teaching Criminal Law in Early Eighteenth-Century Scotland: *Collegia* and *Compendia*," *Fundamina* 20, no. 1 (2014): 90–99, 91.

23. Walter Scott, *The Heart of Mid-Lothian*, ed. David Hewitt and Alison Lumsden (1818; Edinburgh: Edinburgh University Press, 2004).

24. See Andrew Lang, *Sir George Mackenzie, King's Advocate, of Rosehaugh: His Life and Times, 1636(?)–1691* (London: Longmans, Green, 1909), 184–85.

25. Scott, entry for Monday, 20 August 1827, *Journal of Sir Walter Scott*, 341–42. Scott's courtroom in Selkirk remains open to visitors: see www.visitscotland.com/info /see-do/sir-walter-scotts-courtroom-p251761.

26. See Linda Martín Alcoff, "The Problem of Speaking for Others," *Cultural Critique* 20 (Winter 1991–92): 5–32, 8, 17.

27. Miranda Burgess, *British Fiction and the Production of Social Order, 1740–1830* (Cambridge: Cambridge University Press, 2000), 190.

28. A reviewer who believed that Scott remained true to the original ballads praised him for doing so:

> The first merit of an editor, with respect to history, is his *fidelity*. This merit, if we may judge from internal evidence, Mr [*sic*] Scott possesses in eminent degree. . . . Occasional artifices may indeed be justified by the state of public taste. Perhaps, if Dr. Percy had not a little softened down the roughness of his valuable *Reliques*, he would have found neither readers nor followers. But the necessity of deception no longer exists: and Mr Scott has felt that he might confidently publish the rudest of these ballads, in the very state in which they were heard by our ancestors. A few verbal corrections (which we shall presently show to have been injudiciously made) scarcely make an exception to this remark. (Unsigned review of *Minstrelsy of the Scottish Border*, *Edinburgh Review* 48, no. 95 [Jan. 1803]: 396–97)

An otherwise negative appraisal of *Minstrelsy* likewise commended Scott's "fidelity, taste, and learning," despite noting significant editorial alterations Scott made to the ballads. Unsigned review of *Minstrelsy of the Scottish Border*, *Monthly Review*, Sept. 1803, vol. 42, ser. 2, 21–33, 32.

29. Andrew Lang, *Sir Walter Scott and the Border Minstrelsy* (London: Longman, Green, and Sons, 1910), 8–13, 9.

30. Walter Scott, "Essay on Imitations of the Ancient Ballad" [1830], in Walter Scott, *Minstrelsy of the Scottish Border*, ed. T. F. Henderson (Edinburgh: Oliver and Boyd, 1932), 4:10.

31. See, e.g., a defense offered by an early twentieth-century reviewer: "Scott altered, embellished, and sometimes glorified. . . . It is safe to say that when the reviser is a Scott or a Burns all the world may be thankful for their transgressions." Unsigned review of *Minstrelsy of the Scottish Border*, *Edinburgh Review* 197, no. 404 (April 1903): 303–22, 304.

32. Grossman remarks: "In court the barrister had to weave material facts and testimony into a story to bear out the 'whole truth.' . . . In this form of narration telling one's own story in one's own words is a less credible procedure than having one's story reconstructed by an orchestrating third party, namely, the barrister as narrator." Jonathan H. Grossman, *The Art of Alibi: English Law Courts and the Novel* (Baltimore: Johns Hopkins University Press, 2002), 21–22.

33. A number of scholars claim that although he continued for years to publish anonymously, Scott's true identity was, in fact, widely known, as evidenced by playbills identifying him as the "Waverley Author." See Kathryn Sutherland, "Made in Scotland: *The Edinburgh Edition of the Waverley Novels*," *Text* 14 (2002): 305–23, 314. For further

discussion of Scott's reasons for preserving anonymity, see Seamus Cooney, "Scott's Anonymity—Its Motives and Consequences," *Studies in Scottish Literature* 10 (1973): 207–19.

34. Ann Rigney notes that Scott's "decision not to reveal his identity in the face of the overwhelming success of *Waverley*, but to publish the subsequent novels anonymously, only admitting his authorship in 1827, turned out to be a major promotion strategy that helped 'brand' the novel. . . . It was generally known from quite early on . . . that Walter Scott was indeed the Author of *Waverley*." Ann Rigney, *The Afterlives of Walter Scott: Memory on the Move* (Oxford: Oxford University Press, 2012), 212. Pointing to evidence—including European editions of Scott's novels in which his name was printed as author as early as 1822 (identified by William B. Todd and Ann Bowden in *Sir Walter Scott: A Bibliographical History, 1796–1832* [New Castle, DE: Oak Knoll Press, 1998])—Claire Lamont contends that Scott maintained only "partial anonymity." See Claire Lamont, "Walter Scott: Anonymity and the Unmasking of Harlequin," in *Authorship, Commerce, and the Public: Scenes of Writing, 1750–1850*, ed. E. J. Clery, Caroline Franklin, and Peter Garside (New York: Palgrave Macmillan, 2002), 54–66, 55.

35. Monika Fludernik argues: "One of the most significant achievements of narratology is the fact that nowadays we distinguish between author and narrator. Until the late nineteenth century, the author was held to be identical with the authorial narrator. . . . Authorial narrators in English novels of the nineteenth century, those by Scott, for example, sound like tellers of fairy tales, chroniclers of local events, expert historians, satirists, or moralists. This leads one to visualize the respective authors behind their narrative voices. . . . We seem to be face to face with [them]." Monika Fludernik, *An Introduction to Narratology*, trans. Patricia Haüsler-Greenfield and Monika Fludernik (New York: Routledge, 2009), 56.

36. While some of Scott's other novels, including *St. Ronan's Well* (1823), occasionally incorporate missives, those novels do not feature lengthy epistolary sequences similar to the first section of *Redgauntlet*. Among his other writings, *The Visionary* consists of only three letters. Scott's only prior experience with developing a sustained epistolary sequence was his early prose work *Paul's Letters to His Kinsfolk* (1816), which was based on Scott's observations on the Napoleonic Wars.

37. See Mary A. Favret, *Romantic Correspondence: Women, Politics and the Fiction of Letters* (Cambridge: Cambridge University Press, 1993), 12, 34. Robyn L. Schiffman identifies Aphra Behn's *Love-Letters between a Nobleman and His Sister* (1684) and *Redgauntlet* (1824) as the "two works that often bookmark studies of the rise and decline of epistolary novels." Robyn L. Schiffman, "*Werther* and the Epistolary Novel," *European Romantic Review* 19, no. 4 (2008): 421–38, 427.

38. Welsh, *Strong Representations*, 78–79.

39. Favret, *Romantic Correspondence*, 177.

40. English Showalter, *The Evolution of the French Novel, 1641–1782* (Princeton, NJ: Princeton University Press, 1972), 121. Other scholars have challenged Showalter's claims: see, e.g., Janet Gurkin Altman, *Epistolarity* (Columbus: Ohio State University Press, 1982); Elizabeth Heckendorn Cook, *Epistolary Bodies* (Stanford, CA: Stanford University Press, 1996); and Joe Bray, *The Epistolary Novel* (New York: Routledge, 1997).

41. Some older epistolary fictions accommodated the voices of the oppressed. Linda S. Kauffman has shown that "one of the ancient strains of epistolarity . . . is the

trial motif" and that this tradition features a number of female writers who seek redress; in all the examples that she cites, from classical works through twentieth-century fiction, victims at least have the opportunity to communicate via letters. By contrast, most of the lowly characters in *Redgauntlet* are illiterate or otherwise unable or unqualified to represent themselves in writing. Furthermore, I see *Redgauntlet* as subordinating the trial to legally inflected encounters beyond the formal judicial context. See Linda S. Kauffman, *Special Delivery: Epistolary Modes in Modern Fiction* (Chicago: University of Chicago Press, 1992), 54.

42. The elder Fairford was patterned on Scott's father, Walter Scott Sr., who was also a Writer to the Signet. See Walter Scott, "Memoir of the Early Life of Sir Walter Scott, Written by Himself," in John Gibson Lockhart, *Memoirs of the Life of Sir Walter Scott, Bart.*, 7 vols. (Edinburgh: Robert Cadell, 1837–38), 1:1–60, 7.

43. Walter Scott, *Redgauntlet*, ed. G. A. M. Wood with David Hewitt (1824; Edinburgh: Edinburgh University Press/New York: Columbia University Press, 1997), 5. All subsequent citations of *Redgauntlet* refer to this edition and are referenced parenthetically in the text.

44. Walter Scott, "Samuel Richardson" [1823], in Walter Scott, *Miscellaneous Prose Works* (Boston: Wells and Lilly, 1829), 3:7–57, 36.

45. George Philip Krapp, "The Psychology of Dialect Writing," *The Bookman* 63 (Dec. 1926): 522–27, 522. To Peter, with his garbled speech, compare the poor widow Blind Alice in Scott's earlier novel *The Bride of Lammermoor* (1819). As Andrew Lincoln notes, Alice "speaks a dignified English remote from the 'vulgar' idiom of the Scots peasant. In this respect, as in others, she represents an impoverished Scots peasantry by not representing them" (Lincoln, *Walter Scott and Modernity*, 195).

46. Celeste Langan, "Understanding Media in 1805: Audiovisual Hallucination in 'The Lay of the Last Minstrel,'" *Studies in Romanticism* 40, no. 1 (Spring 2001): 49–70, 50.

47. Colin Carman examines "Scott's effort to humanize the mentally disabled," while noting that Scott was a "man of his time" who shared some of the prejudices of his era regarding the mentally ill. See Colin Carman, "Deficiencies: Mental Disability and the Imagination in Scott's Waverley Novels," *Studies in Scottish Literature* 39, no. 1 (2013): 139–61, esp. 141–42.

48. David Brown, *Walter Scott and the Historical Imagination* (London: Routledge and Kegan Paul, 1979), 170–71.

49. Bruce Beiderwell, *Power and Punishment in Scott's Novels* (Athens: University of Georgia Press, 1992), 104.

50. The 1820s and 1830s were pivotal decades in the history of animal rights. Britain's most prominent humane society, the Society for the Prevention of Cruelty to Animals, was founded in 1824, the year that Scott published *Redgauntlet*; it became the Royal Society for Prevention of Cruelty to Animals in 1840. See Andrew N. Ireland Moore, "Defining Animals as Crime Victims," *Journal of Animal Law* 1, no. 1 (2005): 91–108, 93. The Scottish Society for the Prevention of Cruelty to Animals was established in 1839; see Elspeth Attwooll, *The Tapestry of the Law: Scotland, Legal Culture, and Legal Theory* (Dordrecht: Kluwer Academic, 1997), 32. Ian Duncan asserts, "Scott would have been familiar with . . . the notorious claims of Lord Monboddo (ridiculed by Dr. Johnson) that the orangutan . . . could be taught language." See Ian Duncan, introduction to *Rob Roy*, by Walter Scott, ed. Ian Duncan (Oxford: Oxford University Press, 1998), xxv.

51. George R. Jesse, *Evidence Given before the Royal Commission on Vivisection* (London: Basil Montagu Pickering, 1875), 75–76.

52. Michel de Montaigne, *The Complete Essays of Montaigne*, ed. and trans. Donald Frame (Palo Alto, CA: Stanford University Press, 1958), 331.

53. Foxley does not care that Redgauntlet's advocacy and guardianship are fraudulent; the official feels obliged to the laird, who controls his livelihood. Historical evidence indicates that Foxley is not a villainous outlier. The legal historian Douglas Hay notes that eighteenth-century justices of the peace exploited their power to issue judgments to protecting the ruling class's interests. See Douglas Hay, "Property, Authority and the Criminal Law," in *Albion's Fatal Tree: Crime and Society in Eighteenth-Century England*, ed. Douglas Hay, Peter Limbaugh, John G. Rule, E. P. Thompson, and Cal Winslow, 2nd ed. (1975; New York: Verso, 2011), 17–63, 51–52.

Chapter 4 • *Masters of Passion and Tongue*

1. Because the relative scarcity of black voices in the archives of eighteenth-century and Romantic-era writing reflects historical impositions such as legal prohibitions in the antebellum United States against teaching slaves to read, projects that focus on the voices of the black writers who did manage to emerge are often framed—at least to some extent—as reparative measures that honor, if they do not compensate for, the historical trauma of slavery. Reliance on this literature as a means of palliating historical wounds, however, has been challenged. Scholarly focus on antislavery literature has much in common with what Aida Levy-Hussen terms the "therapeutic reading" of post–civil rights era novels in which modern-day protagonists are transported back in time to the era of slavery; Levy-Hussen objects to the use of these fictions "for redressing the ailments of contemporary consciousness." Aida Levy-Hussen, *How to Read African American Literature: Post–Civil Rights Fiction and the Task of Interpretation* (New York: New York University Press, 2016), 5.

2. See Srividhya Swaminathan, *Debating the Slave Trade: Rhetoric of British National Identity, 1759–1815* (Farnham, Surrey / Burlington: Ashgate, 2013), 47.

3. Lynn Festa observes, "Colonial expansion means that readers must find ways of recognizing difference while maintaining other forms of difference. . . . [Late eighteenth-century] sentimental writings thus repeatedly confront the gap between what constitutes a lyric 'person'—emotive, subjective, and individual—and what constitutes a legal 'person'—rational, rights-bearing, and culturally validated." Lynn Festa, *Sentimental Figures of Empire in Eighteenth-Century Britain and France* (Baltimore: Johns Hopkins University Press, 2006), 4. This simultaneous emotional identification and intellectual and legal exclusion was especially pronounced in the decades immediately prior to the abolition of the slave trade. George Boulukos states, "After 1787, those who protest vigorously against the abuse of slaves, but accept the view of blacks as irrationally passionate, are likely the most effective at establishing the conceptual possibility of racial difference for their cosmopolitan readers." George Boulukos, *The Grateful Slave* (Cambridge: Cambridge University Press, 2008), 15. Antislavery literature shares this perception of the enslaved as primarily emotional beings with proslavery works such as *An Inquiry into the Law of Negro Slavery in the United States of America* (1858), in which, as Colin Dayan notes, "Sensibility, passion, affection, and appetite are incorporated into this representation of slaves, while the rational faculties such as the

intellect, will, and the moral sense . . . are excised from this portrayal." Colin Dayan, *The Law Is a White Dog* (Princeton, NJ: Princeton University Press, 2013), 148.

4. I see the relative neglect of proslavery novels, compared to the sustained interest in antislavery works, as attributable in part to concerns similar to those expressed in a recent critical overview of pro-Confederate children's literature: reflecting on Marinda Branson Moore's *The Geographical Reader for Dixie Children* (1863), *Slate* staff writer Ruth Graham repudiated its "noxious brand of Confederacy-worship": "Today, Moore's book is even more painful to read." Graham states that she intentionally decided against linking to online venues where pro-Confederacy fiction could be purchased. Her comments suggest that proslavery works not only inflict "pain" on readers but also expose impressionable readers to racist ideology, and access should be limited accordingly. See Ruth Graham, "What I Learned from Reading Confederate Children's Books," *Slate*, 29 June 2015, https://slate.com/culture/2015/06/books-for-dixie-children-what-i -learned-from-reading-all-the-pro-confederate-kids-literature-i-could-find.html.

5. See Candace Ward and Tim Watson, "Early Creole Novels in English before 1850: Hamel, the Obeah Man and Warner Arundell: The Adventures of a Creole," in *Literary Histories of the Early Anglophone Caribbean: Islands in the Stream*, ed. Nicole N. Aljoe, Brycchan Carey, and Thomas W. Krise (Cham, Switzerland: Palgrave Macmillan / Springer, 2018), 147–70, 155.

6. Karina Williamson, editor of the new edition of *Marly*, believes Stewart could be the author of the novel, but she also notes evidence that could possibly counter this premise. See Karina Williamson, introduction to *Marly; or, A Planter's Life in Jamaica*, ed. Karina Williamson (Oxford: Macmillan Caribbean, 2005), xiv–xv.

7. See Candace Ward, introduction to Cynric R. Williams, *Hamel, the Obeah Man*, ed. Candace Ward and Tim Watson (Peterborough, Ontario: Broadview, 2010), 9–46, 37. I see these distinctions in phrasing as a matter of selective emphasis, similar to the controversial terminology of "prolife"/"prochoice." To be sure, the term *proslavery* may not adequately reflect differences within the coalition or the support for gradual phasing out of the institution. Yet I prefer that term because *proplanter* seems relatively euphemistic, relocating the central emphasis from the grave moral wrong of traffic in human beings to the innocuous activity of planting, labor that most "planters," moreover, did not do themselves. Indeed, both *proplanter* and *antiabolitionist* shift the focus away from the black people at the center of the debate. Another alternative, *ameliorationist*, is obscurantist; only specialists tend to be familiar with it, which impedes discussion beyond academic contexts (I have had to repeatedly explain it), and it also lacks the forthrightness of the other terms. My aim is to place slavery front and center in the terminology connected to it.

8. See Russell Smandych, "'To Soften the Extreme Rigor of Their Bondage': James Stephen's Attempt to Reform the Criminal Slave Laws of the West Indies, 1813–1833," *Law and History Review* 23, no. 3 (Fall 2005): 537–88.

9. See Ramesh Mallipeddi, *Spectacular Suffering: Witnessing Slavery in the Eighteenth-Century British Atlantic* (Charlottesville: University of Virginia Press, 2016), 4–5, 148, 161.

10. For analysis of "paternalist white speech on behalf of the silenced slave" in the antebellum American context, see Jeannine Marie DeLombard, "Representing the Slave: White Advocacy and Black Testimony in Harriet Beecher Stowe's *Dred*," *New England Quarterly* 75, no. 1 (March 2002): 80–106, 81.

11. As Deidre Shauna Lynch has observed, "It is a commonplace that literature took an inward turn at the close of the eighteenth century: that is how it got 'romantic.' [These] inner meanings and psychological depths . . . to many readers have seemed to detach the romantic-period character from mid-century writing's social text." Deidre Shauna Lynch, *The Economy of Character: Novels, Market Culture, and the Business of Inner Meaning* (Chicago: University of Chicago Press, 1998), 6.

12. Paula E. Dumas, *Proslavery Britain: Fighting for Slavery in an Era of Abolition* (Houndmills, Basingstoke, Hampshire: Palgrave Macmillan, 2016), 47.

13. See Christa Dierksheide, *Amelioration and Empire: Progress and Slavery in the Atlantic Americas* (Charlottesville: University of Virginia Press, 2014).

14. See, e.g., Brycchan Carey, *British Abolitionism and the Rhetoric of Sensibility: Writing, Sentiment, and Slavery, 1760–1807* (Basingstoke: Palgrave Macmillan, 2005); Brycchan Carey, "'To Force a Tear': British Abolitionism and the Eighteenth-Century London Stage," in *Affect and Abolition in the Anglo-Atlantic, 1770–1830*, ed. Stephen Ahern (Farnham, Surrey / Burlington: Ashgate, 2013), 109–28; Adam Hochschild, *Bury the Chains: Prophets and Rebels in the Struggle to Free an Empire's Slaves* (New York: Mariner, 2006); and Tobias Menely, "Acts of Sympathy: Abolitionist Poetry and Transatlantic Identification," in *Affect and Abolition in the Anglo-Atlantic, 1770–1830* (Farnham, Surrey / Burlington: Ashgate, 2013), 45–68. David Beck Ryden differs, emphasizing economic factors over moral ones. See David Beck Ryden, *West Indian Slavery and British Abolition, 1783–1807* (Cambridge: Cambridge University Press, 2010).

15. See Elizabeth Ammons, "Heroines in *Uncle Tom's Cabin*," *American Literature* 49, no. 2 (1977): 161–79; Barbara Hochman, *"Uncle Tom's Cabin" and the Reading Revolution: Race, Literacy, Childhood, and Fiction, 1851–1911* (Amherst: University of Massachusetts Press, 2011); Richard S. Newman, *The Transformation of American Abolitionism: Fighting Slavery in the Early Republic* (Chapel Hill: University of North Carolina Press, 2002); and Robyn R. Warhol, "'Reader, Can You Imagine? No, You Cannot': The Narratee as Other in Harriet Jacobs's Text," *Narrative* 3, no. 1 (Jan. 1995): 57–72. Martin L. Hoffman claims, "Harriet Beecher Stowe's empathy may have advanced emancipation by months." Martin L. Hoffman, "Empathy and Prosocial Behavior," in *Handbook of Emotions*, ed. Michael Lewis, Jeannette M. Haviland-Jones, and Lisa Feldman Barrett, 3rd ed. (New York: Guilford, 2010), 440–55, 452.

16. George Boulukos notes that this is a long-standing trend, and he cites literary scholars ranging back to R. B. Heilman in the 1930s and Winthrop Jordan in the 1960s: "It has often been argued—or simply assumed—that sentimental humanitarianism was a driving force behind England's late eighteenth-century antislavery movement" (Boulukos, *The Grateful Slave*, 13). Philip Fisher lauds the sentimental novel for portraying slaves as full human beings: "Sentimentality, by its experimental extension of humanity to . . . slaves, exactly reverses the process of slavery itself which has at its core the withdrawal of human status from a part of humanity." Philip Fisher, *Hard Facts: Setting and Form in the American Novel* (Oxford: Oxford University Press, 1986), 100. More recently, Christine Levecq has argued that eighteenth-century transatlantic black writers "downplay[ed]" corporeality and emphasized emotion for the purpose of obscuring racial difference and gaining support for the antislavery cause. Christine Levecq, *Slavery and Sentiment: The Politics of Feeling in Black Atlantic Antislavery Writing, 1770–1850* (Lebanon: University of New Hampshire Press, 2008), 19.

17. Richard Rorty states, "Progress consists in an increasing ability to see the similarities between ourselves and people very unlike us as outweighing the differences. It is the result of what I have been calling 'sentimental education.' . . . What Harriet Beecher Stowe did for black slaves . . . [is to] make us, the audience . . . feel . . . that [they] are more like us, more like real human beings, than we had realized." Richard Rorty, "Human Rights, Rationality, and Sentimentality," in *Truth and Progress: Philosophical Papers*, vol. 3 (Cambridge: Cambridge University Press, 1998), 167–85, 181.

18. As Elizabeth Barnes observes, whites' sympathy for the enslaved was "contingent upon similarity" of feelings rather than of bodies. Elizabeth Barnes, *States of Sympathy: Seduction and Democracy in the American Novel* (New York: Columbia University Press, 1997), 92. Unless sympathy was cultivated, skin color—as marker of difference—remained the most salient feature: "In the final quarter of the eighteenth century, *skin* suddenly came to be privileged as the primary sign of racial identity." Irene Tucker, *The Moment of Racial Sight: A History* (Chicago: University of Chicago Press, 2013), 7.

19. András Sajó, for instance, contends, "Emotions could change the disposition toward slavery of many people; it would, however, be simplistic and even wrong to argue that the irresistible dictate of constitutional sentiments in the end caused the prohibition of slavery." András Sajó, *Constitutional Sentiments* (New Haven, CT: Yale University Press, 2011), 181.

20. Marcus Wood castigates novelists such as Lawrence Sterne for self-indulgent emotional appropriation: "The empathetic fantasy which attempts to reconfigure the suffering of the slave gives the memory of slavery over to the sentimentalist as aesthetic property." Marcus Wood, *Slavery, Empathy, and Pornography* (Oxford: Oxford University Press, 2003), 18. Brycchan Carey points to contemporary denigration of vehicles of "false sensibility"—literature that cued self-indulgent weeping rather than catalyzing political action. See Carey, *British Abolitionism*, 38–39. For a contrasting perspective, see Mallipeddi, *Spectaular Suffering*, 4–5.

21. George Boulukos, Lynn Festa, and Jamie Rosenthal have argued that authors dwelling on emotion in sentimental writings of the era reinforced perceptions that whites were racially superior to blacks. Boulukos observes that the "untrammeled feelings of grateful slaves contrast with the rational independence of white men, but also with the deeper, more genuine feelings, the much more complex psychic interiority, of white women in late-[eighteenth] century fiction" (Boulukos, *The Grateful Slave*, 26). Citing Janet Schaw's *Journal of a Lady of Quality* (1774–76) as an instance of the "Janus-faced" nature of sentimentalism, Festa argues that "Schaw's text reminds us that acute sensibility and proslavery sentiment may go hand in hand; abolitionists did not possess a monopoly on sentimental feeling" (Festa, *Sentimental Figures of Empire*, 15, 53). Rosenthal argues that Schaw's journal exemplifies how texts by white female authors in the eighteenth-century Caribbean "could use sensibility to differentiate between whites and blacks and to delineate proper and effective forms of slave management." Jamie Rosenthal, "The Contradictions of Racialized Slavery," in *Affect and Abolition in the Anglo-Atlantic, 1770–1830*, ed. Stephen Ahern (2013; New York: Routledge, 2016), 171–88, 173. Even if antislavery literature succeeded in convincing white audiences that black people felt the same emotions as they did, the writers left intact the core claims of racist ideology: intellectual inferiority and emotional immaturity. See also

Amit Rai, *Rule of Sympathy: Sentiment, Race, and Power, 1750–1850* (New York: Palgrave, 2002), xix; and Menely, "Acts of Sentiment," 49–51.

22. Understandably, given their standard methodologies, historians tend to focus on primary documentary records rather than literary texts. In considering the work of "proslavery ideologues" in the antebellum American South, Eugene Genovese searches for their views in "policy statements . . . , in the remarks of travelers, and above all, in the private expressions of planters within their own family circles." Eugene D. Genovese, *Roll, Jordan, Roll: The World the Slaves Made* (New York: Pantheon, 1974), 56, 76. In her account of law, government, and slavery in Jamaica, Diana Paton surveys "information from a variety of sources," including "detailed records from and about houses of correction," "estate records," and "letters between attorneys or overseers and proprietors." Diana Paton, *No Bond but the Law: Punishment, Race, and Gender in Jamaican State Formation, 1780–1870* (Durham, NC: Duke University Press, 2004), 31. For historical scholarship that focuses exclusively on proslavery interests, see Larry E. Tise, *Proslavery: A History of the Defense of Slavery in America, 1701–1840* (Athens: University of Georgia Press, 1987).

23. See Janina Nordius, "Racism and Radicalism in Jamaican Gothic: Cynric R. Williams's *Hamel, the Obeah Man,*" *ELH* 73 (2005): 673–93; Candace Ward, " 'What Time Has Proved': History, Rebellion, and Revolution in *Hamel, the Obeah Man,*" *Ariel* 38 (2007): 49–73; Candace Ward, *Crossing the Line: Early Creole Novels and Anglophone Caribbean Culture in the Age of Emancipation* (Charlottesville: University of Virginia Press, 2017); and Tim Watson, *Caribbean Culture and British Fiction in the Atlantic World, 1780–1870* (Cambridge: Cambridge University Press, 2008). For moments in *Hamel* that complicate interpretation of it as "a monolithic proslavery novel," see Nordius, "Racism and Radicalism," 686.

24. See Elizabeth A. Bohls, *Slavery and the Politics of Place: The Colonial Caribbean, 1770–1833,* repr. ed. (Cambridge: Cambridge University Press, 2017).

25. See Sara Salih, *Representing Mixed Race in Jamaica and England from Abolition to the Present* (London: Routledge, 2010).

26. Ward, *Crossing the Line,* 2.

27. Of the few monographs that devote substantial attention to British proslavery thought, the single full-length volume published in the last three decades is the historian Paula E. Dumas's *Proslavery Britain: Fighting for Slavery in an Era of Abolition* (New York: Palgrave Macmillan, 2016), which gives plot summaries of *Hamel* and *Marly* (111–13). Given her disciplinary focus, Dumas concentrates on historical documents and political events of the period rather than literary works.

28. See, e.g., Edward Long, *The History of Jamaica; or, General Survey of the Antient and Modern State of That Island: With Reflections on Its Situation, Settlements, Inhabitants, Climate, Products, Commerce, Laws, and Government,* 3 vols. (London: T. Lowndes, 1774), 2:364–65.

29. Bryan Edwards, *The History, Civil and Commercial, of the British West Indies* (London: Printed for John Stockdale, 1793), 124–26.

30. Long, *The History of Jamaica,* 2:407.

31. Long, 2:407.

32. Hector Macneill, *Observations on the Treatment of the Negroes, in the Island of Jamaica, Including Some Account of Their Temper and Character, with Remarks on the*

Importation of Slaves from the Coast of Africa (London: Printed for G. G. J. and J. Robinson, 1788), 27–28.

33. Long, *The History of Jamaica*, 2:407; Macneill, *Observations*, 29.

34. *No Rum! No Sugar! or, The Voice of Blood: Being Half an Hour's Conversation between a Negro and an English Gentleman: Shewing the Horrible Nature of the Slave Trade, and Pointing Out an Easy and Effectual Method of Terminating It, by an Act of the People* (London, 1792), 4.

35. *No Rum! No Sugar!*, 4.

36. Anders Sparrman, *A Voyage to the Cape of Good Hope, towards the Antarctic Polar Circle, Round the World and to the Country of the Hottentots and the Caffres, from the Year 1772–1776 [. . .]*, ed. V. S. Forbes, trans. and revised by J. and I. Rudner, 2 vols. (Cape Town: Van Riebeeck Society, 1975), 1:311. On the Khoisan and the "Gunjemans Hottentots," see Richard Elphick and V. C. Malherbe, "The Khoisan to 1828," in *The Shaping of South African Society, 1652–1840*, ed. Richard Elphick and Hermann Giliomee, rev. ed. (Middletown, CT: Wesleyan University Press, 1989), 3–65, esp. 24.

37. Sparrman, *Voyage to the Cape*, 1:346.

38. Sparrman, 1:346.

39. Roger N. Buckley, "The Admission of Slave Testimony at British Military Courts in the West Indies," in *A Turbulent Time: The French Revolution and the Greater Caribbean*, ed. David Barry Gaspar and David Patrick Geggus (Bloomington: Indiana University Press, 1997), 226–50, 228.

40. See Thomas D. Morris, *Southern Slavery and the Law, 1619–1860* (Chapel Hill: University of North Carolina Press, 1996), 229–48, 230–31. Morris considers alternative reasons beyond the theological rationale for prohibiting the enslaved from testifying against whites in the antebellum American South.

41. Buckley, "The Admission of Slave Testimony," 229. For an unusual earlier episode in the West Indies—a 1753 murder trial in St. Kitts—in which a slave's eyewitness account, relayed to the court by a white overseer, was pivotal to the conviction of a white defendant, see Natalie Zacek, "Voices and Silences: The Problem of Slave Testimony in the English West Indian Law Court," *Slavery and Abolition* 24, no. 3 (Dec. 2003): 24–39, 28.

42. An earlier generation of antislavery advocates had called for the plantation system to be placed under stricter legal regulation. Ramesh Mallipeddi notes that Henry Dickson made a case for government oversight after he moved to Barbados in 1773 to serve as private secretary to Governor Edward Hays: "For Dickson, as for many abolitionists, the evils of slavery arose from [its] being a 'private' institution, impervious to external factors like law or public opinion. . . . Hence Dickson's antislavery work, *Letters on Slavery* (1789), aimed to bring the private authority of the masters—'the sovereign arbiters of the liberties and the lives of the enslaved Negroes'—under public scrutiny and, by extension, legal regulation" (Mallipeddi, *Spectacular Suffering*, 1).

43. The historian Helen Taft Manning argued that the opposite was the case: in her account, metropolitan politicians were deferential to West Indian interests through 1815. See Helen Taft Manning, *British Colonial Government after the American Revolution: 1782–1820* (New Haven, CT: Yale University Press, 1933), 143–49.

44. Ronald V. Sires, "Government in the British West Indies: An Historical Outline," *Social and Economic Studies* 6, no. 2, Special Federation Number (June 1957): 109–32, 111.

45. Smandych, "'To Soften the Extreme Rigor of Their Bondage,'" 548. For a recent account of the impact of racial prejudice on the credibility of testimony by African Americans in twentieth- and twenty-first-century contexts, as illustrated through fiction such as *To Kill a Mockingbird*, see Miranda Fricker, *Epistemic Injustice: Power and the Ethics of Knowing* (Oxford: Oxford University Press, 2007), 20–27.

46. Smandych, 537.

47. Just as a slave could be either person or property under the law, depending on circumstance, "evidence" had, at the time, a similar duality—it could be either a person or a thing. While evidence could denote "information given in a legal investigation, to establish the point or fact in question," it could also mean, in a definition flagged as now "obsolete" by the *Oxford English Dictionary*, "one who furnishes testimony or proof; a witness." *Oxford English Dictionary Online*, s.v. "evidence."

48. See Alexander Barclay, *A Practical View of the Present State of Slavery in the West Indies, or, An Examination of Mr. Stephen's "Slavery of the British West India Colonies," Containing More Particularly an Account of the Actual Condition of the Negroes in Jamaica* (London: Smith, Elder, 1826), 6–7, 9–10.

49. Mary Turner, "The British Caribbean, 1823–1838: The Transition from Slave to Free Legal Status," in *Masters, Servants, and Magistrates in Britain and the Empire, 1562–1955*, ed. Douglas Hay and Paul Craven (Chapel Hill: University of North Carolina Press, 2004), 303–22, 304–305.

50. *An Act to Regulate the Admission of the Evidence of Slaves*, in *Papers Presented to Parliament by His Majesty's Command, in Explanation of the Measures Adopted by His Majesty's Government, for the Melioration of the Condition of the Slave Population in His Majesty's Possessions in the West Indies and on the Continent of South America (In Continuation of the Papers Presented in the Year 1826)* (London: R. G. Clarke, 1827), 39–40. The act stipulated that slaves must be Christians and prove that they understood what an oath entailed; among other restrictions, slave testimony could not be admitted against whites in capital punishment cases.

51. Henry Bathurst, Earl Bathurst, to William Montagu, Duke of Manchester, Downing Street, 13 March 1826, in *Papers Presented to Parliament* (see previous note), 2.

52. According to the historian Mary Turner, Great Britain was much less generous than was Spain in opening local avenues for legal complaint by the enslaved in the Caribbean: "The extent to which statutory law afforded the slaves any form of legal redress varied considerably. In British Caribbean representative colonies, there was scant provision. The 1816 Jamaican Slave Code, for example, gave slaves the right to appeal to magistrates only 'wanton' punishments, or workplace punishments in excess of the legal maximum." Mary Turner, *Slaves and Missionaries: The Disintegration of Jamaican Slave Society, 1787–1834* (Jamaica: University of the West Indies Press, 2000), 7.

53. John Stewart, *A View of the Past and Present State of the Island of Jamaica; with Remarks on the Moral and Physical Condition of the Slaves, and on the Abolition of Slavery in the Colonies* (Edinburgh: Oliver and Boyd, 1823), 251–52.

54. Henry Nelson Coleridge, *Six Months in the West Indies, in 1825*, 2nd ed. (London: John Murray, 1826), 310. Coleridge's book was published anonymously, as was the case for a number of British proslavery writings.

55. The new act admitted slaves as witnesses against whites under five key conditions: (1) only baptized slaves were qualified to provide testimony; (2) they had to understand the oath they were taking in court; (3) their credibility was open to question, just as in the case of whites; (4) the evidence of two slaves independently examined was required in order to convict a white person of a crime; (5) the claim must be brought within six months of the alleged deed. See section 128 of *An Act to Alter and Amend the Slave Laws of This Island* (1826) in *Slave Law of Jamaica: With Proceedings and Documents Relative Thereto* (London: James Ridgway, 1828), 134–35.

56. See Nicole N. Aljoe, *Creole Testimonies: Slave Narratives from the British West Indies* (New York: Palgrave Macmillan, 2012), 95–96. The casting of the speech of former slaves as a form of testimony—one that transcended the courtrooms from which it was barred—continued into the late nineteenth century. Shari Goldberg claims, for example, that Frederick Douglass's metaphorical description of himself as "summoned to . . . the witness stand" shows that "Douglass understood his entire antislavery career as the performance of a witness, an offering of testimony, even though his writings encompass a range of genres, from autobiography to political speeches and editorials, and even though no court of law would have recognized them as binding." Shari Goldberg, *Quiet Testimony: A Theory of Witnessing from Nineteenth-Century American Literature* (New York: Fordham University Press, 2013), 57.

57. See Ward and Watson, "Early Creole Novels," 148–51; and Watson, *Caribbean Culture and British Fiction*, 20.

58. [Fortunatus Dwarris], *Substance of the Three Reports of the Commissioners of Inquiry into the Administration of Civil and Criminal Justice in the West Indies* (London: J. Butterworth, 1827), 355–56.

59. Edmund Clarke, "On Framing Petitions to Parliament," *Anti-Slavery Monthly Reporter* 3, no. 69 (20 Oct. 1830): 451–52, 452.

60. Great Britain, William Scott, and John Haggard, *The Judgment of the Right Hon. Lord Stowell, Respecting the Slavery of the Mongrel Woman, Grace, on an Appeal from the Vice-Admiralty Court of Antigua, Michaelmas Term, 1827* (London: W. Benning, 1827), 42.

61. "Pro-Slavery Writings—Jamaica Mortality," *Anti-Slavery Monthly Reporter* 3, no. 54 (Nov. 1829): 146.

62. *Marly; or, A Planter's Life in Jamaica*, ed. Karina Williamson (Oxford: Macmillan Caribbean, 2005), 276. All subsequent citations of *Marly* refer to this edition and are referenced parenthetically in the text.

63. DeLombard, "Representing the Slave," 86–87.

64. Charles Telfair, for instance, styles himself "the father of his flock" whiling away Sundays "in the bosom of his slaves and attachés." He aimed at "overcoming the effects of their mere animal passions." He kept painstaking records (at least eleven volumes) on slaves' activities, including "Black" and "Red" "character books." Charles Telfair, *Some Account of the State of Slavery at Mauritius, Since the British Occupation, in 1810: In Refutation of Anonymous Charges Promulgated against Government and That Colony* (Port Louis, Mauritius: Printed by Jh. Vallet and Vr. Asselin, 1830), 47, 58, 93.

65. Matthew Lewis, *Journal of a West India Proprietor*, ed. Judith Terry (Oxford: Oxford University Press, 1999), 205.

66. Lewis, 347.

67. Lewis, 207.

68. Cynric R. Williams, *A Tour through the Island of Jamaica, from the Western to the Eastern End, in the Year 1823* (London: Hunt and Clarke, 1826), 349.

69. Williams, 21.

70. Lewis, *Journal of a West India Proprietor*, 40.

71. The narrator foreshadows the reversal: "Ambrosio was yet to learn, that to a heart unacquainted with her, Vice is ever most dangerous when lurking behind the Mask of Virtue." Matthew Lewis, *The Monk*, ed. Emma McAvoy (Oxford: Oxford University Press, 2008), 84.

72. Barclay, *A Practical View*, 248.

73. Swaminathan, *Debating the Slave Trade*, 131.

74. Considering the process by which in the Romantic era, "particularized, rounded characters evolved out of eighteenth-century flat ones," Deidre Shauna Lynch observes the rise of "the sensitive reading that plumbs the depths of a character in the novel— the enterprise of 'appreciating' inner lives of beings that cannot be taken at face value" (Lynch, *The Economy of Character*, 126).

75. Lisa Freeman, *Character's Theater: Genre and Identity on the Eighteenth-Century English Stage* (Philadelphia: University of Pennsylvania Press, 2002), 7.

76. Ian Watt, *The Rise of the Novel: Studies in Defoe, Richardson, and Fielding*, 2nd American ed. (1957; Berkeley: University of California Press, 2001), 32.

77. Ward and Watson, "Early Creole Novels," 155.

78. *An Act to Regulate the Admission of the Evidence of Slaves*, 40.

79. Cynric R. Williams, *Hamel, the Obeah Man*, ed. Candace Ward and Tim Watson (Peterborough, Ontario: Broadview, 2010), 57. All subsequent citations of *Hamel* refer to this edition and are referenced parenthetically in the text.

80. Janina Nordius observes, "With the possible exception of Hamel himself, the conspirators are depicted as a frantic mob, driven by feelings of lust and revenge rather than any conscious political aspirations beyond making Combah king of the island." Nordius, "Racism and Radicalism," 679.

81. Ngai observes, "The 'thinging' of the body in order to construct it, counter-intuitively, as impassioned is deployed by both abolitionists [Stowe and Garrison] as a strategy of shifting this body from thing to human, as if the racialized, hence already objectified body's reobjectification, in being animated, were paradoxically necessary to emphasize its personhood or subjectivity." Sianne Ngai, *Ugly Feelings* (Cambridge, MA: Harvard University Press, 2005), 98–99.

82. C. L. Barber, *Shakespeare's Festive Comedy: A Study of Dramatic Form and Its Relation to Social Custom*, new intro. Stephen Greenblatt (1959; Princeton, NJ: Princeton University Press, 2011), 27.

83. Kevin Quashie, *The Sovereignty of Quiet: Beyond Resistance in Black Culture* (New Brunswick, NJ: Rutgers University Press, 2012), 22.

84. For more on how planters in the West Indies perceived missionaries as aiding slaves through literacy acquisition, moral support, and other means, see Edward Rugemer, *The Problem of Emancipation: The Caribbean Roots of the American Civil War* (Baton Rouge: Louisiana State University Press, 2008), 58–64. See also Edward Rugemer, *Slave Law and the Politics of Resistance in the Early Atlantic World* (Cambridge, MA: Harvard University Press, 2019), 88–89: an Anglican missionary, Dr. Fran-

cis Le Jau, complained that South Carolina planters "were generally like those of the West Indies"; in his view, they were uncooperative in missionary efforts and prone to see slaves as akin to livestock rather than as souls worthy of saving.

85. John Pritchard, *Methodists and Their Missionary Societies, 1760–1900* (London: Routledge, 2013), 63.

86. For an instance of a slave girl's testimony in the antebellum American South, and the questioning of her credibility, see Andrea L. Dennis, "A Snitch in Time: An Historical Sketch of Black Informing during Slavery," *Marquette Law Review* 97, no. 2 (2013): 279–334, 324–25; and Scot French, *The Rebellious Slave: Nat Turner in American Memory* (Boston: Houghton Mifflin, 2004), 62–63. French quotes from documents that demonstrate that repudiation of the testimony was based on the witness's slave status and, implicitly, her age.

Hamel's non-eligible witnesses are distinct from Olaudah Equiano and later nineteenth-century "impossible witnesses"—a phrase coined by Dwight McBride to denote slave memoirists, who faced challenges in narrating life under slavery in a way that was true to their own experiences while also representing collective trauma, all while acquiescing to mediation by antislavery supporters. See Dwight A. McBride, *Impossible Witnesses: Truth, Abolitionism, and Slave Testimony* (New York: New York University Press, 2001), 10, 98.

87. In its original context, Alex Woloch's phrase does not refer to race; it describes the situation of minor characters in general with regard to the "overtly asymmetric nature of the . . . character-field" in nineteenth-century novels by Jane Austen and Charles Dickens (319). See Alex Woloch, *The One vs. the Many: Minor Characters and the Space of the Protagonist in the Novel* (Princeton, NJ: Princeton University Press, 2003), 145.

88. Unsigned review of *Hamel, the Obeah Man, The Scotsman*, 21 April 1827, 249.

89. Unsigned review of *Hamel, the Obeah Man, Westminster Review* 7 April 1827, 444–64, 463, 451.

90. The 1826 legislation was designed in response to political pressure for more humane conditions after antislavery activists claimed that the 1816 Jamaican Slave Act did not go far enough to assuage their concerns. See William A. Green, *British Slave Emancipation: The Sugar Colonies and the Great Experiment, 1830–1865* (Oxford: Clarendon, 1976), 108–9.

91. William Huskisson, "Dispatch from His Majesty's Principal Secretary of State for the Colonial Department," 22 Sept. 1827, repr. in *Slave Law of Jamaica*, 145–58, 153. Huskisson had previously supported planters' rights and shepherded the safe passage of Barbados's Consolidated Slave Act of 1826. Although he cited the Jamaican act's failures to comply with certain stipulations for amelioration mandated by the 1824 Trinidad law of evidence, which was supplemented by the 1824 Order in Council, Huskisson proclaimed that he would have approved the Jamaican act nonetheless, had it not included one key proviso: he was an avid proponent of religious liberty, and he did not approve of the act's stipulation of a sentence of whipping for those who preached without their owner's permission.

92. When supporters of slavery claimed that cheery reactions were evidence that enslaved people were humanely treated and satisfied with their lives, they were sometimes met with skepticism. Marcus Rediker comments on the plantation heir John Riland's *Memoirs of a West-India Planter* (1827):

Soon after the captain had secured his "living cargo" on the African coast, he informed Riland that now he would see that "a slave-ship was a very different thing from what it had been represented." He referred to the abolitionist propaganda that had changed public opinion in England and abroad. Against all that he would show his passenger "the slaves rejoicing in their happy state." To illustrate the point, he approached the enslaved women on board and said a few words, "to which they replied with three cheers and a loud laugh." He then went forward on the main deck and "spoke the same words to the men, who made the same reply." Turning triumphantly to Riland, the captain said, "Now, are you not convinced that Mr. Wilberforce has conceived very improperly of slave-ships?" He referred to the parliamentary leader who had trumpeted the horrors of slave transportation. Riland was not convinced. But he was intrigued, and he was eager to learn whether the captain might be telling the truth. (Marcus Rediker, *The Slave Ship* [New York: Viking, 2007], 67)

Rediker quotes from John Riland, *Memoirs of a West-India Planter, Published from an Original MS. With a Preface and Additional Details* (London: Hamilton, Adams, 1827).

93. Catherine Gallagher, "The Rise of Fictionality," in *The Novel*, vol. 1, *History, Geography, and Culture*, ed. Franco Moretti (Princeton, NJ: Princeton University Press, 2006), 336–63, 337.

94. In privileging the perspective of white authorities instead of the testimony of the enslaved, the proslavery strategy differs significantly from the antislavery approach to eyewitness reporting. Dwight McBride describes the antislavery enthusiasm for slave narratives: "It was common for the slave narrators to deliver their testimonies orally on the abolitionist 'lecture circuit' before the accounts were committed to paper.... This black body that testified on stage was somehow more truthful than the word of white abolitionists, who were mere witnesses one step removed.... Even eyewitness accounts on the part of white abolitionists did not make them authentic in this regard—not authentic in the way abolitionists wanted, needed, and desired to have 'real' black bodies on stage telling their 'real,' authentic stories" (McBride, *Impossible Witnesses*, 4–5). See also Didier Fassin's distinction between the "first-hand" testimony of the "survivor witness" and the "proxy testimony" of the "humanitarian witness." Didier Fassin and Richard Rechtman, *Empire of Trauma: An Inquiry into the Condition of Victimhood*, trans. R. Gomme (Princeton, NJ: Princeton University Press, 2009), 143.

95. William Shakespeare, *Othello*, The Arden Shakespeare Third Series, rev. ed., ed. E. A. J. Honigmann, new intro. Ayanna Thompson (London: Bloomsbury, 2016), 5.2.340–41, 334.

96. See Richard K. Fleischman, David Oldroyd, and Thomas N. Tyson, "Plantation Accounting and Management Practices in the US and the British West Indies at the End of Their Slavery Eras," *Economic History Review* 64, no. 3 (August 2011): 765–97, 794; and Donald L. Horowitz, "Color Differentiation in the American Systems of Slavery," *Journal of Interdisciplinary History* 3, no. 3 (Winter 1973): 509–41, 512, 524.

97. Ruth Graham, "I Don't Feel Your Pain," *Boston Globe*, 15 June 2014, https://www.bostonglobe.com/ideas/2014/06/14/don-feel-your-pain/cIrKD5czM0pgZQv7PgCmxI

/story.html. See also Joanna Bourke, *The Story of Pain: From Prayers to Painkillers* (Oxford: Oxford University Press, 2014), 194.

98. Such privileging of bodily evidence over narrative witnessing continues today. In their study of the European Commission's Medical Committee for the Exiles (COMEDE), Fassin and Rechtman question reliance on corporeal evidence to validate stories of torture: "On close examination, however, the physical body has little to say. . . . Exhaustive enumeration and detailed descriptions of scars are both tedious and offer little in the way of proof. They speak of injury, but usually without confirming its origin" (Fassin and Rechtman, *Empire of Trauma*, 257). Notably, Sancho's death is attributed vaguely to "disease"; this etiological finding appears to rule out the direct role of whites in Sancho's death, but it not only fails to explore whether multiple beatings immediately before his death hastened his demise; it also does not fully exculpate the whites from involvement in other factors, such as malnutrition or overwork, that may have precipitated it. No slaves in *Marly* die from abuse at the hands of whites.

99. Saidiya V. Hartman, *Scenes of Subjection: Terror, Slavery, and Self-Making in Nineteenth-Century America* (Oxford: Oxford University Press, 1997), 43–44.

100. Tanya Batson-Savage, "A Voyeuristic View of Plantation Society," review of *Marly, Jamaica Gleaner,* 19 March 2006.

101. *The Parliamentary Debates: Forming a Continuation of the Work Entitled "The Parliamentary History of England, from the Earliest Period to the Year 1803,"* published under the superintendence of T. C. Hansard, n.s., vol. 14, *Comprising the Period from the Second Day of February, to the Seventeenth Day of March, 1826* (London: Pater-noster Row Press, 1826), 1014.

102. *Parliamentary Debates,* 14:1014.

103. In Edgeworth's tale, a slave named Caesar must decide who deserves his loyalty when he hears of plans for a slave rebellion: "Caesar's mind was divided between love for his friend and gratitude to his master: the conflict was violent, and painful. Gratitude at last prevailed: he repeated his declaration, that he would rather die than continue in a conspiracy against his benefactor." Maria Edgeworth, "The Grateful Negro," in *Popular Tales,* 3 vols. (London: J. Johnson, 1804), 3:193–240, repr. in *Popular Tales; Early Lessons; Whim for Whim,* ed. Elizabeth Eger, Clíona Ó Gallchoir, and Marilyn Butler, vol. 12 of *The Works of Maria Edgeworth,* ed. Marilyn Butler, 12 vols. (London: Pickering and Chatto, 2003), 49–63, 55.

104. Unsigned review of *Marly,* attributed to James Silk Buckingham, ed., "Memoirs of a Planter," *The Athenaeum,* 25 March 1828, in compendium of issues, 2 Jan. 1828–23 July 1828, 279–80, 279.

105. The review ends as follows: "The volume contains some curious examples of West Indian reasoning on the subject of the Slave Trade, but we believe the arguments employed have all, by one channel or the other, found their way to England. The information the work contains is the best argument which could be brought against the nefarious system; for it proves, beyond all contradictions, that the miserable beings who are kept in slavery, because said to be unfit for freedom, are only made unfit for it through the influence of Slavery itself" ("Memoirs of a Planter," 280).

106. Unsigned review of *Marly, London Weekly Review; and Journal of Literature and the Fine Arts,* 1828.

107. Unsigned review of *Marly*, *The Atlas*, Sunday, 23 March 1828, 187, British Newspaper Archive online database (in partnership with the British Library).

108. John Riland, *Memoirs of a West-India Planter* (London: Hamilton, Adams, and J. Nisbet, 1827), iv–v.

109. Review of John Riland, *Memoirs of a West-India Planter*, in "Select List of Books Recently Published, Chiefly Religious," *Wesleyan-Methodist Magazine*, Oct. 1827, 685–93, 690.

110. Michael McKeon, *The Origins of the English Novel, 1600–1740*, 15th anniv. ed. (Baltimore: Johns Hopkins University Press, 2002), 419.

Epilogue • Abiding the Law

1. David Cameron, "Cameron's Speech on the European Court of Human Rights in Full," 25 Jan. 2012, *The Guardian*, www.theguardian.com/law/2012/jan/25/cameron -speech-european-court-human-rights-full.

2. Cameron does note quote Blackstone verbatim. Also, he chooses to cite the first published version of the passage rather than the one added by Blackstone to subsequent editions of the *Commentaries*, in which the jurist hedges: "and so far becomes a freeman; though the master's right to his service may *possibly* continue." See William Blackstone, *Commentaries on the Laws of England*, 4 vols., *Book 1: Of the Rights of Persons*, ed. David Lemmings (Oxford: Oxford University Press, 2016), chap. 1, sec. 123, 86.

3. Lynn Hunt, *Inventing Human Rights: A History* (New York: Norton, 2007), 39.

4. Steven Pinker, *Enlightenment Now: The Case for Reason, Science, Humanism, and Progress* (New York: Viking, 2018), 284.

5. William Rees-Mogg and James Dale Davidson, *The Sovereign Individual: How to Survive and Thrive during the Collapse of the Welfare State* (New York: Simon and Schuster, 1997), 16.

6. Cameron was responding to a recent controversy: overruling British courts, the European Human Rights Court had recently blocked the extradition from England of a Muslim cleric suspected of fomenting terrorism. The Court averred that Jordan, the nation that supported the extradition, permitted the admission of evidence acquired by torture and that the cleric's right to a fair trial was at risk. See Sonia van Gilder Cooke, "Britain Seethes as Radical Islamic Cleric Released from Prison," *Time*, 14 Feb. 2012, http://content.time.com/time/world/article/0,8599,2106807,00.html.

Other politicians use similar rhetoric. A contemporaneous report noted that "senior Conservative politician Peter Bone said Britain should put the safety of its citizens over the 'so-called rights of an extremist terrorist.'" Murray Wardrop, "Abu Qatada's Mother Calls for Hate Preacher Son to Be Deported to Jordan," *The Telegraph*, 14 Feb. 2012, https://www.telegraph.co.uk/news/uknews/law-and-order/9080924/Abu-Qatadas -mother-calls-for-hate-preacher-son-to-be-deported-to-Jordan.html.

During a parliamentary debate on immigration in 2014, Philip Davies suggested that the government was granting legal agency to undocumented persons while neglecting the needs of citizens: "Surely anybody who enters this country illegally should not be able to remain here with indefinite leave or be granted asylum, but should go through the proper processes. Will the minister explain how many such cases have occurred as a result of the Human Rights Act, dating back to 1997? Is it not the case that that Act, rather than giving any meaningful rights to decent, law-abiding citizens in this country, is a charter for illegal immigrants? Is it not time that that wretched Human Rights Act was scrapped?" "Illegal Immigrants," UK Parliament, House of Commons Hansard, 13 Oct. 2014, vol. 586, hansard.parliament.uk/Commons/2014-10-13/debates/1410134000016/illegalimmigrants.

7. Ronald Reagan, "Excerpt of Remarks by Governor Ronald Reagan—Sacramento Host Breakfast" (7 Sept. 1973), 5, in folder "Speeches—Governor Ronald Reagan, 1973 [09/01/1973-12/31/1973]," box P19 of the collection "Reagan, Ronald: Gubernatorial Papers, 1966–74: Press Unit," in *Ronald Reagan Presidential Library Digital Library Collections*, Ronald Reagan Library, https://www.reaganlibrary.gov/sites/default/files /digitallibrary/gubernatorial/pressunit/p19/40-840-7408624-p19-003-2017.pdf.

8. James Conaway, "Looking at Reagan," *Atlantic Monthly*, Oct. 1980, 32–45, 35.

9. The contrasting but similarly facile versions of eighteenth-century history offered by Reagan and Cameron have persisted in subsequent decades. Leftist politicians have largely failed to devise alternatives with broader appeal. Jeremy Corbyn, the leader of the Labour Party, gave a treacly and reductive synopsis of what he described as eighteenth-century values: "I have this eighteenth-century religious view that there is some good in everybody. . . . Because I've never had any higher education of any sort, I've never held in awe those who have had it or have a sense of superiority over those who don't. Life is life. Some of the wisest people you meet are sweeping our streets." Greg Heffer, "Labour Leader Jeremy Corbyn: I Have an 18th Century View," *Sunday Express*, 22 Dec. 2015, https://www.express.co.uk/news/politics/628786/Labour-leader -Jeremy-Corbyn-18th-century-fearless-university-degree-Trident-interview.

10. Benjamin R. Barber, *A Passion for Democracy: American Essays* (Princeton, NJ: Princeton University Press, 2000), 16n5.

11. David van Mill, "Civil Liberty in Hobbes's Commonwealth," *Australian Journal of Political Science* 37, no. 1 (2002): 21–38, 21.

12. *Marly; or, A Planter's Life in Jamaica*, ed. Karina Williamson (Oxford: Macmillan Caribbean, 2005), 62.

13. *Marly*, 280, 277.

14. The political scientist Kirstine Taylor traces the apparently "racially neutral" language of "law and order" from Nixon through Reagan to Donald Trump at the end of her article "American Political Development and Black Lives Matter in the Age of Incarceration," *Politics, Groups and Identities* 6, no. 1 (2018): 153–61.

15. See Donald J. Trump tweets: "Democrats and liberals in Congress want to disarm law-abiding Americans at the same time they are releasing dangerous criminal aliens and savage gang members onto our streets. Politicians who put criminal aliens before American Citizens should be voted out of office!" (4 May 2018); "Republicans believe our Country should be a Sanctuary for law-abiding Americans—not criminal aliens" (2 Nov. 2018); and "If you want to protect criminal aliens—VOTE DEMOCRAT. If you want to protect Law-Abiding Americans—VOTE REPUBLICAN!" (3 Nov. 2018), Trump Twitter Archive, http://www.trumptwitterarchive.com/archive.

16. The characterization of the middle class as law-abiding is at least a century old: in his classic 1899 study of economic thought, the economist and sociologist Thorstein Veblen identified the middle class with "law-abiding citizens": "Indeed, it is becoming something of a commonplace with observers of criminal life in European communities that the criminal and dissolute classes are, if anything, more devout, and more naively so,

than the average of the population. It is among those who constitute the pecuniary middle class and the body of law-abiding citizens that a relative exemption from the devotional attitude is to be looked for." Thorstein Veblen, *The Theory of the Leisure Class: An Economic Study of Institutions* (New York: Macmillan, 1912), 320. Susanne Karstedt and Stephen Farrall note that "politicians have professed to be enacting criminal justice policies in a bid to protect the 'law abiding majority' . . . the middle classes who do not appear [cast as perpetrators] in government crime rhetoric." Susanne Karstedt and Stephen Farrall, "Law-Abiding Majority? The Everyday Crimes of the Middle Classes," *Center for Crime and Justice Studies [King's College London] Briefing* 3 (June 2007): 1–8, 1. Karstedt and Farrall suggest that policy makers reconsider the yoking of middle-class and "law-abiding" identity, citing survey evidence that the majority of middle-class people engage in law-breaking behavior, albeit involving minor crimes.

17. Oliver Wright, "David Cameron to 'Scrap' Human Rights Act for New 'British Bill of Rights,'" *The Independent*, 1 Oct. 2014, https://www.independent.co.uk/news/uk /politics/conservative-party-conference-cameron-announces-plans-to-scrap-human -rights-act-9767435.html.

18. Joe Watts, "Theresa May Responds to Donald Trump's Tweet by Saying She Is Fully Focused on Extremism," *The Independent*, 30 Dec. 2017, www.independent.co.uk /news/uk/politics/theresa-may-donald-trump-twitter-islamic-terrorism-britain-first -latest-a8084421.html.

19. Results obtained for a search for "law-abiding" in 1800 through 2018 using the Hansard archive search tool at https://hansard.parliament.uk/search/Contributions ?startDate=1800-01-01&endDate=2018-08-08&searchTerm=%22law-abiding%22&partial =False. The thirty-seven times the term was used in June of 2018 is exceeded only by June of 1997 (sixty-one times) in recorded Parliamentary archives since 1800.

20. The concept appeared still earlier, albeit in different phrasing, in medieval texts that discuss the need to "abyde" the law.

21. John Bisset, *Christ the Covenant of the People. A Sermon on Isaiah XLII.6. Designed to Have Been Preached in the East-Church of Aberdeen, . . . 1756. By the Late Reverend Mr. John Bisset, . . . Found among the Papers of the Deceased; . . . with a Preface by his Son, the Reverend Mr. John Bisset* (Aberdeen: Printed and sold by J. Chalmers, 1756), 31. For a subsequent instance of Bisset's usage of the term, in which he describes Christ as "law-abiding," see Bisset, 34.

22. James G. Birney, *Letter on Colonization, Addressed to the Reverend Thornton J. Mills, Corresponding Secretary of the Colonization Society* (New York: Office of the Anti-Slavery Reporter, 1834), 25 (emphasis in original).

23. *Marly*, 325.

24. Walter Scott, *Redgauntlet*, ed. G. A. M. Wood with David Hewitt (1824; Edinburgh: Edinburgh University Press / New York: Columbia University Press, 1997), 357. For Scott's complex characterization of the prince, see also Julian Meldon D'Arcy, *Subversive Scott: The Waverley Novels and Scottish Nationalism* (Reykjavík: University of Iceland Press, 2005), 205–7.